VENGEANCE

India after the Assassination of
Indira Gandhi

Also by Pranay Gupte

The Crowded Earth: People and the Politics of Population (Norton)

VENGEANCE

India after the Assassination of Indira Gandhi

PRANAY GUPTE

W · W · NORTON & COMPANY · New York · London

Published simultaneously in Canada by Penguin Books Canada Ltd, 2801 John Street, Markham, Ontario L3R 1B4
Printed in the United States of America.

The text of this book is composed in Avanta (more commonly called Electra), with display type set in Codex. Composition and manufacturing by The Haddon Craftsmen, Inc. Book design by Nancy Dale Muldoon

First Edition

Portions of this book have appeared, in slightly different form, in the *New York Times* and in *Vanity Fair* magazine.

Library of Congress Cataloging in Publication Data

Gupte, Pranay.
Vengeance: India after the assassination of Indira Gandhi.

Bibliography: p.
Includes index.
1. India—Politics and government—1977-2. Gandhi, Indira, 1917- —
Assassination. I. Title.
DS480.853.G86   1985   954.05'2   85-7207

ISBN 0-393-02230-7

W. W. Norton & Company, Inc., 500 Fifth Avenue, New York, N. Y. 10110

W. W. Norton & Company Ltd., 37 Great Russell Street, London WC1B 3NU

1 2 3 4 5 6 7 8 9 0

I dedicate this book to the memory of my father,
Balkrishna Trimbak Gupte,
17 October 1909 — 5 February 1985.

Dhanyavad
—With gratitude for the gift of Life, Love, and Laughter.

Contents

A FOREWORD

From Mahatma Gandhi
to Rajiv Gandhi

by James W. Michaels

I AM a relic, one of the few still active American newsmen who
covered the events leading to Indian independence, knew the
personalities involved, and stayed on to report on the bloodshed and
on the gradual settling down that followed. I have visited India
frequently in the years since and followed her progress both through
reading and personal contacts.

However, in writing this foreword at Pranay Gupte's request, my
intent is not to reminisce, but to draw upon my very personal experience to help readers transcend the cultural differences between India
and the West. The differences are profound. But so are the similarities, the common ground. India is in just about every sense of the
word a political democracy. Respect for human rights and toleration
of cultural diversity are not foreign importations to India but as
deeply rooted in culture and history as in the West. A Westerner's
first impression of India is: how different this place is. But closer

observation yields a quite different insight. Democracy in India is a living breathing reality—blemished, but reality usually is.

We live in an era when democracy is in general retreat. It has been rejected in most of the Islamic world. It has been trampled upon in the name of Marxist-Leninism in Eastern Europe and in many former colonial countries. In Nicaragua, a left-wing despotism has replaced a right-wing despotism. Democracy is barely struggling for life in Latin America. China, for all the recent reforms, remains a tightly controlled society. But in India, as in most of Western Europe and the United States, people are still free to be human—providing they do not too flagrantly break the law.

Here are 800 million people, half of them under the age of twenty. They speak languages which are often undecipherable to one another —it is common in Delhi and elsewhere to observe a South Indian speaking in English to a North Indian waiter because it is the only language they have in common. Religions? Hindu and Muslim have a history of strife that makes Catholic and Protestant in Northern Ireland seem like a couple of neighbors squabbling over a back fence. Yet this polyglot, polyracial, polyreligious mass of people has maintained under ferociously difficult conditions what I believe to be the only freely elected government among the dozens of countries which shed imperial rule after World War II. India's army has left its barracks only to fight foreign enemies or to restore order when the police were overwhelmed. Unlike its counterpart in next-door Pakistan, the army in India does not pretend to embody national legitimacy; it exists only to defend that legitimacy. For all her flaws, modern India is a magnificent and humane accomplishment.

My personal passage to India began forty-two years ago. It was the India of the British Raj, of colonial subjugation. The late Paul Scott has described the last days of British rule far better than I could; and television viewers have glimpsed that period in the magnificent series, *The Jewel in the Crown,* based on Scott's *Raj Quartet.* In those four novels, and in a fifth, *Staying On,* Scott has brought a dead society back to life and shown the strange mixture of attraction and antagonism that differentiated British rule in India from colonial rule in most other places.

The significant thing is this: while Indians finally rose against the worst features of British rule, they ended adopting some of the better features of British democracy and fair play. Why did this happen in India when so many other former colonial countries fell back into one form or other of autocracy? I think because Hindu culture, which is dominant in India under the veneer of Westernism, is basically tolerant and respectful of individual eccentricity; it is thus extremely fertile ground for democracy. (Many of my Indian friends would prefer that I say "Indian" culture is tolerant, but I see no evidence of democracy taking strong hold in Islamic nations.) India was not a tabula rasa on which the British etched new patterns. In a major sense the British simply helped make legible again that which was already written there.

All this—the mutual sympathies, the fertile ground for democracy —came as an almost total surprise to me when first exposed to India, because, like most Westerners, my first impression of India was of uncrossable, unfathomable gulfs.

I first had a sense of crossing these gulfs on a stifling premonsoon morning in Delhi four decades ago. June 6, 1945, to be precise. I awoke that sweltering morning in New Delhi to the frightening news that President Franklin D. Roosevelt had died in Hot Springs. The preeminent leader of the Free World was gone. What did his passing mean to the world? Indeed, what it did portend for me?

I was one of the tens of millions whose lives had been disrupted and changed by World War II, which caught me on the eve of my graduation from Harvard and deposited me, at twenty-two, in India, a country of which I knew almost nothing. In 1943 and part of 1944 I served as an American Field Service volunteer ambulance driver with the British-Indian army that was slowly pushing the Japanese back into Burma. Later I graduated from the mud and blood of India's eastern frontier in Manipur to an interesting but scarcely taxing office job for what was then the United States Office of War

Information in Delhi. From the small room I shared with another American in the old Cecil Hotel (Europeans Only) I bicycled daily the four miles or so to the USOWI office in New Delhi's Connaught Circle area. My path took me through the crowded Chandni Chowk, Old Delhi's street of moonlight. Then as now Chandni Chowk was framed on one side by the crowded bazaar, but in those days when India's capital had scarcely 10 percent its present population the broad street opened on the other end to a stunning vista of the red sandstone Mogul fort, the Lal Qila, across what was then a vast parade ground.

I had already experienced two years of India and had, like Kipling's Kim, traveled the Grand Trunk Road from Bombay to Calcutta. I had even learned enough Hindi—in the military mode—to converse with ordinary Indian soldiers. For all this I as yet knew only a little of the country or its culture. It was British India then and as an employee of the United States government I was discouraged from mixing socially with Indians; our British allies, not yet reconciled to the loss of the jewel in the King Emperor's crown, did not like our doing so. Franklin D. Roosevelt had already irritated the British Tories on the subject of India's freedom; so much so that FDR's personal emissary to India had been booted out by the British authorities. FDR's Four Freedoms had nourished the growing hope for independence in the minds of those Indians literate enough to know what was going on. The American press was loudly and sometimes ignorantly critical of British imperialism. The last thing the imperial authorities wanted was a lot of naive young Americans running about and getting the natives stirred up.

Yet to the extent I could do so without endangering my job and without seeming queer to my fellow Americans, I quietly made a few Indian contacts. A charming pandit, whose family was steeped in Delhi history, whose mouth was red from betel-chewing, came weekly to my room to give me Hindi lessons. He brought with him Indian food—then almost unobtainable by foreigners in this heart of India—from the bazaar. Over a bottle of sherry which he loved but could not himself afford we talked Indian history and culture and the virtues and vices of British rule, then in its last few years. These evenings were, for me, a rare and almost forbidden pleasure. By and large, Indians and Westerners felt clumsy in one another's company, and remained so well after independence.

And so, though I liked the few Indians I had gotten to know I was not at all prepared for what happened as I cycled to work on that sweltering morning of June 6, forty years ago. Chandni Chowk was always crowded in the morning, a time when the temperature was still only in the low 90s. This particular morning it was extraordinarily crowded. I had to get off my cycle and push it. Only slowly did it dawn on me why the street was thicker with people than usual. I suddenly realized: people aren't ignoring me as usual. Recognizing by my uniform that I was an American, people were offering condolences at the death of my president—a powerful foreigner who seemed to understand their yearnings for freedom. A grizzled, burly middle-aged man blocked my path. What did he want? Only to embrace me, tears in his eyes. In his few words of English he said: "We have lost a friend." That done, he let me pass. Other Indians were crying. People wanted to touch me, to show me, any American, their sorrow at the death of the English-speaking statesman who championed their cause against that of his own British allies. A common sorrow united us. FDR had plucked the same sympathetic strings in those "strange" Indians as in so many Westerners. We were divided by culture and economic status but united by the Four Freedoms. For the first time, I sensed that Indians and Americans had more in common than was commonly supposed.

At this time Mahatma Gandhi and his protegé Jawaharlal Nehru were agitating furiously for Indian independence from British colonial rule. Like many Americans, I was ambivalent about Indian nationalism. It was bred into Americans that one nation ought not rule another and the arrogant discrimination against brown skins was irritating and stupid to most of us. But there was another side to British imperialism, at least in those twilight days. The unfairness, the irrationality of one nation ruling over another was tempered by the British sense of fair play and respect for law. From a political point of view such rule is no longer acceptable. But say this for it: respect for individual and human rights in British India was of a far higher order than respect for individual rights is today in many so-called Islamic and Marxist-Leninist states.

But individual rights were not the main issue in India then. Political freedom was. In the middle of World War II, when both the Western powers and the Soviet Union were in mortal battle against an evil enemy, the Indian National Congress declared that independence came before cooperation in the war against Hitler. Without a firm promise of freedom Indians would not only not support the war effort, they would impede it. And impede it many of them did. But with few exceptions, there was no sympathy for the Axis powers: it was America's—Roosevelt's—call for freedom that Indians in general resonated to, not to Japanese propaganda about Asian solidarity. When the British finally conceded Indian independence, there was, therefore, surprisingly little bitterness in spite of the sometimes brutal history of British rule.

Mahatma Gandhi, Jawaharlal Nehru, Maulana Abdul Kalam Azad, Vallabhbhai Patel. All dead now, these were the men who led India to independence and to a reconciliation with the former colonial master. In 1946 and later, as a young reporter for United Press International, I met them all, these founders of Independent India. Gandhi, who knew how to sway simple peasants and rouse them to a sense of nationhood. Nehru, Cambridge-educated, smooth, a graceful writer and speaker in English, urbane—Gandhi's seeming opposite yet Gandhi's choice for leading independent India. Azad, a courtly, neatly bearded Muslim who represented the Indian soul of the Indian Muslim and opposed the creation of Pakistan. Patel, ugly as a toad, but tough and smart, and to some observers the most able of the nationalist leaders; Patel lost in the power struggle to Nehru because he seemed to represent Hindu India rather than the secular India which the more cosmopolite Nehru stood for. I shall never forget the day when, from a distance, I watched Mahatma Gandhi gently shaking his finger at Patel, who like a child hung his head. Gandhi opposed the creation of Pakistan but once it was a fact he insisted that India carry out her agreements with Pakistan to the letter. Patel advocated a tough line to Pakistan but relented under the Mahatma's scolding.

The two nations were born, India and Pakistan, amidst terrible bloodshed—bloodshed directed not toward the departing colonialists but inwardly, Indian slaughtering Indian. For the Indian revolution took a strange turn. Not only did the colonial power leave of his own will, he actually sent one of his most influential and charming personalities, Lord Louis Mountbatten, to make sure that independence did not get delayed by bickering among the endless shades and gradations of Indian nationalism. Had the British suddenly seen the error of their old ways? It wasn't just that. They had no stomach for a fight—the war had bled them dry—and did not want to get caught in the middle as the various factions struggled for the prize of power that was now sure to fall. The British may not have left willingly but they left gracefully. In scenes unparalleled elsewhere at a time when colonialism was unraveling throughout the world, the last viceroy, Lord Louis, drew cheers from the Indian crowds almost rivaling those for Jawaharlal Nehru. The British left India, not with the lion's tail between his legs, but proudly and with general good grace.

Unfortunately, independence did not come peacefully. Deflected from resentment of the former oppressors, revolutionary ardor turned inward and Muslims and Hindus did some settling of ancient scores. Millions were uprooted from ancestral homes and literally hundreds of thousands died in cruel, senseless mutual slaughter. Pakistan, which was first conceived as little more than a bargaining chip in a grab for power by the brilliant and enigmatic Mohammed Ali Jinnah, was torn from India to hasten the independence timetable; it was as if the mothers in the King Solomon tale had agreed to settle their differences by putting the baby to the knife. Jinnah, the father of Pakistan, was not even a good Muslim; he smoked, drank, ate pork, and emulated in his style of life the English gentleman. Never mind that he didn't really represent Muslim India as Maulana Azad did; he understood power, understood that he could capitalize on Britain's desire to get out and on the nationalist mainstream's desire for democracy. Pakistan made no sense geographically, historically, or economically but there it was and there it is.

Would this truncated, bleeding India hold together? Probably not. Could it develop in relative peace? The chances looked slim. But it wasn't my problem. For me it was a thrilling opportunity to practice my journalistic trade on a grand scale at an early age. I was just a greenhorn journalist but I was recording history. Good fortune had me on the scene at Birla House in New Delhi within minutes of Mahatma Gandhi's assassination and UPI broke the story to the world press. Trekking through the hills and mountains of Pakistan I became the first foreign journalist to report from the spot the fighting between India and Pakistan over Kashmir in 1947, a conflict that smolders still. It seemed that India, born in bloodshed, would not last long.

But India did hold together. It has had wars with Pakistan and China, a runaway population growth, an oil crisis and riots and separatist movements based both on language and religion. Corruption festered, encouraged by the bureaucratic socialism that breeds corruption wherever it exists. Resources were wasted on grandiose state projects. Yet the center held. There were no coup d'etats—just free elections. India made huge advances in technology, industry, trade. The statistics show only modest economic growth since independence. I do not believe the statistics, which are likely to be understated in a society where nobody quite trusts the bureaucracy. Low though it still is on average, the Indian standard of living has made leaps forward since independence and a huge middle class has been created where hardly any existed before. Upward mobility is strong now in a society which for a millennium was in the static grip of caste. Though the government's economic policy was, by and large, atrocious, the natural industry and talent for business of the Indian people managed to shine through.

It is March 1977. Thirty-two years have passed since I wheeled my bicycle through the crowds in Chandni Chowk on the morning after FDR's death. Delhi has swollen to almost ten times its former size. Except for the grand old Imperial buildings and the still resplendent uniforms of the President's Guard, Paul Scott's India is gone. Delhi is no longer British and Mogul. It is all commerce and politics now, a sprawling industrial center as well as the capital. It is a Punjabi city now, its character transformed by the hundreds of thousands of Hindu and Sikh refugees who fled east after Pakistan was carved from India's flesh. I am dining at the home of old Indian friends. They have a visitor, another old friend who lives to the north in the hills above Almora. There he owns a small fruit orchard, employing about three dozen workers. The man from Almora is puzzled. All the polls, all the newspapers are predicting that Indira Gandhi will win the general election, that her party will win in a landslide.

The prime minister had been ruling under a State of Emergency which gave her government extraordinary powers to arrest, to censor, to punish, and to suspend civil liberties. By and large, these powers were used sparingly but there were certainly abuses. Indira's youngest son, Sanjay, had launched a powerful campaign to bring down India's birthrate. This was not a brutal dictatorship as we see it today in so-called Marxist-Leninist countries but neither was it the usual Indian state of live-and-let-live. India was flirting with totalitarianism. Just flirting, mind you. Stung by criticism of her use of the new powers Mrs. Gandhi had called the election, confident that the masses would be sufficiently pleased by her government's somewhat heavy-handed progress against crime, corruption, and inflation that they would forgive the relatively minor infringements against personal liberty.

Which was why my friend from Almora was puzzled. Everybody thought Mrs. Gandhi would win. But the illiterate men who tended his orchard told him privately that they intended to vote for the opposition. Why? Well, they said, they appreciated all Mrs. Gandhi had done for the country but they were angry because recently, under the Emergency, the police had come at night to a neighboring village and carted off the village schoolmaster who had been openly critical of Sanjay Gandhi's male sterilization campaign. My friends wondered: could the polls and the experts be wrong? Could Mrs. Gandhi possibly lose?

Lose she did and overwhelmingly. Indira Gandhi even lost her own seat in Parliament. Her party was swept from office. The experts were scarlet-faced. But would she accept defeat? Would she mount a coup? She went quietly from office. I later spoke to several fairly ordinary Indians. How did they feel about the election results? A significant number said the same thing: they had voted against her only to teach her a lesson; they did not want her to lose but they did not want her to win so strongly that it would go to her head and give and her son too free a hand.

So the 1977 elections showed clearly that India was no pushover for totalitarianism even when it was exercised in the name of the masses. The voters firmly rejected it. They were not about to follow anyone blindly, not even the tough daughter of Jawaharlal Nehru, hero of independence. There clearly would be no Khomeinis in India, no Castros, no Qaddafis. Indians had reacted to a power grab, no matter how moderate, pretty much as Americans and Western Europeans would.

The opposition, now in power, made a terrible mess of things and Indira Gandhi was prime minister again in 1980. But she had learned a lesson: in her comeback period she ruled democratically, and was ruthless where she had to be, but she was always aware of the limitations on her ability to exercise power. In the end she was removed from power, undemocratically, by traitors' bullets. Even this tragedy did not seriously damage democracy in India. Although terrorism continued to flicker, the country regained its balance as surely as the United States did after the assassination of John Fitzgerald Kennedy. Mrs. Gandhi's successor, her older and sole surviving son, Rajiv, was confirmed overwhelmingly by the voters, but he is already learning the limits of power in a democracy.

A strange kind of democracy you may say. One family has ruled for thirty-five of the nearly forty years since independence. Rajiv Gandhi succeeded his mother; Indira Gandhi, after a lapse of a couple of years, succeeded her father, Jawaharlal Nehru, as prime minister; and Nehru reigned from independence until his death in 1964. Nehru's father, a wealthy Allahabad lawyer named Motilal

Nehru, had been head of the nationalist party long before independence. And although Mohandas K. Gandhi, the Mahatma, had
stirred and roused the masses to clamor for freedom, he never exercised real power, giving instead his blessing to Nehru. A royal family?
Four generations of them. Maybe, but Americans would do well to
remember how close our country came to making the Kennedys a
royal family. We should remember, too, that even Nehru had to live
with the constraints and frustrations that democracy and the rule of
law imposes upon a government.

How will history judge Indira Gandhi? One can only guess, and I
confess to being an admirer. Her flaws were obvious: her tendency
to surround herself with nonthreatening nonentities, her occasional
ruthlessness. She was political to her very soul; while campaigning on
an "eliminate poverty" platform, she did little to stimulate the economic growth that can alone reduce poverty in a developing economy. Politics interested her; economics was secondary.

Grant all this, but examine the other side of the balance sheet. This
fragile woman held India together. Given the centrifugal tendencies,
she may have been right to emphasize politics over economics. She
had a shrewd sense of timing, rarely making major moves until she
felt the swell of public opinion behind her. When she did move it
was with overwhelming force. Take the war with Pakistan over Bangladesh. She held her hand while millions of refugees poured into
India, while Pakistani troops committed atrocities in what was then
East Pakistan; she seemed to remain passive despite the clamor for
action from the electorate. But she was not being passive; just waiting
for her case to build. India won an overwhelming victory. Again with
the Sikhs: Hindus were screaming for the government to stop the
Sikh terrorists; why did she fail to act? She was giving the extremists
the rope they needed to hang themselves—which they obligingly did.
Foreigners, with scant knowledge of India, were surprised when she
ordered the army into the Golden Temple in Amritsar. But most
Indians wondered why she waited so long.

That India held together in spite of such horrendous strains is, I
think, largely due to Indira Gandhi's leadership. That she had to pay

with her life for this determination to hold the country together is a measure of the irrationality of the forces any Indian leader must deal with.

I spent an hour interviewing her in early 1984, when she had less than a year to live. She was in a philosophical mood, dwelling on the difficulties of working needed change in an ancient, impoverished society. I shall never forget her words: "Although India doesn't present the tidy picture we would like to have, you can't deny the forward movement." No, you can't. Nor can you deny her dominating presence in that movement.

One of the greatest obstacles to forward movement is what Indians call communalism and we, in slightly different context, call racism. Both are more often swear words than accurate descriptions of attitudes. When an Indian deplores communalism he means the practice of favoring one's own community over other communities, putting community before nation. Communalism, carried to extremes, leads to bloody riots. In practice, the term is almost always coupled with "Hindu," since the Hindus, being 80 percent of the population, are expected to be more tolerant than the minorities—for whom one is supposed to make allowances. One is supposed to be particularly gentle with Muslims and solicitous of their sensibilities. Since the central government is bound by the very Constitution to secularism, any assertion of Hindu rights or of Hindu virtues tends to be regarded as communalism. Thus we see the spectacle of an overwhelming majority having to behave with great restraint in its own land. When Sikh extremists were massacring innocent Hindus in the Punjab, throwing bombs into wedding parties, and pulling travelers from buses and hacking them to pieces, a devotion to secularism forced many Indian intellectuals into a position of criticizing Mrs. Gandhi's government for ignoring the "legitimate demands" of the Sikhs— although nobody really knew what these demands were.

Ridiculous as these arguments sometimes become, there is virtue in them. They force the majority to lean over backward to protect the rights of minorities. That India's overwhelming Hindu majority accepts, though sometimes grumblingly, these restraints is one more sign of India's underlying commitment to tolerance and to democracy.

With regard to the question of the Sikhs, I disagree with Pranay Gupte. It seems to me that Mrs. Gandhi could not negotiate effectively with the Sikhs because the moderate decent Sikhs dithered while murderous fanatics emerged from the shadows of Sikhdom. Nobody can negotiate with the IRA provos, the Red Brigades, or Khomeini terrorists—and nobody could conduct rational negotiations with the Sikh killers. In May of 1985 a remnant of the terrorists surfaced and showed their prowess by massacring innocent people. In so doing they put their own people in jeopardy from revenge-seeking Hindus. Deliberately so. Your average Sikh is a loyal and proud Indian; he or she cannot support a movement whose main support comes from a reactionary fringe of their community. The terrorist game is to incite Hindu against Sikh so that the mass of Sikhs will be driven into the extremist arms. It is a filthy game and I hope it does not work.

Remember this about the Sikhs: they are no downtrodden minority but a group who by dint of hard work and common sense have earned an economically and politically privileged position in India. They are an admirable people ill-served by a rotten leadership; one is tempted to think of Germany in the 1930s. What is sad is that many Sikhs in Britain and the United States, secure in their sanctuaries, egged on and financed the fanatical leadership and helped bring suffering on their people in India.

Americans who know little about India are frequently antagonized by India's foreign policy. India calls herself a democracy, yet on international issues aligns more frequently with the Soviet Union than with the United States. Why has India not taken a stronger stand against the Soviet invasion of neighboring Afghanistan? I put that question to Indira Gandhi during my interview with her last year. Her answer, though not entirely satisfactory, had a certain logic. She said that, quite simply, the Soviet Union had been a great friend of India. That is hard to deny. The Soviets have sold India oil below the world market price, and they sell sophisticated arms that the United States denies to India. When India gets in international trouble its government can almost always count on the Soviets to support it in international forums. Moreover, the Soviets have carefully abstained from encouraging the strong Indian Communist parties from turning violent in what is clearly an explosive situation. Obviously, the Soviets do not act out of the goodness of their hearts. With India as an ally of sorts, Soviet claims to be a friend of the nonaligned countries sounds less hollow. And it is worth something for the Soviets to keep India out of the Western camp.

As an American friend of India, of course I resent this hobnobbing with a superpower that is the declared enemy of political freedom. I resent, too, the frequent portrayals in the Indian press of the United States as a rambunctious bully and cesspool of moral decadence. However, when I pointed this out last year to an American Embassy man in New Delhi, he smiled and said: "Okay, but look at the long lines outside the U.S. visa office. You won't find any lines outside the Soviet visa office." True, and the few Indians I met in Moscow a few years ago looked miserable and out of place. Contrast this with the hundreds of thousands who prosper in the United States and now feel at home there as in their native Punjab or Andhra Pradesh or Kerala.

From the Indian viewpoint, the so-called East–West struggle is not the primary issue. The primary issues are the political vulnerabilities of India's geographical position, its struggle for economic development and a deeply felt if possibly exaggerated desire to continue to be militarily much stronger than Pakistan.

Keeping this in mind, we would be wise not to expect too much of the young government of Rajiv Gandhi. In the economic sphere he will certainly move India away from some of the bureaucratic socialism that has hobbled the nation's economic growth. His grandfather, Jawaharlal Nehru, believed in socialism à la London School of Economics. His mother, Indira Gandhi, was to some degree imbued with her father's ideas. Rajiv belongs to a generation for whom socialism is synonymous with corruption, bungling, chronic inefficiency, and oppression. His sympathies lie clearly with the West. But he will have to move slowly to a freer economy because this, after all, is a democracy.

Rajiv Gandhi will probably abandon his mother's nasty habit of blaming the CIA for everything from lack of rain to communal riots ("CIA" is a curse word in India; if the KGB even exists you wouldn't know it from reading the Indian papers). The bigger reality, though, is that he will be unable to break India's close trade, military, and international political association with the Soviet Union. Some people had unrealistic expectations for a reorientation of Indian foreign policy under Rajiv. They were surprised when Rajiv went to Moscow in May, praised the Soviets, skirted the Afghan issue, and took a swipe or two at the United States. That's realpolitik. In the long run, India's survival as a democracy is more important to world freedom than Indian support for U.S. policies in the United Nations.

It is almost impossible to end an essay like this without comparing India with China, ancient civilizations both, similarly afflicted by too many people and too little capital. China has gone the Marxist-Leninist way, India the democratic way. Which has done better? By just about any standard I would say India. We currently see the Chinese moving cautiously toward a freer economy—which means a freer society. In the meantime, India has managed to avoid paying the terrible price in human suffering that China had to pay during the failed Cultural Revolution. So far as economics are concerned, I see no evidence that China's industrial and agricultural progress has been faster than India's. Totalitarianism has brought China more misery than benefit; democracy has cost India something but has brought great benefits.

How does one measure human happiness in the mass? I do not know. But I suspect that in human happiness, as well as in real gross national product, India's has been the better path. May India stay on that path and may we in the West, whatever our differences, help her stay on it.

What happens now to the Third World's only major working democracy? Much is hopeful but the population figures, projected a few years out, are sheer horror. With the obstetricians and midwives working overtime, with the population growing 15 million souls a year, will the generation that Rajiv Gandhi represents be able to maintain democracy? In the chapters that follow, Pranay Gupte tries to provide some answers.

Born and raised in India, Gupte is transplanted to New York where he distinguished himself at a relatively young age in the highly competitive business of newspaper and magazine reporting and book writing. As an author, and as a New York Times foreign correspondent, he has traveled and reported widely in Africa, China, Iran, Cuba, and just about any other place you can mention.

Like Rajiv Gandhi, who belongs to the same generation, Pranay Gupte represents a new and worldly India. He and I disagree on a number of points, the Sikh troubles being one. Our differences are not so much philosophical as generational. He, being younger, is less patient with injustice and corruption; and I, being older, tend to take a longer view. Yet I firmly believe that what he reports here on the human face of democratic India is of great importance to those of us who are both worried and hopeful about the future of the free world.

PROLOGUE

"This Is Vengeance"

THAT morning, I went to see my father in his hospital room in Bombay. A doctor had already told him about the shooting of Mrs. Gandhi. He pointed to a sheet of paper on which he had written something. Since his tracheotomy he had lost his voice.

"I knew this would happen," my father wrote. "It was destined on the day she launched the attack on the Golden Temple in Amritsar. This is vengeance."

"Vengeance?" I said.

"What do you expect?" my father wrote out on his shiny white pad. "You send in troops to the temple, you take untold lives. You don't know how fanatical Sikhs are. What is the Biblical saying—an eye for an eye, a tooth for a tooth? This is one life avenged for a thousand lives taken in June. But this life was worth more than all of them. This life was priceless."

"How do you know she is dead?" I asked. The early reports had only said that the prime minister had been shot and wounded in her garden by two Sikh security guards.

"Vengeance," my father wrote, slowly. "When you shoot someone in vengeance, you shoot to kill. She must be dead. What a tragedy, what a loss to this nation. Nehru's daughter dead. What will happen to India now?"

INTRODUCTION

India After Indira

THE murder of Indira Gandhi in her own garden by two trusted Sikh security guards on October 31, 1984, changed forever the political landscape of India. It touched off a holocaust in which thousands of ordinary Sikhs were massacred by Hindu mobs. The very idea of secularism, ardently espoused by Mrs. Gandhi's father, Jawaharlal Nehru, and so eloquently enshrined in the Indian Constitution, was suddenly threatened. Government in the capital city of New Delhi was paralyzed. The question on everyone's mind was: will India, the world's biggest democracy, survive as one nation?

On the day that the prime minister was assassinated, I happened to be in Bombay. There was no massive outpouring of grief in India's biggest commercial city for Mrs. Gandhi, nor in most other places across this huge country. There was, of course, alarm over the brutal manner in which she was murdered by her own security guards, and Sikhs at that—but about Indira Gandhi herself there was a noticeable ambivalence. Shops and offices shut down, and people welcomed the opportunity to go home early. Other than her Congress Party associates and sycophants who now stood to be deprived of her patronage, most people simply did not shed tears for her.

I recalled the day Mrs. Gandhi's father, Jawaharlal Nehru, India's first prime minister, died in 1964. I was in high school then. The whole nation shook with shock and sadness; people cried openly. Nehru, the father of modern India, drew hero worship and affection from the masses as no one before him, perhaps not even Mahatma Gandhi, Nehru's mentor and the man who more than any other helped obtain for India her independence after one hundred and fifty years of British colonial rule. Nehru's daughter was less loved by ordinary Indians, although there were periods—after the 1971 victory over in the Bangladesh War, for instance—when Indira Gandhi enjoyed overwhelming popular support. She lacked his public warmth, his affability, and his gift of laughter. She lacked his conviction that ultimately people would respond to enlightened leadership with good civic behavior. Throughout her years of stewardship, Indira Gandhi came across mostly as a grim woman of unbridled ambition who would stop at nothing to gain and consolidate power.

There was more to it than that. Both Mahatma Gandhi—who was not related to Indira Gandhi—and Nehru gave enough play to the essential plurality of India; they sought consensus, they solicited diverse counsel, including from those politically and ideologically opposed to their own positions. These tactics obtained for Nehru, especially, widespread popular admiration. His daughter, instead, had imposed on the national scene the will of one person. It was, of course, a matter of style, and maybe of circumstance. Rajni Kothari, one of India's most distinguished political scientists, puts it this way: "That she wanted 'national unity' and strove for it, there need be no doubt. But the politics that she pursued to achieve her goal left deep scars on the country's communal, regional, and political framework. One reason why many of her admirers, as well as some among her critics, thought that there was no alternative to Mrs. Gandhi was that she had succeeded in creating a number of problems that she convinced everyone only she could handle. Now she is gone but the problems are very much there."

What Indira Gandhi did since her swearing-in as prime minister on January 24, 1966, was to undertake a definite transformation in the manner in which political power was exercised in India. Rather than seek popular and secular appeal as Nehru had, she often sought to rouse—however subtly—the chauvinistic sentiments of the country's Hindu majority, especially in her last years. Hindus constitute nearly 80 percent of India's population of nearly 800 million people, and Mrs. Gandhi considered their electoral support vital to her political survival. "My father was a statesman, I am a political woman," Mrs. Gandhi once said, in a rare moment of candor. "My father was a saint, I am not."

The name of her game was always political survival. She moved from her father's policy of seeking national consensus to one of confrontation. Confrontation, of course, was her way of keeping her opponents constantly off-guard. The creation of problems was a key aspect of her style—because then she could demonstrate that only she could solve those problems. So what Indians were left with were situations like the Punjab, where Mrs. Gandhi refused to grant relatively straightforward demands by Sikh leaders for more economic benefits for a state that continues to be India's granary. She refused to accept the legitimacy of an opposition government in another strategic border state, Kashmir, and she actively undermined and subsequently toppled that administration. She alienated the sensitivities of southerners when she authorized a clumsy—and unsuccessful—attempt to overthrow a legitimately elected opposition government in the state of Andhra Pradesh. In short, Indira Gandhi could tolerate no opposition of any kind: she wanted to be unchallenged. It was not necessary to create these problems, and Mrs. Gandhi was not able to manage them—and now they remain to haunt her son and successor, Rajiv Gandhi.

In the end, Indira Gandhi fell victim to the very poisons she injected into the Indian system. And so, in the days following her assassination, India mourned, but it did not cry for Mrs. Gandhi.

It occured to me that October day that the assassination of Indira Gandhi in her New Delhi garden nevertheless brought to an end a special era, just as Nehru's death by natural causes at the age of seventy-four had. It was an era dominated by an ongoing confrontation between Mrs. Gandhi and the opposition parties, but it was also the era of a charismatic leader whose style and character had been forged in the freedom struggle against the British. Later that day, October 31, it was announced that Mrs. Gandhi's son, the forty-year-old Rajiv Gandhi, would become prime minister. His ascension has opened the door for a generation of political leaders who were born or who grew up after independence in modern India and who are likely to be more technologically oriented and receptive to modern business strategies than Mrs. Gandhi and politicians of her generation, who were encrusted in outdated socialism.

On December 24 and 27, nearly 300 million voters participated in elections for the national Parliament—and Rajiv Gandhi's ruling Congress Party won an unprecedented 401 out of 508 seats contested. The young Gandhi, a former pilot with Indian Airlines, the main domestic carrier, had campaigned promising change, but he provided few specifics. When the election results were announced on the morning of December 29, the stunning majority that Indian voters handed to Rajiv Gandhi was widely interpreted not as an endorsement of Indira Gandhi's policies, nor only as a sympathy vote. Gandhi was seen as having received a mandate to institute accelerated change; he was seen as the man to fulfill the aspirations of a young population, 75 percent of whom were born after Independence. For this post-Independence generation, Rajiv Gandhi, despite his political inexperience, is clearly India's hope for the future.

His triumph also reflected the widespread disenchantment of Indian voters with the national opposition parties, which they see as being disunited, petty-minded, and aimless. It was the first time since independence in 1947 that a massive negative vote had been cast by Indians not against a government in power but against an opposition. It was not an especially heartening campaign: more than $300 million was said to have been spent by Gandhi's ruling Congress Party, among other things on an advertising spree that stirred up voters against any public dissidence by raising the specter of disintegration —the opposition parties were cleverly portrayed as promoting disunity at a time of deepening national crisis over issues such as

Punjab and Kashmir; the Congress message was that the Indian nation was in danger and that Rajiv Gandhi's party alone was capable of saving India from anarchy.

I followed the December election campaign quite closely. It was clear that the Congress Party appealed to the deep-rooted communal instincts of India's Hindu majority, particularly in the so-called Hindi-speaking Belt in the states of Uttar Pradesh, Haryana, Bihar, Madhya Pradesh, and Rajasthan. It was not just that India's 14 million Sikhs felt alienated; India's Muslim population of nearly 80 million—which is the largest in the world after Indonesia, Bangladesh, and Pakistan—felt similarly shut out of the political process.

Many Indians I met in recent months talked about their gathering uneasiness with what was happening in the country's mainstream politics. They said that after a long period of pluralistic existence, the very spirit of accommodation and tolerance on which the Hindus prided themselves was being abused. During my travels I met Hindus who said openly, and with resentment, that in fact it was the Hindus who were being shafted! These Hindus said that, in effect, India's "minorities"—from Muslims and Sikhs to tribal communities in Assam—were being pampered. I was surprised how many Hindus echoed the sentiments of one Calcutta brahmin who said to me: these minorities have had a good thing going for them in secular India—they got the benefits of state patronage, they got special job slots and educational privileges, and here we were, the so-called majority, left high and dry.

Rajiv Gandhi's message to the electorate was not just of Mister Clean but of a shrewd combination of that image with the rhetoric of confrontation of a nation in peril. His election rhetoric was cleverly packaged: the opposition was illegitimate, we can do without one; there were serious threats from Pakistan and China, India's traditional enemies, and from the unidentified "foreign hand" that guided antinational forces. Gandhi's advertising campaign was prepared by a Bombay firm called Rediffusion: it was a slick, hip, and hyped-up campaign. It worked, and Indians gave Rajiv Gandhi an unprecedented mandate.

His mother's death had brought him to leadership. However, I believe that had Mrs. Gandhi voluntarily retired from politics, and had the trauma of her death not gripped the nation, such a massive mandate would not have been possible. The challenge Rajiv Gandhi faces now is the need to overcome his mother's political legacy of communal discord and regional hostilities.

Indira Gandhi was a consummate practitioner of the politics of confrontation, both along communal and regional lines, and within the country's bewilderingly complex party system. She left behind an atmosphere of anxiety and insecurity about where India was headed. Rajiv Gandhi does not possess his mother's overwhelming personality, nor her charisma, and probably not her ruthlessness. So how is he going to do it? How is he going to tackle the problem of Sikh separatism in the Punjab? Of tribal discord in Assam? Of Muslim dissatisfaction in Kashmir? How is he going to reassure India's diverse minorities that their welfare will be looked after? How is he going to arrive at some working accommodation with Pakistan and Bangladesh and Sri Lanka, neighboring nations that have long felt that Big Sister India behaves like a bully and actively works to destabilize their own nations under one pretext or another?

And what about the thorny business of relations between the central government and the states? India's twenty-two states are certain to demand greater devolutionary powers, and they are certain to ask for a larger share of tax revenues (recognizing this, Rajiv Gandhi's new budget, which was unveiled on March 16, promised an increase of 39 percent in federal assistance to state coffers). These states, after years of being treated like stepchildren by Indira Gandhi, are certain to demand more equitable treatment. The only way that Rajiv Gandhi will be able to deal effectively with such demands is to federalize India's political system even more and to decentralize authority. But his mother, who was indifferent to the question of states' rights, has left behind an extremely centralized system.

The great theme in India in the years ahead is likely to be one of the management of power in a multicultural nation–state given to what the Indian press likes to call fissiparous tendencies. Will Rajiv

Gandhi be willing to devolve power when his mother has left him a heavily centralized administration? Will he interpret his huge election victory as a justification for more concentrated authority in New Delhi, or as an opportunity to share power with the states? Will the Delhi–states power nexus consist of an iron chain emanating out of the prime minister's office in the capital's magnificent sandstone complex from where Britain's viceroys ruled so haughtily barely forty years ago? Or will this nexus consist of a silken thread?

It was to find answers to such questions that I undertook an extensive reporting trip through India in the weeks following the assassination of Indira Gandhi. What gifts did she bequeath to her country? I wanted to see for myself what lasting impact her style had had on the lives of everyday Indians, and where they now saw their lives going. I wanted, if not a portrait, then at least a sense of where my country stood at a particular point in time.

I traveled from the snow-capped heights of Kashmir in the north to the sandy beaches and dazzling green rice paddies of Kerala in the south. I went to villages, small towns, and big cities. I talked to people of all religions and ethnic persuasions. I observed first-hand the December 1984 national elections in which Rajiv Gandhi's ruling Congress Party won by a landslide unseen in all the years since India became independent from Britain in 1947. Most authors suffer from a twenty-twenty hindsight, and now of course I wish I had visited all twenty-two states and had spoken to more people in the rural areas.

I rediscovered the hugeness of my land—1,269,340 square miles, or twice the size of Alaska. I heard the cadences and cacophonies of India's fifteen major languages and of many of its estimated 874 regional dialects.

Everywhere there were crowds: when India achieved independence in 1947, there were 350 million Indians; now there are more than twice that number, and they are procreating so rapidly that in another fifty years there will be three times as many Indians as there are today. Everywhere there also were cattle: India has 200 million of them, or a quarter of the world's bovine population. More than seven tenths of Indians depend on farming for their livelihood, but although agriculture constitutes almost 45 percent of India's gross national product of $180 billion, farmers enjoy a per capita income of considerably less than the national average of $250.

I found that fewer than half of India's 576,000 villages—where 70 percent of the country's population lives—were electrified. Literacy was also low in villages: only one woman in four can read and write; only half of India's males have gone to primary school. I was told that more than a third of the world's illiterates live in India. Despite widespread health care, the infant mortality in India is 129 per 1,000 —one of the highest in the world—compared with 92 in Brazil, 56 in China, 28 in the Soviet Union, and 14 in the United States and Britain. Life expectancy is 54 years, according to the government, but Indians in many parts of the country survive fewer years than that.

I found out that there were 100 million "untouchables" in India, the economically backward and socially shunned people whom Mahatma Gandhi called Harijans, or God's children. Of India's current estimated population of nearly 800 million people, 85 percent are Hindus and 10 percent are Muslims; there are also 20 million Christians, 14 million Sikhs, 5 million Buddhists, and almost 4 million Jains, members of a sect who abhor violence so much that most wouldn't even dream of crushing a cockroach.

I was encouraged by people's general and perhaps superficial optimism concerning Rajiv Gandhi, who was widely perceived as a young and fresh-faced man untainted by the corrosive political practices of his predecessor and mother. I was also encouraged by the fact that in a period of general political decline, missed economic opportunities, and authoritarian tendencies under Mrs. Gandhi, popular Indian culture nonetheless flourished: the fine arts and performing arts were thriving robustly; and several grassroots organizations had sprouted to serve everyday needs of deprived people in towns and villages, whether such needs concerned the supply of potable water or the provision of legal advice.

I repeatedly asked Indians about the effect Indira Gandhi's helmsmanship had on their individual lives. One bitterly cold evening in

New Delhi, Romesh Thapar, an incisive political and social analyst, shared tea and his thoughts with me. "Indira Gandhi has left behind an extraordinary record of mercurial, manipulative, conspiratorial, and brilliant leadership," he said. "Everything she did affected the entire political system." But how did her actions touch India's everyday people? Had she been an agent of change for the better?

I posed other questions as well, questions that sometimes rose out of conversations as I moved through the country: How did a society that set out on a particular model of integration find its secular vision collapsing? How has popular disenchantment with traditional politics led to a growing belief in the value of modern managerial techniques to bail the country out of its woes? Will "technology and science" —the new buzzwords in India—really clean up the country's sociopolitical mess? I looked into the economic "liberalization" that was being instituted: how widely will India open itself to Western investment, and how useful will such investment be for India's economy? I felt that unless the purchasing power of ordinary Indians was increased, the standard of living in the country simply would not improve. Would the new economic "liberalization" quickly increase the purchasing power of the common man?

I asked whether the enormous problems of poverty were being tackled correctly. Had "development" failed in India? Had land reform worked? Has the emphasis on rapid heavy industrialization led to intolerable deforestation and destruction of the ecology? How can such institutions as Parliament, the police, and the judiciary, which were weakened during Indira Gandhi's rule, now be revitalized and strengthened? A big question: With India expected to contain more than two billion people within the next fifty years, what urgent steps will be taken to slow down population growth without violating human rights?

And perhaps the biggest question: Will Prime Minister Rajiv Gandhi be able to hold India together?

What follows in this book is an account of the India I saw at a particular point in time. By experiencing—or, I should say, re-experiencing—the heat and dust of the places I traveled to, I was able to understand freshly and interpret India in the light of the above questions. But India is exhausting!

My starting point is the day Indira Gandhi was assassinated. Two lines of inquiry suggested themselves at the very outset: although the identities of her assassins have been established, why was Indira Gandhi really killed? And will India survive? I have highlighted two regions, the Punjab and Kashmir, which preoccupied Mrs. Gandhi and whose politics were a source of frustration for her. I have reconstructed the assassination with details I obtained during my research; I was myself a witness to some of the ugly aftermath. The manner in which Indians reacted to the assassination sheds light not only on the cultural, geographical, and political diversity of India—but also on the kind of society Indira Gandhi had helped to shape during the long years she was on center stage. If October 31, 1984, was a day of darkness for India, the days that followed were darker still.

Nations, like people, do overcome tragedies, of course, and life does go on. National attention in India is already focused on different things. The Indian cricket team, after being thrashed by a visiting English squad, traveled to Australia in March and surprised everybody by winning a "World Series" championship—defeating, among others, the same English team that had inflicted such humiliating losses on the Indians only weeks before. The Indian captain, Sunil Gavaskar, became—at least for the moment—as popular in his home country as Prime Minister Gandhi: only a short while back, Gavaskar was widely vilified as the man who had lost India's honor in cricket!

Rajiv Gandhi came out on March 16 with a $82.7 billion budget that called for drastic reduction in personal and corporate taxes, and a paring of the bureaucratic regulations that have long hampered industry. The prime minister says he wants to assist the corporate sector to mobilize resources through the stock market and thus reduce its dependence on public financial institutions. In India's business circles, the Gandhi budget was hailed as an entrepreneur's dream. The *Wall Street Journal,* in an editorial titled "Rajiv Reagan," said: "The budget amounts to a minor revolution for a country long enamored of the socialist mirage, and it continues a revolution in economic ideas that we've noticed in much of the developing world." I, for one, whole-heartedly endorse Rajiv Gandhi's seeming preference for free enterprise. All over the Third World there is the growing realization that a state-controlled, centralized economy does not promote rapid growth. The license system breeds corruption; socialism in the Third World has had a proven record of failure.

The Indian newspapers are applauding the Gandhi budget, but some of them are also warning of the consequences of rapid industrialization and inadequate monitoring of such growth. The newspapers are still filled with articles about various investigations into the Bhopal tragedy in December 1984, in which more than two thousand people were killed when methyl isocyanate, a deadly chemical used to make pesticides, escaped into the air from a faulty valve at a Union Carbide plant: it was the largest industrial accident in history, and in addition to those killed, thousands more men, women, and children were permanently blinded. Union Carbide has been accused of gross negligence in the maintenance of its Bhopal plant.

Elections were held in early March for legislative assemblies in eleven states, and Gandhi's Congress Party retained control of eight of those states but was unable to make inroads in the key southern provinces of Karnataka and Andhra Pradesh, which are controlled by opposition parties. In subsequent by-elections to Parliament and states assemblies in April, Gandhi's Congress Party was able to capture only nine out of 28 seats. Already, the political honeymoon has ended. Gandhi got some sobering news in Bombay in the spring: his Congress party was routed in the local municipal elections, winning only 37 of the 170 seats in the governing civic council of India's most important commercial city. The Congress lost to a local Hindu-based communal party called the Shiv Sena, which has frequently spread hateful propaganda against Muslims. The loss was interpreted not necessarily as a diminishing of Rajiv Gandhi's national popularity but as a sign that in municipal polls parish-pump politics are often more important than national issues. The Shiv Sena's campaign emphasized that Bombay, long a cosmopolitan city that drew hundreds of thousands of out-of-state migrants each year, was losing its native Maharastrian characteristics—and that "native" Bombayites were being muscled out of rightful jobs by the newcomers; the Shiv Sena wants a ban on the inflow of people from other states into the city, and its leaders also want to expel out-of-state emigrants who moved to Bombay in the last decade.

The clangor and clamor of India continues unabated. In the western state of Gujarat, troops were brought in to maintain law and order following riots to protest job and education quotas for disavantaged castes and tribes. The riots led to a statewide strike by Gujarat's 700,000 civil servants; and in a bizarre turn of events, what had started off as a students' protest against the local government's affirmative-action policy, turned into an ugly confrontation between Hindus and Muslims. Scores of people died in the agitation.

And the Punjab is heating up again. The Gandhi government, in an effort to break the impasse over the Punjab, released from jail several top Sikh leaders; Rajiv Gandhi even promised to hold an inquiry into the massacre of Sikhs following the assassination of his mother last year, and, in response to demands by leading members of the Sikh community in the Punjab, he lifted the ban on a radical group called the All-India Sikh Students Federation. But Sikh terrorism escalated in May: more than a dozen bombs were set off in New Delhi, and in the neighboring states of Haryana, Uttar Pradesh, and Rajasthan. Nearly a hundred people, some of them children, were killed. Officials said that Sikh terrorists had once again mounted a well-coordinated operation to create communal disharmony. Some analysts are saying that the Sikh radicals want to incite Hindu revenge against the general Sikh population in order to create chaos—so that the only solution then would be the establishment of an independent Sikh state in what is now the Indian Punjab. Once again, too, suspicion has flared against Pakistan: government officials as well as media pundits have renewed their contention that the Sikh extremists were being convertly inspired, financed and assisted by Pakistani agents. Many intelligence officials are now also saying that fund-raising for radical Sikh activity has been accelerated in the United States, Canada, Britain, and Scandinavia. These officials point to the fact that many Sikhs in these countries are affluent businessmen, farmers, and professionals who were drawn to the Khalistan cause by such events as the army assault on the Golden Temple and the holocaust against Indian Sikhs in the aftermath of the murder of Indira Gandhi.

Another troubling development was the disclosure that a fresh plot to assassinate Rajiv Gandhi had been set into motion in the United States by Sikh expatriates. William H. Webster, director of the Federal Bureau of Investigation, said in Washington on May 13 that his agency had foiled a plot by Sikh terrorists to kill Prime Minister Gandhi during his scheduled state visit to the United States in June 1985 to inaugurate the "Festival of India." These Sikhs, five of whom were arrested in May in New Orleans, also planned guerrilla-type operations against Indian diplomats and Indian government facilities, according to the F.B.I. These Sikhs had sworn vengeance against the Gandhi family for the invasion of the Golden Temple in June 1984. Indians once again began worrying that should anything happen to Rajiv Gandhi or any members of his family, there would be a new, and perhaps genocidal, bloodbath against the Sikhs in India. At about the same time that the Sikh plot in America came to light, the surviving assassin of Mrs. Gandhi, Satwant Singh, and two alleged coconspirators went on trial in New Delhi.

As if his plate weren't already heaped with domestic political and economic problems, Rajiv Gandhi has also had to contend with the growing ethnic strife in neighboring Sri Lanka. Guerrillas who have been fighting to establish an independent Tamil state in the northern region of the pear-shaped island nation raided majority Sinhalese areas in May and killed scores of people. The Sinhalese retaliated by murdering Tamils. The Indian government has long been suspected by the Sri Lankan administration of President Junius R. Jayewardene of aiding and harboring the Tamil guerrillas, although Rajiv Gandhi has denied any complicity. Still, India has to accept thousands of Tamil refugees who fled Sri Lanka; there are influential members of the Indian Parliament who say that the only way the Sri Lankan situation can be resolved is for India to militarily assist the Tamils to carve out their own state in northern Sri Lanka—much in the manner of the Bangladesh affair in 1971, when Indian troops, responding to pleas from local guerrillas who were fighting to break away from Pakistan, overran what was then East Pakistan and helped create the new nation of Bangladesh.

National attention is also focusing these days on Rajiv Gandhi's anticorruption campaign. There is talk of establishing special courts to try tax evaders. Income tax authorities have raided homes of many wealthy people to recover "black money"—illegally held currency that is supposed to account for more than a third of the cash now in circulation. There have been indictments handed up against officials accused of large-scale peculation and corruption. The chief executives of several top nationalized banks have been dismissed for their alleged role in granting multimillion-dollar unsecured loans to overseas friends who are suspected of absconding with the money.

Besides pledging a vigorous fight against corruption, Rajiv Gandhi and Company are now increasingly talking of a new scientific age in India, of the need to employ sophisticated computer technology and industrial methods to catapult India into the twenty-first century. Gandhi's budget, in fact, proposes extraordinary concessions—such as tax-free import of certain kinds of computers—for the scientific and technology communities. Change is in the air.

A long time ago, Rajiv Gandhi's illustrious grandfather, Jawaharlal Nehru, wrote: "To endeavor to understand and describe the India of today would be the task of a brave man—to say anything about tomorrow's India would verge on rashness."

I feel both brave and rash. What I saw and heard during my passage through India caused me to share the excitement that many of my friends said they felt in post-Indira India. There is a definite sense that a new era of a rejuvenated political leadership is here. There are those who see Rajiv Gandhi leading India well into the next century, barring another tragedy.

The India he leads remains, in global terms at least, among the poorest countries, yet one endowed with great resources that have not been sufficiently explored. India has 15.5 percent of the world's population, but only 1.5 percent of its income. Neighboring China is able to produce 400 million tons of food grains annually with 100 million hectares of cultivable land; but India, with 166 million hectares of cultivable land, can produce just about 150 million tons. India is said to possess the largest acreage of such crops as cotton-seed, peanut, and flax-seed—but its yield is the lowest in the world! While such Asian neighbors as Singapore, Taiwan, South Korea, and Hong Kong raced ahead because of their market-oriented policies of economic development, India stagnated because of misguided and often foolish economic policies that were shaped by socialist statism. The number of known jobless people in India today is nearly 50 million, with 130,000 new entrants to the unemployment rolls every month. The potential here for new social tensions is tremendous.

Protection of the market seemed like a reasonable idea in the aftermath of Independence. The notion that unbridled free enterprise would inevitably lead to economic colonialism won many adherents in the first flush of freedom. But the statist system quickly deteriorated; corruption became endemic in India's "Socialist" society. It got to a point where one needed to bribe railway and airline clerks to get tickets on government-run trains and planes. The "licence Raj" of the Nehru–Shastri–Indira Gandhi years spawned an all-encompassing subculture where businessmen, for instance, spent their time and resources fashioning contacts in government and learning how to bend the law. The "licence Raj" created a national climate where the most appropriate technology for India's development became—a modern mind! There was, of course, a positive side to all this: Indians came to realize that lack of competition was a menace. By the time Rajiv Gandhi came on the national scene, everyone was desperately looking for a fresh breeze, for a way out of the general economic mess.

The question in my mind is whether Gandhi will falter as the immensity of India and its problems engulfs him. And the answer to this will depend a great deal on whether Rajiv Gandhi eventually settles down to governing through a sycophantic coterie as his mother did, or through a multilayered and self-renewing apparatus of intellectuals, technocrats, and specialists of merit. Given the right environment, India and Indians can achieve extraordinary things.

A new political era may have dawned—but the challenges are also economic in nature. Will this new era really bring better times for India's teeming millions, who have waited patiently and who have been kept hoping for so long? And how soon will the better times arrive?

Part One

THE NEWS

1

The Assassination of
Indira Gandhi

O N the morning of Wednesday, October 31, 1984, Indira
Gandhi woke up, as usual, at six o'clock and rang for her valet,
Nathuram, who fetched her a pot of piping hot tea. Mrs. Gandhi,
barely a month short of her sixty-eighth birthday, then quickly
scanned a variety of local Hindi and English-language newspapers—
another daily practice. Most of the papers carried front-page articles
about her swing, the previous day, through the eastern state of Orissa,
where she had made a number of appearances at political rallies. It
was dully cold in her bedroom—few Delhi homes are equipped with
central heating—and the portable electric heater seemed to work
unsatisfactorily. Mrs. Gandhi rose and spent a few minutes on limber-
ing yoga exercises, bathed, put on a bright orange saree, and joined
her grandchildren Priyanka and Rahul, and Rajiv Gandhi's wife,
Sonia, for breakfast. Rajiv was in West Bengal that morning on a
political mission for his mother, the prime minister, who was widely
expected to announce soon the date for India's national parliamentary elections.

The morning meal consisted, as usual, of toast, cereal, boiled potatoes, freshly squeezed orange juice, eggs, and tea, after which the children would set off for school. Mrs. Gandhi asked Rahul and Priyanka how they felt, for the previous evening the car in which they had been riding was rammed by a van that shot through a red light not far from the prime minister's official residence at One Safdarjung Road in New Delhi. The children weren't hurt, and the security staff attached to the prime minister's house reported that there was nothing sinister about the accident. As Mrs. Gandhi spoke with the children, who seemed in good spirits, her aides entered the dining room. One was Rajendra Kumar Dhawan, a short, pleasant forty-seven-year-old man with slickly oiled hair that appeared permanently plastered down on his scalp. Dhawan had served Mrs. Gandhi for almost twenty years and was probably her most trusted subordinate. It was nearly time to leave for her appointment, Dhawan told the prime minister, who smiled, then kissed and hugged her grandchildren, and walked into her small study to flip through a pile of government files that Dhawan had already placed on her desk.

On her desk, too, was something Mrs. Gandhi had written in her own hand. It was a sort of last will and testament. Of her aides, only Dhawan had seen it, even though the document wasn't quite complete. He had once asked her about it, and Mrs. Gandhi had merely shrugged the question away. But Dhawan, like some others who worked in close proximity to the prime minister, was aware that she had lately seemed rather distracted, and once or twice had even reflected aloud about the possibility that some harm might befall her. Mrs. Gandhi's mood worried people like Dhawan, who had been concerned about her safety since the Indian Army's assault in June 1984 on Sikhism's holiest shrine, the Golden Temple in Amritsar. The army had successfully flushed out the Sikh terrorists who had holed up in the temple, but not before hundreds of men, women, and children who came as pilgrims to Amritsar died in the crossfire between the terrorists and the military. Mrs. Gandhi had been determined not to yield to the terrorists' demand for a separate nation, which they wanted carved out of the northwestern state of Punjab, India's granary. Although the majority of the country's 14 million

Sikhs did not support the separatists, the army's action in Amritsar was widely deplored in the Sikh community not only because of the loss of lives but also because of extensive damage to the Sikh shrine.

Among Mrs. Gandhi's aides, as among Indians all across this vast country of 800 million people, there was, since the Amritsar event, a growing conviction that it would be only a matter of time before Sikhs took revenge against the prime minister.

Was she herself seized by some premonition about her death?

Dhawan glanced quickly at the handwritten note. This is what Mrs. Gandhi had written:

"I have never felt less like dying and that calm and peace of mind is what prompts me to write what is in the nature of a will. If I die a violent death as some fear and a few are plotting, I know the violence will be in the thought and the action of the assassin, not in my dying—for no hate is dark enough to overshadow the extent of my love for my people and my country; no force is strong enough to divert me from my purpose and my endeavor to take this country forward.

"A poet has written of his 'love'—'How can I feel humble with the wealth of you beside me?' I can say the same of India. I cannot understand how anyone can be an Indian and not be proud—the richness and infinite variety of our composite heritage, the magnificence of the people's spirit, equal to any disaster or burden, firm in their faith, gay spontaniety even in poverty and hardship."

Dhawan reminded Mrs. Gandhi of her first appointment of the morning, which was with Peter Ustinov, the actor. Ustinov had planned to produce a documentary on her and, indeed, had followed the prime minister around on some of her travels across India. The feature on Mrs. Gandhi was to be part of a series tentatively called *Ustinov's People.* Now he had scheduled a final interview with Mrs. Gandhi and was waiting with his film crew on the lawns behind the Safdarjung Road residence, on the side facing Akbar Road. Mrs. Gandhi had a special liking for men and women of the arts, and Peter Ustinov was one of those whose career she had followed with interest. Moreover, Ustinov, a stout jolly Santa Clause in mufti, was heavily involved in a cause that the prime minister herself vigorously supported—the plight of children. In fact, Ustinov had come to India wearing two hats: as a film producer, and as a fundraiser for UNICEF, the United Nations Children's Fund. "I wanted to ask her how as a single child she came to terms with loneliness," Ustinov said later.

Ustinov's interview was scheduled for 9:20 A.M. He thought the Akbar Road lawn would be an ideal spot because of its picturesque location. It was a cool, late fall morning, with just a nip in the air, and the roses in Mrs. Gandhi's garden were in full bloom. Behind the lawn was the prime minister's residential office, where she often received visitors in the morning before her usual journey to the more formal prime ministerial office in South Block, near Parliament House; this building, and a tall hedge next to it, separated the Akbar Road area from Mrs. Gandhi's living quarters at One Safdarjung Road.

At 9:15, Mrs. Gandhi stepped out of her home, with Narain Singh, a New Delhi policeman, holding an umbrella over her head to shield her from the sun. Dhawan was behind them. And behind him were Rameshwar Dayal, a local police sub-inspector, and Nathuram, Mrs. Gandhi's valet. She walked briskly, as was her custom, toward the Akbar Road office. As she neared a hedge, she spotted Beant Singh, a Sikh policeman who had been part of her security guard for six years. She smiled at the twenty-eight-year-old Beant. The tall bearded Sikh was still attached to her personal security force because the prime minister herself had resisted pleas from aides to have him transferred in the wake of the assault on the Golden Temple. "I have nothing to fear from Sikhs," Mrs. Gandhi told them.

Beant moved up to Mrs. Gandhi, whipped out a pistol, pointed it at her, and fired three shots into her abdomen. Without a word, Mrs. Gandhi started to fall to the ground. But before her body slumped, another Sikh guard, Satwant Singh, twenty-one years old, emerged from the hedge and opened up with a Thompson automatic carbine. Mrs. Gandhi's body was nearly lifted from the ground by these powerful bullets; she spun around, then crashed to the ground. In the space of twenty seconds, thirty-two bullets had been pumped into her small, frail body. It was now 9:17 A.M.

The body lay on the ground for nearly a minute before anyone took action. Her bodyguards had dived for cover. Rameshwar Dayal had been shot in the thigh from the round fired by Satwant Singh. When Dhawan and the others rose, they saw Beant and Satwant standing with their hands raised; they had dropped their weapons.

"We have done what we set out to do," Beant Singh said, in Hindi. "Now you can do whatever you want to do."

But no one attempted to grab the assailants. Mrs. Gandhi's aides looked at her body and started shouting orders to one another. At this point, Sonia Gandhi ran out of the house barefoot and still in her dressing gown, her hazel-brown hair still wet from a wash.

"Mummy! My God! O Mummy!" Sonia screamed.

Then Sonia shouted: "Get a car!"

"Madam, there is an ambulance here," someone responded.

A specially equipped ambulance was parked near the Safdarjung Road exit; the vehicle was kept there on a twenty-four-hour stand-by for emergencies. But on this morning, with Mrs. Gandhi bleeding profusely and bits of her bones and flesh spattered on the ground, no one could find the ambulance driver. Someone said he'd gone off to get some tea; someone else said the driver hadn't reported for work at all; there were no keys in the ignition switch.

Sonia Gandhi and Rajendra Kumar Dhawan then lifted Mrs. Gandhi's body, with the assistance of Narain Singh, Nathuram, and Dinesh Bhatt, a security official, and carried her toward an Indian-made Ambassador car that was parked nearby. She was placed on the backseat, with Sonia cradling her head as she crouched on the floor. Dhawan, Bhatt, a house physician named Opeh, and an aide named M. L. Fotedar also got in. Dhawan ordered the driver to rush to the All-India Institute of Medical Sciences.

The institute was a good twenty minutes away by car; other medical facilities were closer to the prime minister's house, such as the Ram Manohar Lohia Hospital on Baba Khark Marg. But the institute, known locally as AIIMS, kept a special supply of Mrs. Gandhi's O group Rh negative blood type, along with her complete medical record. The Ambassador car darted toward AIIMS, but the mid-morning traffic was fairly heavy and it was not until ten o'clock that the vehicle finally reached the hospital, some four kilometers away from the prime minister's home. Dr. Opeh administered artificial respiration, but he could already see that there were few signs of life in Mrs. Gandhi.

Back at One Safdarjung Road, meanwhile, it had not occurred to anyone to telephone AIIMS to warn hospital authorities that Mrs. Gandhi was being brought there. Various security guards scurried about the area where Beant Singh and Satwant Singh still stood, their weapons on the ground. Then someone suggested that the two men be arrested. They were led off to a nearby guardhouse by members of the elite Indo-Tibetan Border Police. Within twenty minutes, shots were heard inside the guardhouse. Beant and Satwant both had been shot by their guards; Beant died instantly, while Satwant suffered serious injuries to his spine and kidneys. It was later explained by the government that the two Sikhs had tried to wrest away their guards' weapons in an effort to escape. But at least three officials present at the scene have testified that the Indo-Tibetan guards abused the Sikhs verbally and then shot them.

When the prime minister's car arrived at the emergency entrance of the All-India Institute of Medical Sciences, there was no reception committee. In fact, it took the sentries more than three minutes to even open the gates leading up to the emergency section, for the guards had not been informed that the prime minister was in critical condition. Once at the emergency unit, Dhawan and Fotedar jumped out to alert medical personnel that Mrs. Gandhi lay gravely wounded outside. But no stretcher could be found. Someone got hold of a hospital gurney.

As the body was placed on the gurney, the young intern in charge of the emergency room became hysterical.

"Madam! Madam!" he started shrieking, nearly collapsing over Mrs. Gandhi's crumpled, blood-covered body.

Another physician who was present in the room said to himself: "This cannot be Indira Gandhi. She looks like a child wrapped in a washerman's sheet. Is this really the prime minister of India?"

This doctor rushed to a house phone and dialed the number of the institute's senior cardiologist. Within minutes, a dozen of the institute's top physicians gathered in the emergency room, including Dr. J. S. Guleria, a veteran professor of medicine, and Dr. Balram, the senior cardiothoracic surgeon on duty that morning. They tried to massage Mrs. Gandhi's heart. A quick electrocardiogram test showed faint traces of a heartbeat.

"Her pupils were dilated—so we knew that her brain was already affected," one physician recalled later. "Even if we had clinically revived her, there already was permanent brain damage." There was no pulse. One medical aide inserted an endotracheal tube—a rubber tube that is pushed down the mouth and windpipe—to pump oxygen to Mrs. Gandhi's lungs, mainly to keep the brain alive. Two intravenous lines were set up for blood transfusion.

At this point, the decision was made to take Mrs. Gandhi to the eighth-floor operation theater. There, in Operation Theater Number Two, surgeons labored to remove bullets from her body. More than eighty pints of blood were pumped into her, or several times the body's normal blood content. The surgeons linked Mrs. Gandhi's body to a heart-lung machine, which assumed the function of pumping and purifying her blood. The surgeons wanted to ensure that her body's metabolism rate slowed down and that her blood pressure dropped—this was done through the heart-lung machine, which cooled the blood from the normal 37 degrees centigrade to 31 degrees.

Present in Operation Theater Number Two were the finest of the physicians and surgeons attached to the All-India Institute of Medical Sciences, which has long been the country's showcase medical teaching and research facility. In addition to Dr. Guleria and Dr. Balaram, there were cardiothoracic surgeons P. Venugopal and A. Sampat Kumar; and general surgeons Shukla, Dhawan, and M. M. Kapoor. The anaesthetist was G. R. Gode. They quickly found that the bullets Beant Singh and Satwant Singh pumped into her had ruptured the right lobe of Mrs. Gandhi's liver. There were at least twelve perforations in the large intestine and there was extensive damage to the small intestine. The heart was intact, but one lung was shot through. Blood vessels, arteries, and veins had burst. Bones and vertebrae were shattered. The spinal cord was severed.

Nothing that the surgeons could do would bring Indira Gandhi back to life.

"She was already far, far gone by the time she was brought to the Institute," one surgeon said later. "In fact, Mrs. Gandhi probably was dead by the time she hit the ground in her garden at Safdarjung Road."

At two-thirty that afternoon, five hours after she was shot in her garden, Indira Gandhi was officially declared dead.

On the morning of Wednesday, October 31, Vichitra Sharma was preparing to leave her home in New Delhi's Maharani Bagh for her office in Connaught Place, the capital's bustling downtown section. The thirty-year-old Sharma lives with her parents in one of Delhi's rich residential neighborhoods; it is uncommon for single women to live away from home, even in sophisticated urban India, and besides, Delhi at the moment was experiencing a dreadful housing crunch.

Vichitra Sharma is what her colleagues call a star. Her star shines at the *Hindustan Times,* one of Delhi's leading English-language dailies. She is a small woman, with large expressive eyes that can bore into a subject's face until he confesses all. Her reporting assignments have taken Sharma all over India, but in the last year or so she had been focusing especially on labor and political issues in Delhi. She had recently written an acclaimed series of articles on medical politics at the prestigious All-India Institute of Medical Sciences.

At ten-thirty on this morning, just as Sharma was about to step out of her parents' two-story house, the telephone rang. The caller was A. R. Wig, Sharma's immediate superior and the newspaper's "chief reporter." Wig asked Sharma to go immediately to the All-India Institute of Medical Sciences.

"Indira Gandhi's been hurt," he said. "We think she was taken to the Institute. You know a lot of people there. Why don't you try and get in there and see what you can find out?"

Sharma recalls that her first reaction to Wig's call was that perhaps the prime minister had been injured at some political rally. Sharma was scheduled to cover one of Mrs. Gandhi's forthcoming campaign swings through the neighboring state of Uttar Pradesh, and a colleague at the *Hindustan Times* had cautioned her to expect stone-throwing incidents in that politically volatile province where Mrs. Gandhi was not universally popular.

Sharma hailed a taxi outside her home. The thirteen-kilometer ride to the institute took nearly thirty minutes. There were no signs of any unusual activity at the hospital's gate, no crowds had gathered. Sharma wandered for a few minutes around the institute's academic block, hoping to spot a familiar face. She met a young physician who'd been a source for her recent articles on the institute. He'd been in the emergency room assisting the surgeons who tried to revive the mortally wounded prime minister.

"Look, the whole eighth-floor area has been sealed off by security guards," the physician, Dr. Rizvi, said to Sharma. "If you want to go anywhere near the area where Mrs. Gandhi is, then go as a blood donor. We badly need the O Group Rh negative type blood."

"She's not dead, then," Sharma said.

"She's in very bad shape," Dr. Rizvi said.

Vichitra Sharma slipped into the institute's main building. She was stopped by a security guard on the main floor.

"No one allowed," the guard said.

"But I'm going to give blood," Sharma said.

"Then you may enter," the guard said. "The blood bank is up ahead."

Sharma knew enough about the building's layout so that she could circumvent the blood bank and head toward the stairwell that would take her to the eighth floor. Over the next ten hours, this stairwell, which surprisingly was unmanned by security guards, would be Sharma's repeated route back and forth from the eighth floor operation theater to the main floor, where Delhi's most important people would gather.

As Sharma climbed the stairs, she ran into a woman who was rushing down. The woman was in tears.

"She's gone, she's gone!" the woman cried.

"How could it be?" Sharma said.

"I saw it upstairs. The doctors have given up."

Once upstairs, Sharma found the eighth-floor corridor outside Operation Theater Number Two filled with guards and various hospital personnel. No one tried to stop her. She surreptitiously took notes. Now there was a crescendo of murmurs. People began arriving. Sharma recognized a woman named Shehnaz Hussain, Mrs. Gandhi's personal beautician. Miss Hussain wore a long, flowing yellow evening dress. Sharma also recognized several members of Parliament belonging to Mrs. Gandhi's ruling Congress Party. Socialites started showing up; some junior cabinet ministers followed.

Sharma decided to check out the scene downstairs on the main floor. There she found that many senior cabinet ministers were ensconced in a conference room. Some of them were weeping, most seemed numb.

Someone tapped Sharma's shoulder.

"Excuse me, but can you do me a favor?" a man asked Sharma. "My boss, the health minister Shri Shankaranand, is in that room. Can you tell him that his driver is waiting outside and wants to know if the boss will come home for lunch?"

"Why don't you go in yourself?" Sharma said.

"I cannot do that. I am only a lowly employee."

Sharma delivered the message, but Shankaranand seemed too distraught to understand what she was saying. It struck Sharma that these cabinet ministers had slid into a kind of collective coma.

"What kind of men were these?" Sharma would say later. "I realized then that she had made puppets out of every one of them —and now she was no longer around to pull the strings. In her years of power, she'd taken away the manhood from every one of these men —so now they were like zombies, not knowing what to do, no initiative coming from them. It occurred to me how propitious a time it was for some determined military man to seize power at this very moment."

Upstairs, the surgeons kept pumping blood into Mrs. Gandhi's body. They furiously kept trying to remove the bullets, trying to revive her—knowing full well that she was long dead. But no one had ordered them to desist—so they kept up their efforts.

At four o'clock in the afternoon, Rajiv Gandhi, Mrs. Gandhi's son and heir apparent, arrived at the All-India Institute of Medical Sciences. At the time when Mrs. Gandhi was brought into the eighth-floor operation theater, the forty-year-old Gandhi was addressing a huge rally more than a thousand miles away in Contai, in the state of West Bengal. It was an hour or so later, on his way to yet another political rally, that Gandhi's motorcade was stopped by a police jeep at a place called Heria. It was there that a police inspector told him about the assassination attempt.

A number of Congress Party workers around him started to weep, but Rajiv Gandhi kept his poise and even comforted some of them. A police officer told him that an Indian Air Force helicopter was waiting at a place called Kolaghat to transport Gandhi to Calcutta or some nearby military air base from where an air force jet would speed him back to New Delhi. But when Gandhi's motorcade reached Kolaghat, there was no helicopter there. Apparently it had already been despatched to Mahisadal, which would have been the next destination on Gandhi's schedule that morning. A policeman rang Mahisadal urging that the helicopter be sent back to Kolaghat.

While he waited, clad in a homespun white shirt called the kurta and in loose pyjama trousers, with his trademark Kashmir woolen shawl draped around his shoulders, Rajiv Gandhi appeared to the men and women around him a picture of cool composure. He fiddled with the dials of his portable Sony transistor radio and finally raised the BBC. The British Broadcasting Corporation's overseas service was already saying that Indira Gandhi was dead. But Rajiv Gandhi had also tuned in to the All-India Radio network, which was playing Hindi film music.

"It's all very confusing," Gandhi said, to no one in particular.

There was confusion, too, at the All-India Institute of Medical Sciences when he eventually arrived. Government officials were fluttering about like pigeons, arguing among themselves whether the government-owned radio and television networks should announce the prime minister's death. There were angry comments about Sikhs in general, and about Mrs. Gandhi's Sikh assailants in particular. There was some discussion also about whether Indira Gandhi's body should remain at the hospital or be taken back to One Safdarjung Road.

Rajiv Gandhi stayed inside Operation Theater Two until about six o'clock in the evening. By now the corridor outside was thick with Congress Party workers, cabinet ministers and their families, and assorted hangers-on.

Sharma stood next to a group of wealthy Delhi socialites.

"I must go inside to show my face to Rajivji," one of these socialites said. "He must know we took the trouble to come here at a time like this." Sharma thought: in India it is so important to be seen doing the right thing in front of the powers-that-be.

When Rajiv Gandhi left, the corridor was quickly emptied of people. A physician who knew Sharma told her that Gandhi had said he would return at 7:30 P.M. to collect his mother's body.

By 9:30 P.M., he had not come back. Sharma went into the operation theater to look at the body. Indira Gandhi lay there, alone and dead and unattended, on a cold steel table. No family member was present, just some curious medical orderlies who occasionally slipped into the room.

"I was in tears," Sharma said later. "Here was a woman who ruled India, who was so powerful until that very morning. And now she lay there cold and lifeless. And no one was there to pay her the courtesy of guarding her body. It was pathetic.

"I felt numb. Before me lay a woman who once was so majestic. Now she was a mere body, crusted with blood and surrounded by ugly tubes and bottles and equipment. Right before my eyes I saw that an era had ended, that something had gone from our lives for all time."

2

"What Now?"

I T was a typical Bombay morning: the sky was cloudless and blue, the sunlight was strong and the humidity heavy. The roar of automobiles, scooters and lorries, accompanied by the tinkling of a thousand bicycle bells, rushed in through the open windows of a friend's apartment where I was staying; I could hear polyglot hawkers outside, proclaiming the fine virtues of their fruit or fresh fish or vegetables, and there were also the dull drumbeat and rhythmic mantras of a sadhu, a mendicant with his sacred brahma bull for makeshift worship by Hindu pedestrians as they trudged to their offices. Somewhere in the neighborhood, a muezzin's voice was being broadcast by a public-address system perched on a mosque's minaret: faithful Muslims were being summoned to prayer. The fragrance from a magnolia tree outside floated into the apartment as well, mixed with the fumes from the traffic.

I had slept badly. The air conditioner had stopped working, and someone in an adjacent apartment in this ancient block of flats had played cacophonous Hindustani film music through much of the night. The first order of the day was, as is for every Hindu, the morning ablution, and as I showered away the night's accumulated sweat from my skin, the telephone rang.

It was Malavika Sanghvi, the wife of one of my closest friends, Vir Sanghvi. Vir was the editor of *Imprint,* a general circulation magazine, and Malavika herself was fashioning a reputation as a writer.

"Can you come over?" Malavika said. "It's quite important."

"Are you both all right?" I said, alarmed by the tone of her voice.

"Yes, yes, we are okay," she said. "There's nothing wrong with us. But come over if you can. I can't tell you over the phone, but I think something terrible has happened."

I got dressed, hurried out of the apartment, and hailed a taxi. The Sanghvis lived several miles away on Carmichael Road, in a swank residential neighborhood of Bombay. The driver was a jolly man of the local Maratha community named Ramchandra Moray. Like most Bombay taxi drivers, he was used to breakneck driving, which is to say that there was no need for me to tell him that my journey was urgent. Moray cheerfully cursed the thick traffic in his native language of Marathi, he cursed in Hindi, he even cursed in English. He very nearly plowed into a bullock cart near Marine Drive, the long, curving corniche that links south Bombay to the northern, hilly neighborhoods of Malabar Hill and Carmichael Road. Moray challenged other taxis in a series of spurts through the dense traffic. I held on to the worn leather handles of the back door, too terrified to think much about why Malavika Sanghvi had called me. Each time I tried to reflect on my conversation with her, Moray would jerk his taxi to within millimeters of a major accident. Moray deposited me in front of the Sanghvis's building in eleven minutes. I asked him to wait for me, for taxis were ordinarily hard to get in this part of town during the busy morning hours.

Malavika Sanghvi, a tall, striking woman of twenty-six, was ashen-faced when she opened the door of her apartment.

"Indira Gandhi has been shot," Malavika said.

I looked at my watch, a reporter's habit. It was ten-fifteen.

"What? How do you know this?" I asked Malavika.

"A family friend telephoned my father," she said. "My father phoned me. Vir left for an appointment before my dad's call, so I thought I'd see if you could find out more about this."

"How did this family friend get the news?"

"She's the wife of a top government official and she happens to be in Bombay at the moment. Her husband phoned her from Delhi. She didn't tell my dad anything more. All she knew was that Mrs. Gandhi was shot in her garden just after nine o'clock this morning. Can you find out more?"

I reached for my briefcase, which I always carry—another old habit —and retrieved my phone book. I looked up the number of Hari Jaisingh, the editor of the Bombay edition of the *Indian Express,* the country's largest English-language newspaper. He, if anyone, would have the latest news. I had his direct number at the newspaper office; Jaisingh answered the phone himself.

I identified myself.

"Where are you?" Jaisingh asked.

"In Bombay," I said.

"Welcome, welcome," he said, ever the gracious Indian.

"Thanks. Now tell me, is it true that Mrs. Gandhi has been shot?"

There was a slight pause.

"Yes, we just got the news on the ticker. Two security guards. We think they were Sikhs, who else? But no confirmation yet. Come over to the office, if you can. We should soon know more. But I must tell you, it's pandemonium here."

I asked Malavika where we could reach Vir.

"He's probably already reached his astrologer's office by now," Malavika said.

"Vir believes in astrology?" I said. I hadn't known about this aspect of my friend's life.

"Devoutly."

"Let's call him."

Malavika dialed the astrologer's number. Vir was summoned to the phone.

"Vir, we've heard that Mrs. Gandhi was shot just a while back," I said.

"You're joking," Vir said.

"No," I said. "I just talked with Hari Jaisingh at the *Express* and he said the news is already on the ticker."

"You're joking."

"No, really."

"God, I don't know what to say."

"Let's meet later in the day. I'm off to the *Express* office to get more details."

"I'm absolutely stunned," Vir said. "I just don't know what to say."

"Ask your astrologer what's in store for India," I said, and immediately regretted my flippancy.

We agreed to meet for lunch at one o'clock at Chopsticks, a Chinese restaurant in the Churchgate area, not far from Vir's office. Chopsticks had become a haunt for Bombay's journalists. Malavika promised to join us there.

Downstairs, Moray was listening to his transistor radio. A small, plump man with a handlebar mustache and betel leaf–stained teeth, he was drenched in sweat, and for a moment I thought he'd heard the news on the radio. But it was the humidity. Moray had been enjoying Hindi film music on All-India Radio. It would not be until six o'clock that evening that India's government broadcasting station would formally announce the death of Mrs. Gandhi, almost nine hours after the shooting; the station's bureaucrats waited because none of their superiors would take the initiative and give the go-ahead to broadcast the dreadful news until a cabinet minister had personally given permission—but, as it happened on this day, the entire cabinet was paralyzed and unable to act.

I was tempted to tell Moray what I'd heard, but I resisted the impulse. Had I said anything to him, he would no doubt have asked me how I knew, and then I'd have to explain and elaborate, and my Marathi was simply not good enough to sustain an entire conversation—I'd lived in America for twenty years, and this had pretty much eroded my native vocabulary.

I directed Moray to the *Indian Express* building at Nariman Point, a good five miles from Malavika Sanghvi's apartment. I also asked

him to drive more slowly this time. I wanted to observe the scene,
I said.

"Scene? Sahib, what is there left to see in Bombay?" Moray said.
"The city has become so ugly. All tall buildings, no space left. Ugli-
ness everywhere. Too many people. Eight million, nine million people, and still growing. You want to see scenery? I will take you to the
Hanging Gardens on Malabar Hill. About the only open space left
in this city. You wish to go to the gardens?"

He drove, the radio on low volume. Still the Hindi songs, and no
word about Mrs. Gandhi's condition. Indira Gandhi shot? Had
Malavika Sanghvi and Hari Jaisingh together been playing a practical
joke on me? But how would Malavika have known that I'd telephone
Jaisingh for confirmation concerning the shooting? One thought kept
turning in my head: Indira may not have been very good for the
country, and she may even have been disastrous. But she was always
splendid.

There were rivers of people on the pavements of Bombay, men and
women and children and beggars and sadhus and urchins. They
cascaded through the streets of Bombay. Spindly men pushed two-
wheeled carts laden with cartons and crates. Cats scratched in gar-
bage mounds. When my taxi stopped for red lights, miserable women
would come running toward my vehicle, thrusting at me babies with
bloated bellies and watery eyes. "Babu, a paisa for food," the women
would say, each echoing the other in what seemed to be a rehearsed
refrain. An occasional mangy dog tried to cross the flood of traffic,
only to return frightened and yelping to the pavement. The interiors
of the small clothing shops in various neighborhoods were brightly lit,
and even at this relatively early commercial hour seemed to be
packed. Salesmen and customers were haggling, and as I drove past,
they seemed like characters in some pantomime; the mithai shops,
with their garish hand-painted signs, had already begun attracting
customers lured by their assortment of greasy, ghee-dripping sweetmeats.

There were no anxious knots of people gathered in the street
around someone's transistor radio, as happens in India when some

momentous event is being announced on the air. Life seemed to go on as if nothing had happened. And why should it not? How many of those people would have heard about the shooting? In most Third World countries, the radio is about the only instant source of news for most people—and in most Third World countries the radio network is usually operated by the government, which is not inclined to broadcast unfavorable news with any alacrity. As Moray took me down Hughes Road, then through the access road leading into Marine Drive, I saw newsboys peddling the early editions of *Midday* and the *Free Press Bulletin,* Bombay's afternoon tabloids. I strained to see the headlines as we passed the urchins, but there was nothing about the shooting.

On the morning of Wednesday, October 31, Ramchandra Moray was in a particularly good frame of mind. The previous day, he had paid off the last installment of a 60-thousand-rupee (the equivalent of about $6,000) bank loan to buy his Fiat taxi, and now the vehicle was no longer, as Indians like to put it, "hypothecated" to the Bank of Baroda; the car was all his. The previous week, Moray's wife had given birth to a boy they named Santosh—their first son, after six daughters—and Moray, who had recently turned forty, was convinced that the stars were finally aligned just right for him.

Moray lives with his wife, Anasuya, and their children in the Colaba section of Bombay, a neighborhood of fashionable apartment buildings in whose shadow sit blocks upon blocks of squat, squalid tenements, known locally as chawls. The Moray family occupy two rooms in one of these chawls; their apartment is scrunched above a small restaurant off a street named Allana Marg. The restaurant specializes in idlis, the rice pancakes favored by many people in South India, where rice is the main crop. Ramchandra Moray has no particular liking for idlis; he is a good, robust consumer of mutton and chicken dishes, which he insists that Anasuya prepare for breakfast.

On this morning, there was no Anasuya around to prepare breakfast. She was a hundred miles away in her hometown of Alibagh, where she'd given birth. Also with her were the six Moray daughters

—ages sixteen to seven—and Ramchandra was alone in his dwelling. He woke up at eight o'clock, which was an hour later than usual for him, and pumped the kerosene stove in the alcove kitchen and made himself a strong brew of tea: he put sufficient sugar into his teacup so that the spoon was virtually cemented into place, erect. He then bathed in the tiny communal bathroom just outside his apartment, lit several aggarbattis, or joss sticks, at the small altar above his bed and prayed for fifteen minutes before the pictures of the Hindu gods Krishna and Shiva. The prayers were of gratitude over the fact that he was now the father of a son: the Moray family name was now assured of continuity. At the end of his devotional session, Moray applied a little tikka on his forehead, a dab of red vermilion which signifies that a Hindu man has performed a religious duty.

Ordinarily Moray leaves home at about eight o'clock every morning. He checks the engine of his taxi, lights another aggarbatti in front of a small picture of Shiva on the dashboard, and is off. He drives till noon, returns home for lunch, takes a nap for an hour, and is back driving his taxi until seven or eight in the evening. This effort nets him about 200 rupees every day, or the equivalent of $20. This is a relatively handsome income in a country where the per capita income statistically is $250, but where annual incomes of less than $100 are the lot for most people.

On this day, Moray decided to relax. He slipped on a pair of chappals, the hardy, thonged sandals favored by many Bombayites, and went for a walk. Around the corner from his home, on Colaba Causeway, he stopped at a roadside news stand and bought a copy of *Navakal,* a local Marathi-language newspaper. One of the articles on the front page was about Prime Minister Indira Gandhi. She had toured the eastern state of Orissa the previous day and visited a number of military facilities. At a place called Gopalpur, she laid the foundation stone of a new military school for guided-missile training.

That same day, Moray read in the newspaper, Indira Gandhi spoke at a rally in Bhubaneshwar, the capital of Orissa State. It was a typical political rally, which is to say that hundreds of thousands of people had gathered in an open-air parade ground to get a glimpse of her and to applaud her, no matter what she said. In her thirty-minute speech in Hindi, Mrs. Gandhi spoke about the dangers of communalism and about external threats to India's security. Then she recalled that in some quarters there was considerable political hostility to her and that sometimes the situation got out of hand. She recalled that only the previous day, someone had hurled a stone at her at a rally.

"But I am not afraid of these things," the newspaper quoted Mrs. Gandhi as saying. "I don't mind if my life goes in the service of the nation. If I die today, every drop of my blood will invigorate the nation. Every drop of my blood, I am sure, will contribute to the growth of this nation to make it strong and dynamic."

Moray, not a man to be especially moved by political rhetoric, shrugged as he read the newspaper. He did not think that Indira Gandhi's seventeen-year tenure had been all that beneficial for India's poor; she certainly hadn't done much for his own hometown, Alibagh, where farming was on the decline because of high production costs—a situation that forced people from peasant backgrounds, such as himself, to flee from India's 576,000 villages to big cities like Bombay in order to earn any kind of living. Moray had been lucky in being able to buy a taxi and become self-reliant; but some of his folk from Alibagh hadn't even found permanent jobs, drifting from one household to another as temporary naukars, or servants.

Moray walked back to his taxi and drove off. At about ten o'clock, at the point where Colaba Causeway meets Sohrab Bharucha Lane, a man in a brown safari suit furiously flagged down Moray's taxi. I was that man.

On the way to the *Indian Express* office, I stopped to see my parents at the Bhatia Hospital, where my father had taken a private room. I told them that I would probably extend my stay in India and not return to New York within a day or two as planned. As I entered Moray's waiting taxi just outside the Bhatia Hospital, I found him fiddling with the dials of his transistor radio. He seemed agitated.

"I am trying to get some foreign station called the BBC," Moray said.

"Why the BBC?" I said.

"These young fellows who were just walking by a minute ago said the BBC is saying that Indira Gandhi has been shot. Do you know how to get the BBC?"

"Does your radio have a shortwave band?"

"What is shortwave?"

"If you don't know what shortwave is, then your radio probably doesn't have it."

I was right. No BBC would be available on Moray's transistor, which had only the local radio bands. The BBC world service had broken the news of the shooting within minutes of the event. By eleven o'clock, the BBC was saying that Mrs. Gandhi was reported to be dead.

"Is it true?" Moray said. "Is she dead?"

"I don't know if she's dead. But she was shot a little while ago in her garden in Delhi."

"What fate! I was reading only a little while ago in *Navakal* about her speech yesterday in Orissa. She said something about not minding death in the cause of the nation. Do you believe in fate, sahib? All these things are ordained."

I nodded, intrigued by the speech to which Moray referred. He had already discarded his copy of the Marathi newspaper.

"Did the Sikhs shoot her?"

"That is what's being said."

"Are you going to Delhi?" Moray suddenly asked.

"No, why should I? I would now like to go to the *Indian Express* building."

"If the Sikhs shot her, there will be bloodbaths everywhere. I hope for the sake of the Sikhs that whoever shot Indira was not a Sikh."

"I agree."

"Sahib, do you think the Sikhs are really Indians?"

"Of course they are. Why shouldn't they be?"

"Then why did they kill Indiraji?"

"We don't know for certain if she was killed by Sikhs."

"Tell me, sahib, if the BBC is a foreign station, how did they get this news so fast? My All-India Radio station is still playing Hindi songs."

I told Moray that the BBC had the best radio news service in the world, that it had painstakingly carved for itself over the years a reputation for being impartial and fair—and for often being first with the news. The BBC, although a British government corporation, was rarely partisan. Such was its reputation that officials in New Delhi frequently called up the BBC's India correspondent, Mark Tully, for information and insights concerning political developments in the country. While the BBC and Radio Australia—each of whom had excellent local sources in Delhi—were broadcasting details about the Gandhi assassination, All-India Radio's executives were still awaiting orders from higher-ups about when to release the news of the death. But these higher-ups themselves did nothing until a new prime minister was selected. As I spoke with Moray, I could not have known anything about the paralysis that had gripped the capital of New Delhi, a thousand miles to the north. Moray drove in silence the rest of the way to the *Indian Express* building. I looked for signs of unusual crowd activity. The street peddlers and beggars and urchins and cart pushers were still busily going about their business. The shops were still open. Bombay was still its usual self.

Moray drove me along Marine Drive. We passed six- and seven-story buildings where Bombay's wealthy live, their bedrooms and balconies facing the vast expanse of the Arabian Sea. We passed the open maidans, or grounds, of the Hindu, Islam, and Parsi gymkhanas, the clubs set up by ethnic community leaders well before India's independence from the British in 1947 to counter the whites-only policy of the Britons' own exclusive recreation establishments. We passed the Bal Bhavan, the children's center, where my father brought me when I was a toddler so that I could be exposed to books and games and educational films. How the years had flown—the Bal Bhavan remained to nourish and nurture successive generations of children, but I had fled India.

At one point, there was a traffic jam: one of Bombay's 26,000 black-and-yellow taxis had come to grief against a lamppost, and a crowd had gathered out of curiosity, even though no one seemed to have been hurt—I was merely seeing one of some 5,000 traffic accidents that occur daily in Bombay, a city of eight million people and a million vehicles. Moray told me he'd never been involved in a major accident.

"How can I afford to bang up my car?" Moray said. "It provides me my livelihood. I have to save up for the sake of my son, Santosh."

"Why are you already worried about your son? He's only a week old."

"Yes, but they grow up so fast—and the cost of living moves up even faster," Moray said. "I went to my village last week to see the boy after his birth—and do you know how expensive the mithai was? But I had to distribute the sweetmeats. It is the tradition, especially when a son comes into the family. I feel very happy, sahib—a son after six daughters."

The offices of the *Indian Express* are located on the second floor of a skyscraper known as the Express Towers. The skyscraper is situated in Nariman Point, on land that was reclaimed about ten years ago from the Arabian Sea. The newspaper is published daily in English at ten centers around the country, but Bombay's is clearly the flagship edition. The paper's owner, Ramnath Goenka, is an irascible old man of eighty who seems fitter and more youthful than many of his far younger employees. Perhaps that is because he pays them badly. When Indira Gandhi imposed her "emergency" in 1975 and subjected the Indian press to censorship, Goenka was one of the media barons who continued to criticize her. It took courage to do so, and Goenka suffered a great deal of harassment—his books were frequently audited by the tax authorities, his buildings were raided by the police, his presses were sometimes stopped in mid-edition.

His building here has not aged well; large shards of plaster have peeled from its outer walls, creating a unintended illusion of rust. The stairwells have been so thoroughly soaked in urine that the tiles have eroded. The elevators creak. In many places the electrical wiring lies exposed. Across the street from the newspaper's offices is the Hotel

Oberoi Towers, a luxury facility whose coffee shop, called Samarkand, is frequented by *Express* staffers, who are given discounts by the management. Many an *Express* employee, shouted at by Goenka, has sought refuge in a beer bottle, or two, at this coffee shop.

On this morning, the Samarkand was empty. India's bush telegraph—word of mouth—was already at work, and those who could manage it had flocked into the newsroom of the *Express*. By the time I reached Express Towers, security guards were posted at the entrance to the paper's offices. I elbowed my way through a thick throng struggling to get into the premises.

"No one allowed now," a burly guard in a brown beret said, standing squarely in the middle of the doorway to the newsroom. He tried to push me back.

"I have an appointment with Mr. Hari Jaisingh," I said.

"In that case, welcome!" he said.

There was a murmur in the crowd behind me.

"Why is that man being allowed in?" someone shouted, in Hindi. "We all have appointments with this Mister Jaisingh. Let us in!"

"Go away!" the guard shouted back.

"But our prime minister has been shot," someone protested. "All we want is the real story. Is that too much to ask of a newspaper?"

By this time, I had slipped past the guard and was well into the cavernous newsroom. I could see immediately what Hari Jaisingh had meant when he told me earlier on the phone that it was "pandemonium" there.

Virtually everyone in the room had gathered around the bank of teletype machines. People yelled every time a fresh bulletin appeared on the ticker. Sometimes they gasped. Hari Jaisingh was frenetically trying to get some of these people to leave the teletype area and return to their desks.

"Come, let's sit in my cabin," Jaisingh said to me, giving up on the idea of re-establishing his authority in the newsroom. "What's the use of shouting at them? People will be people."

Jaisingh is a large man with a broad forehead and tired eyes. He wore a gray safari suit that morning, and it was badly ironed. He was a bit agitated, but he did not overlook his hostly duties: he gave me a cup of tea.

"A very high-up source just telephoned me from Delhi with very sad news," Jaisingh said, presently. "I am afraid that she is no more with us. Indira Gandhi is gone."

I started to say something, but Jaisingh had swiveled his chair around to face the window. He looked out at the vast blue sea, then said:

"The question is, what now?"

Chopsticks was crowded. Among those enjoying ersatz Chinese food were a couple of movie actors; there was Rekha Mehta, editor of *Woman Today*, a hip, slickly produced magazine; and there was Rauf Ahmed, an amiable local publishing executive. The restaurant, uncomfortably air-conditioned, was abuzz with conversation. As I walked in at about one o'clock, I overheard people talking:

"There will now be a massacre of the Sikhs."

"Rajiv is sure to become Prime Minister."

"Rajiv will impose another Emergency—a permanent one this time."

"Will we still be a democracy tomorrow morning?"

"Maybe she's not really dead. All-India Radio is still playing film music."

"She must be dead. No one can survive after being shot at such close range."

"How do you know about the close range?"

"The BBC said so."

"She'll be a martyr. Maybe Rajiv will win the elections now."

"That's right. Indira would never have won the next election."

"Can you imagine? A pilot as our leader?"

"He's not become PM yet. Maybe they'll pick someone else."

"Who? Who is there? They're all old farts. He's the only decent chap."

"How could she have let Sikhs stay on as her bodyguards?"

"Sheer stupidity of her staff. They should all be arrested."

Vir and Malavika Sanghvi were already seated at a table toward the rear of the restaurant and were eating soup. Chopsticks was one of their haunts, and so they'd already ordered from the menu for me. Neither looked especially distraught; Malavika, in fact, now appeared a great deal less pale than when I last saw her in the morning. I filled them in on what I'd picked up at the *Indian Express.*

Vir Sanghvi, a slim man with an intense face and large, soulful eyes, is a whiz kid of Indian journalism. A product of Bombay's exclusive Campion School and Ajmer's Mayo College, he went on to the Mill Hill School in London, and then obtained a master's degree in politics, philosophy, and economics at Oxford University's Brasenose College. He'd started writing for Indian publications while he was at Oxford. Upon his return to India, Sanghvi helped start Bombay's first city magazine, one modeled vaguely after *New York* magazine. It is called *Bombay,* and he guided it for three years. It is still flourishing as a guide to this cosmopolitan city's arts and entertainment and trend-setting activities and activists; and people still call up Sanghvi pleading to be featured in the magazine, even though he now has moved on to the editorship of a far more serious journal, *Imprint,* which runs long, thoughtful articles on national affairs and enjoys a dedicated readership all over India. And Vir Sanghvi is only twenty-eight years old.

"Are you going to miss Indira?" I asked.

"I think it's fair to say that most people of my generation were ambivalent about Indira Gandhi," Sanghvi said. "In 1966, when she first became prime minister, we were too young to realize what she stood for—I was only ten then. But by 1971, when she fought a national election and won by a landslide—after having first broken away from the Congress Party bosses who'd installed her in the first place—we were all on her side. Then she won state assembly elections all across the country in 1972 and established her credentials as India's most powerful leader, one who did not need the support of any party machine.

"My disillusionment came later. By 1974, things had begun to go badly wrong: inflation, lawlessness, corruption—these were all on the rise. Still, I retained a sneaking admiration for her until 1975, when she declared the Emergency and suspended the Constitution and jailed thousands of her political opponents. Even then, I was prepared to buy her story: that the Opposition, through its unruly, disruptive agitations, had left her with no choice. By late 1976, though, when her younger son Sanjay rose to be heir apparent, it was impossible to defend Indira Gandhi. She was clearly establishing a dynasty, and this became even clearer after Sanjay's death in an air crash in 1980— Indira insisted that Rajiv give up his pilot's career and enter politics, even though he seemed extremely reluctant to do so at that point. For most of the last eight years of her life, I was opposed to Indira Gandhi and much of what she stood for."

Did he feel any sadness at all at her death?

"Of course," Sanghvi said, "an old woman was shot to death in her own garden. There is sorrow in that. Indira did contribute to India. She provided firm, strong leadership, she ran a shrewd and intelligent foreign policy, and she believed in India as an entity, often rising above caste and communal divisions."

What impact did she have on Indian life, I asked Sanghvi, how would he assess her legacy? I realized that it was probably much too early to ask such a question, but I wanted to try it out on him.

"She did a lot of damage," Sanghvi said, as if he had expected the question. "In retrospect it seems clear that she either destroyed or subverted most of the institutions of Indian democracy. She pretty much killed the Congress Party, which was one vehicle, especially under her father, Nehru, of ensuring that a vast country like India was ruled by consensus. She destroyed the powers of state chief ministers and damaged the federal structure. She pressurized the judiciary and sapped its independence by appointing mediocre judges and transferring to inconsequential and uncomfortable outposts those judges who dared to assert their independence. She damaged the independence of the bureaucracy by calling for a 'committed civil service.' She politicized the army by using it for civilian purposes and by manipulating promotions. She turned the cabinet into a joke by vesting unprecedented and sweeping powers in her personal staff and in her sons. And she prevented any rivals from emerging within the party—peopling it, instead, with thieves and scoundrels, in comparison to whom her older son, Rajiv, seems positively angelic."

What impact did Indira Gandhi's life have on his own life, I asked Sanghvi?

He reflected on that a bit, fiddled with the fried rice on his plate, then said:

"I feel tremendously let down. I came back to India with great hopes and a sense that good would prevail. But what I encountered was a cynical leader whose only concern was political survival.

"I think people now, and certainly myself included, simply have no faith in their national government. We've seen how corrupt those in government have become. It seems to me that if Rajiv becomes prime minister, he simply will have to institute major political reforms—he will have to fashion a new climate of hope and political cleanliness—if people are to trust their leaders again. I don't think his task is that difficult. Unlike a lot of other Third World countries, we still have such institutions in place as a judiciary, a parliament, a strong press. We have the two-thousand-odd officers of the Indian Administrative Service who can be galvanized into efficient service. The answers are already there—no need for Rajiv, or whoever becomes prime minister, to appoint commissions to search for solutions. I say, stop interfering with the judiciary, depoliticize the bureaucracy, lift the stifling controls over industry—and stop trying to run every little thing directly from the prime minister's office in Delhi. Let people be."

Malavika Sanghvi had been listening attentively to her husband. I asked her how she viewed Indira Gandhi's death and the likely ascension of Rajiv Gandhi to India's political throne.

"I can't help but feel in my bones that exciting times lie ahead," she said. "I know, of course, that Indira herself had a wonderful opportunity back after the 1971 elections to bring about massive changes. She blew it. So I'm cautious about the prospects of any leader to succeed. But there is one side of me that desperately wants Rajiv—and I hope it will be him in the prime minister's seat—to succeed. After all these years of bad news, we need good things to happen in India."

3

The Succession

AT nine-forty on the morning of Wednesday, October 31, 1984, Murli Deora was saying farewell at Bombay's cavernous Victoria Terminus to nearly a thousand elderly citizens who were about to board a train for the northern city of Allahabad. They were all "freedom fighters," men and women who had struggled alongside Mahatma Gandhi and Jawaharlal Nehru and Indira Gandhi against India's British colonial rulers. On this morning, they were about to travel to Mrs. Gandhi's hometown of Allahabad to observe the fiftieth anniversary of the founding of their particular freedom fighters' unit. In his capacity as president of Bombay's Congress Party organization, Deora had arranged the trip.

Deora is a short, slim man with a ready smile and quick wit. He is a self-made businessman who parlayed his high school savings into a personal fortune. He has served as Bombay's nonexecutive mayor. Married to an interior designer named Hema Phansalkar—who is the mother of the Deoras's two sons—Murli Deora is seen at every event that "matters" in Bombay, but most especially he makes it a point to attend events that attract the city's political and commercial elite, whose darling he has become. His attraction to them, Deora explains with a twinkle in his eyes, is largely because of his own personality and charm. Not so. Bombay's high-and-mighty are fully aware of Deora's powerful connections in New Delhi. He was very close to Indira Gandhi; and he has personally taken her son, Rajiv Gandhi, to participate in management seminars in Western Europe, where Deora has business associates. That Deora had survived as a Gandhi friend was the subject of much discussion in Bombay society. Normally, those who billed themselves as "close" to Indira Gandhi lasted in that position for about an hour after the characterization came to Indira's attention. She had a way of exiling from her inner circle those who capitalized on their friendship with her. And there was no shortage of such people. A former chief minister of Maharashtra State, A. R. Antulay, even collected millions of rupees for a dubious social-welfare society, telling his industrialist donors that his friend, Mrs. Gandhi, had blessed his endeavor. Antulay was eventually cut adrift by the prime minister.

On this morning, Deora mingled with the "freedom fighters" and addressed the group briefly in Hindi.

"You are going to a historic place to observe a historic anniversary," Deora said. "You are going to the very home of Nehru and our beloved leader, Indiraji."

The group applauded vigorously. Deora wished them well in their journey and left for his business office in Khetan Bhavan, a blue-facaded building located in Bombay's commercial district of Churchgate. He ordered a cup of tea, then settled back in his high-backed vinyl chair to scrutinize the morning's mail. Behind his chair was a large montage showing a sylvan setting of green woods and sun rays streaking through foliage. The office had a yellow sofa and armchairs to match, and little else.

At 10:15 A.M., one of the four telephones next to Deora's desk rang. It was Girilal Jain, the Bombay-based editor in chief of the *Times of India* chain.

"I've just learned that the prime minister was shot in her home," Jain said. "She's not dead, as far as I know. I thought I should inform you."

Deora leaped out of his chair.

"Thank you for telling me," he said, replacing the receiver in the cradle.

As Deora recalls it, his first reaction was of total disbelief. He suddenly thought of telephoning a local physician friend, Shantilal Mehta. The physician had long ago operated on both Nehru and on Mrs. Gandhi, and was still occasionally consulted by the prime minister. Deora reached Dr. Mehta at Bombay's Jaslok Hospital.

"You are familiar with Indiraji's health," Deora said to Mehta. "Perhaps you can be of assistance to the doctors in Delhi."

The two men decided they would fly to Delhi at once. Deora told Mehta that he would collect him at the hospital in thirty minutes and that meanwhile he would book them both on whichever flight was available.

As it turned out, while Deora was on the phone with Dr. Mehta, someone called Deora's office on behalf of two key Gandhi aides, Dr. P. C. Alexander, her principal private secretary, and Dr. Krishnaswamy Rao Sahib, the cabinet secretary. These two men had happened to be in Bombay that morning, and now a special Indian Airlines plane was being readied to transport them to Delhi. The caller urged that if Deora wanted to fly to Delhi, he should be at Bombay's Santa Cruz Airport no later than eleven o'clock.

Deora informed his wife, Hema, that he was on his way to Delhi. She herself had just heard the news of the shooting from Harry Cahill, the United States Consul General in Bombay, and she'd been trying unsuccessfully to reach Deora by phone.

Deora collected a small overnight suitcase that was kept fully packed in his office closet, then drove off to Jaslok Hospital, where Dr. Mehta was waiting for him, with his own overnight attaché case. Deora's driver sped to the airport. But by the time they reached Santa Cruz, which is located in the northern suburbs of Bombay, some 30 kilometers from Deora's South Bombay office, it was almost 11:20. The Boeing 737 jetliner chartered by Dr. Alexander and Dr. Rao Sahib had taken off. No regular flight from Santa Cruz to Delhi was scheduled until 5 P.M.

Deora found out, however, that there was an Air India Kuwait-bound flight out of nearby Sahar Airport—which is actually the international wing of Santa Cruz—scheduled to stop in Delhi. That flight would leave at 1:30 P.M. So Deora and Dr. Mehta rushed to Sahar.

There they found an assembly of local officials who'd already booked themselves on the Air India flight to Delhi. Among those gathered at the check-in counter were Vasantdada Patil, the chief minister of Maharashtra State (of which Bombay is the capital), and Margaret Alva and Saroj Khaparde, both members of Parliament.

"Somebody had a transistor on, but All-India Radio was still giving no news about the shooting," Deora recalled later.

The men and women gathered at the airport exchanged views about the shooting. There was general agreement, Deora recalls, that the assassination attempt was part of a conspiracy by the Sikhs.

"Among us, there was gloom, sadness—and growing anger that something like this had been allowed to happen," Deora said later.

Everybody aboard the Air India flight was tense during the one hundred five-minute ride to Delhi. Deora walked up to the cockpit several times to request the pilot to radio for additional news concerning Mrs. Gandhi. Virtually everyone on board refused the meal offered by Air India's stewardesses.

"When we landed in Delhi, the atmosphere of gloom at the airport was so heavy that I just knew she had died," Deora recalled. "I just broke down and cried."

Dr. Shantilal Mehta, who was almost thirty years older than Deora, put his arm around the younger man and consoled him.

"We just have to accept what happened," the physician said.

The two men were driven by Saroj Khaparde in her car to the All-India Institute of Medical Sciences. It was her driver who told them about Mrs. Gandhi being taken there. Deora saw that several foreign embassies, including the United States Embassy, had already lowered their flags to half-mast—but the flags at Indian Government offices were still flying loftily. Huge crowds had gathered in front of the Institute. Security guards were using lathis—the bamboo sticks favored by Indian policemen—and batons to keep people from entering the hospital's compound. But in India, dignitaries like Members of Parliament enjoy almost divine status, and so Mrs. Khaparde's car was allowed to enter the premises.

It was 4:15 P.M. Deora, Dr. Mehta, and Mrs. Khaparde went up to the eighth-floor operation theater where surgeons had tried to revive Mrs. Gandhi. They were informed that the prime minister had been officially declared dead at 2:30 P.M. Deora was crying without control. He saw Rajiv Gandhi disappear into Operation Theater Two, where Mrs. Gandhi's body was kept, and then reappear to comfort some friends who waited outside in the corridor.

"But I just did not have the heart to go up to Rajiv," Deora recalled.

Deora composed himself and continued to linger in the area outside Operation Theater Two. At 5:15 P.M., there was some commotion. President Zail Singh, who'd been in North Yemen on an official visit, had arrived directly from Delhi Airport. Rajiv Gandhi greeted him and escorted the bearded Sikh head of state into the operation theater. Deora spotted Karan Singh, the Hindu former Maharaja of Kashmir, and Pupul Jayakar, India's cultural czarina and probably Mrs. Gandhi's closest friend. He saw Rajiv Gandhi's close friends and aides, Arun Singh and Arun Nehru.

"Rajiv Gandhi was the most calm and collected person there," Deora recalled to me. "Everybody else was weeping or howling. He was comforting others."

As Deora waited, he thought about the last time he'd seen Indira Gandhi alive. It was during her visit to Bombay on October 5. He arranged a Congress Party meeting for her, and then, as he drove with her to Santa Cruz Airport, he casually mentioned that her elderly uncle, Raja Hutheesing—who was married to Nehru's sister, Krishna—was grievously ill and confined to his home in Navroze Apartments on Altamount Road.

"He would be very happy to see you," Deora said to the prime minister. "With someone as old as he is, you never know what can happen."

Mrs. Gandhi's first response was that Deora should have suggested this earlier. But then she grew silent.

"You're right," she suddenly said to Deora. "You never know what's going to happen to any of us. Let's go and see him." The prime minister's motorcade was ordered to turn around. Mrs. Gandhi hugged Hutheesing warmly. As she left, after a ten-minute visit, she said to him: "Get well soon!"

Was it a premonition of her own death that made her decide to see Hutheesing? Deora pondered this as he waited outside Operation Theater Two, where Indira Gandhi now lay, her body rendered lifeless by assassins' bullets.

It was now well after six o'clock. Saroj Khaparde suggested to Deora that they go to her home so that he could rest for a while. Deora decided instead that he would stop off at the Taj Mahal Hotel, where a room had been booked for him by his Bombay office. He showered, napped briefly, then went to Maharashtra Sadan—the Delhi bureau of the Maharashtra State government—to meet Chief Minister Patil. At around 10:30 P.M., the two men drove to One Safdarjung Road to meet Rajiv Gandhi. They didn't know that he had already been sworn in as the new prime minister of India.

"He was very composed," Deora recalled. "He was consoling every visitor. I thought to myself, what class! The torch had been passed to a new generation."

Gandhi told Chief Minister Patil that he should at once return to Bombay.

"I want all state chief executives to be at their station," the prime minister said. "If any trouble occurs around the country, I want you all to be back where you belong."

The directive obviously applied to Deora as well, for he was head of the influential Bombay unit of Rajiv Gandhi's Congress Party.

As Patil and Deora left One Safdarjung Road at around 11:15 P.M., they ran into B. K. Nehru, an uncle of Gandhi and a former ambassador to the United States. Many years ago, One Safdarjung Road used to be Nehru's private residence when he held a government post in

Delhi; Nehru now was governor of the western state of Gujarat.

"Why did she reinstate those Sikh guards?" Deora recalls Nehru asking. Mrs. Gandhi had insisted that Beant Singh and Satwant Singh be brought back as her personal security guards after they had been transferred in the wake of the Indian Army's assault on the Golden Temple in Amritsar. Indian intelligence officials believed that a plot to kill the prime minister had been devised by radical Sikhs following the army's action on June 6, 1984, as vengeance for the hundreds of Sikhs who died in the military operation.

That night, at the luxurious Taj Mahal Hotel on Mansingh Road, Murli Deora slept fitfully. He wondered what sort of prime minister Rajiv Gandhi would make. He worried that there would be a backlash against India's minority Sikhs. Would there be trouble in Bombay? And in Delhi?

Deora fell asleep not knowing that the massacre of Sikhs in India's capital city had already started.

At about the same time that Murli Deora was fading off into his troubled sleep, Swraj Paul was disembarking from Air India's Flight 104, which had brought him nonstop from London to New Delhi. The journey had taken eight hours, and Paul had sat through most of it in uncharacteristic silence. He is ordinarily an extrovert, an irrepressible man, given to loud laughter and continuous chatter. At fifty-three, he'd established himself as the wealthiest Indian immigrant entrepreneur in Britain; he bought steel mills and foundries, and now was into electronics, publishing, and shipping. But it was not because of his self-made millions that Paul had become well known in both Britain and India. His fame—some would say notoriety—was more the consequence of his much-publicized friendship with Indira Gandhi and her family.

There were those who apportioned sinister underpinnings to that friendship, whispering that Paul was the foreign-based manager of the Gandhi family's ill-gotten fortune. In truth, the Paul–Gandhi relationship was far less complex, Swraj Paul would say. According to him, it was based simply on one man's unswerving loyalty to the

Nehru–Gandhi dynasty because he believed in its greatness. His explanations did not silence critics, some of whom wondered in print whether Paul's close ties with the Gandhis had resulted in pecuniary gains for him; no one, of course, was able to produce a shred of evidence to support such speculation.

Indira Gandhi profited from knowing Swraj Paul. Between 1977 and 1980, when she was out of office and a political pariah during the opposition Janata Party's years in power, it was Paul who invited her abroad and arranged many public appearances for the former prime minister. Those appearances helped sustain her confidence in her own ability as speech maker; Mrs. Gandhi also used the travel to keep up to date on international affairs. And the travel got her widespread media coverage, always a restorative for a politician's spirits, especially a politician who was then being vilified in her native land.

At four-forty-five that Wednesday morning, the phone rang in Swraj Paul's bedroom in his fourth-floor apartment on Portland Place, a fashionable residential district of London.

"Swraj, sorry to tell you this—but the prime minister has been shot," the caller said.

Paul's first thought was that the call sounded like a long-distance one. He was right. The caller was a friend named Ralph Buultjens, who was telephoning from New York. Buultjens was at least as close to Indira Gandhi as Paul was; Buultjens, in fact, was widely said to be her most influential foreign policy adviser, even though he was a Sri Lankan who made his living as a political scientist in the United States. Buultjens had heard the news on American television at around 11:30 P.M. in New York on Tuesday night (Eastern Standard Time is generally ten and a half hours behind Indian Standard Time).

Swraj Paul woke up his wife, Aruna, who had slept soundly through his brief conversation with Ralph Buultjens. Her response to the news was one of disbelief. She suggested that Paul at once telephone New Delhi.

Paul direct dialed the prime minister's residence. The phone was picked up by Mrs. Gandhi's information advisor, H. Y. Sharada Prasad.

"Is it true?" Paul asked.

"Yes, I'm afraid," Prasad said, glumly. "The news is very, very bad."

Paul recalls that he took this to mean that Mrs. Gandhi was dead, although even as Sharada Prasad spoke with him the prime minister was being treated by physicians at the All-India Institute of Medical Sciences in Delhi and had not been officially pronounced dead.

Paul started to cry. So did Aruna. They decided to catch the next available flight to New Delhi. But within minutes of Buultjen's call, members of London's Indian community as well as Britons began telephoning the Pauls to inquire about Indira Gandhi. The Pauls' friendship with the prime minister was well known. Aruna Paul thought it would be best if she stayed behind in London to attend to such calls.

Air India's Flight 104 left London's Heathrow Airport at nine-thirty-five that morning. As Swraj Paul lowered his six-foot frame into his first-class seat, he wondered if Rajiv Gandhi had been selected by the ruling Congress Party to succeed his mother.

People like Swraj Paul seldom have to bother with details such as immigration and customs in India. These things are taken care of for them. A special car whisked Paul from Delhi's international airport to One Safdarjung Road. Rajiv Gandhi and Swraj Paul embraced each other.

Paul spent several hours in the prime minister's house. He watched Rajiv deal with scores of visitors and thought how poised and collected the young man seemed. Paul recalled another Gandhi family tragedy some years back when Rajiv's younger brother, Sanjay, was killed in a plane accident. Then Indira Gandhi had said to Swraj Paul: "My father once said to me that people in public life cannot afford personal tragedies."

Paul went to the dining room where Mrs. Gandhi's body now lay, smothered in flowers. Incense wafted from joss sticks. Paul thought about the last time he had met with Indira Gandhi. It was in August 1984, when he had flown in from London to present Mrs. Gandhi with a copy of his pictorial biography of her.

"I really enjoyed doing this book—and I hope you like it," Swraj Paul had said to Mrs. Gandhi.

"I'm sure I will," she had replied, with a soft smile. Then, turning the pages of the lavishly illustrated volume, the prime minister said: "I appreciate what you have done here."

The conversation had taken place in the same dining room where Indira Gandhi now lay.

On that Wednesday morning, Ralph Buultjens, like Swraj Paul, spent many hours remembering Indira Gandhi.

Swraj Paul's friendship with Mrs. Gandhi was of relatively recent vintage: in 1969, she had helped with arrangements to transport Paul's younger daughter, Ambika, to London for treatment of leukemia (Ambika subsequently died). But Buultjens had known the Nehru family for nearly thirty years, ever since he traveled to New Delhi after his education in Colombo to obtain an interview with Mrs. Gandhi's father, Prime Minister Jawaharlal Nehru. So close did Buultjens and Mrs. Gandhi become that they spoke on the phone regularly. Buultjens, a Sri Lankan social scientist and authority on Asian politics, would meet up with Mrs. Gandhi in New Delhi or during one of her periodic travels abroad. They discussed not only foreign affairs and politics but also history, literature, poetry, the theater. Buultjens would frequently arrange for Mrs. Gandhi to have private meetings with Western intellectuals, whose company he says she relished.

When Buultjens first heard a bulletin about the Gandhi shooting in New Delhi—where it was already Wednesday morning—through a late-night phone call from India to New York on Tuesday, he could not believe the news.

His first thought: This is a very bad joke.

But then a producer from the American Broadcasting Corporation telephoned him, asking that Buultjens appear on a television news show on Wednesday morning. Shortly thereafter, a producer from the National Broadcasting Company called, and after that someone from the Columbia Broadcasting System. On Wednesday, Buultjens, who was already known to television and radio producers as an authority on the Indian subcontinent, would be one of the most sought-after sources for the American media.

In between the media queries, Buultjens—still in bedclothes—telephoned friends in India to get the latest news concerning Mrs. Gandhi. His phone bill for the night of October 30–31 would amount to nearly $900.

"I kept wondering what was going to happen to the whole region now," Buultjens said later. "I was always telling Mrs. Gandhi during our phone conversations to be careful of her security."

He recalled being in her Delhi office on June 1, the day the prime minister had given her generals the go-ahead for Operation Bluestar—the army assault on the Golden Temple in Amritsar. Mrs. Gandhi had said to Buultjens: "You know, this is the most difficult decision of my political career. This is a kind of war with our own people."

A couple of months later, Buultjens had accompanied Mrs. Gandhi to Delhi's Red Fort, from whose ramparts she delivered her annual Independence Day speech on August 15. He noticed that the sixty-seven-year-old prime minister became a bit breathless as she climbed the steep stairs to the rostrum.

"It must be very tiring to go up all those steps," Buultjens later said to Mrs. Gandhi.

"I may never have to do it again," she replied.

And only two days before the assassination, Buultjens had spoken with Mrs. Gandhi about the continuing controversy concerning the army action in Amritsar.

"Things are rather grim. We're besieged on all sides," Mrs. Gandhi said to Buultjens. "But we will pull through this one."

And a few weeks before that conversation, Buultjens had telephoned the prime minister to relay the news that he'd been selected recipient of the Toynbee Award, which is given annually to a distinguished social scientist. Buultjens requested Mrs. Gandhi to hand out the award formally (an request had already been sent to her office by the Toynbee Award Committee).

"I'd be delighted," Mrs. Gandhi said. Then she added: "But I may not be around to give it to you."

On the morning of Wednesday, October 31, Ralph Buultjens told the press that he thought the real test of a political leader was how he or she tackled his society's problems. "Did the leader leave the country in better shape than when he or she found it?" Buultjens said. "By that criterion, Indira Gandhi did very well."

Buultjens said that under Mrs. Gandhi's helmsmanship, India coped well with many difficulties: the Bangladesh War of 1971; the global oil crisis of the 1970s; the economic slump that followed; the Emergency of 1975–77. "She managed to keep the unity and integrity of India under great pressure," Buultjens said. She was responsible for making India a self-sufficient country in food, he went on, and she instilled in the country's poor a consciousness that they had the right to a better life. Mrs. Gandhi, Buultjens said, took personal interest in promoting such things as science, technology, and higher education, items she saw as the "bedrocks" of India in the future.

"She was also a real secularist," Buultjens said. "She really believed that people of all religions could co-exist within the boundaries of a modern state.

"She was the single most exposed and heard political figure in the twentieth century," Buultjens continued. "Just think of the millions in India who saw her at rallies, on television, who heard her voice on radio. And think of her own life—she'd met virtually every major political figure of this century: Gandhi, Nehru, of course, Churchill, De Gaulle, Adenauer, Mao, Chou En Lai, Kennedy, Eisenhower."

It was largely because she was her father's daughter, of course, that Mrs. Gandhi initially gained such exposure. Between 1947 and 1964, she served as Prime Minister Jawaharlal Nehru's official hostess and occasional adviser. Her mother, Kamala, had died in 1936. Nehru, although he enjoyed dalliances with a number of women, never remarried. Indira's own marriage in 1942 to a Parsi named Feroze Gandhi floundered: she and her two sons, Rajiv and Sanjay, lived with

Nehru at the prime minister's official residence in New Delhi, while
Feroze Gandhi camped in a house reserved for parliamentarians (he
died in 1960 of a heart attack).

Those years at Nehru's side, Buultjens recalled, were invaluable.
She learned statecraft. As president of his Congress Party, she played
a leading role in forging a coalition in Kerala that upset that state's
ruling Communist government. She traveled the length and breadth
of India, getting to know grassroots party workers everywhere. She
often accompanied her father on his frequent trips abroad; she attended summit meetings, she sat in on his sessions with that group
of Third World leaders such as Tito of Yugoslavia and Nasser of
Egypt who had formed the nonaligned movement. This experience
more than made up for her lack of a completed university education.
She was very well prepared to handle power.

Buultjens, who someday intends to write a biography of Mrs.
Gandhi, based on his huge collection of conversational notes with
her, pointed out to questioners that it was not until after Nehru's
death in 1964 that Indira Gandhi fully came into her own. She was
selected by Nehru's successor, Prime Minister Lal Bahadur Shastri,
to serve as a minister for information and broadcasting. Shashtri died
in Tashkent of a heart attack on January 10, 1966; fourteen days later,
Mrs. Gandhi was sworn in as prime minister.

She was initially chosen, Buultjens said, because the Congress
Party's aging but still powerful leaders—known collectively as The
Syndicate—thought Indira Gandhi would be extremely amenable to
their manipulations. No one suspected her of possessing a steely will.
She outmaneuvered these party bosses, broke with from the old
Congress leaders to establish her Congress Party, and flourished.

How would Indira Gandhi be remembered?

"As a political giant," Buultjens said, on one of the television
programs on Wednesday morning. "As a superb political strategist.
As a leader who genuinely cared for her people and worked selflessly
for them."

That evening he boarded an Air India flight for New Delhi. As the
Boeing 747 jetliner took off from New York's Kennedy International

Airport, it struck Buultjens how Orwellian a year 1984 had turned out for India: there was the tribal massacre in Assam; there were the tensions in the Punjab; there was the army assault on the Golden Temple; there were assorted political crises in Kashmir and Andhra Pradesh; and now there was the assassination of Indira Gandhi.

And as the plane roared into the night, Buultjens thought of something else. How ironic it was that once again, as at Independence in 1947, people were asking aloud if India would survive as one nation. History, Ralph Buultjens thought, had come full circle.

In Britain, where there are said to be nearly 500,000 Sikhs, there was jubilation in the Sikh community over Indira Gandhi's death.

Jagjit Singh Chauhan, the self-appointed "president" of Khalistan, gave several television interviews when the news of the assassination broke in London.

"She was doomed to die," said Chauhan, a physician with a long white beard and a gentle manner. "She deserved to die."

What about Rajiv Gandhi, an interviewer asked, would he now also be killed?

"He's definitely a target," Chauhan said.

Sikhs took out processions in Southall, the London neighborhood that Britons call Little India. They distributed sweetmeats and chocolates. Sikh women danced in the streets. Non-Sikhs recoiled in horror. Hindus conducted special mourning services in temples. In New York City, too, many Sikhs were ecstatic over the event. They bought hundreds of dollars worth of candy and distributed it to passers-by in front of the Indian grocery stores on Lexington Avenue in Manhattan. They drank champagne. They gave out roses. They tore up photographs of Indira Gandhi and spat on the Indian flag. Like Chauhan across the Atlantic, they appeared on television programs and said they were delighted about Mrs. Gandhi's death.

If tensions between Hindus and Sikhs had built up in India because of the Punjab problem, these frictions until now were rarely mirrored in relations between the two communities in Britain. Hindus and Sikhs had mostly lived in harmony here. They were, after all, both strangers in a land where whites attitudes concerning nonwhite immigrants were becoming guarded, even hostile. Britain, which once hired the poor men of its former tropical possessions in the West Indies and India for its textile and metal-fabricating industries, now was withdrawing such welcome: Britain's economy was languishing; the great foundries of the midlands were shutting down, as British metal products lost out in the face of sharp competition from Western Europe, Japan, Taiwan, even Singapore; unemployment was in excess of 12 percent—in a country of barely 53 million people. (Total immigration into Britain in 1983, in fact, was 12,000, the lowest annual figure in recent years.) The immigrants from the Indian subcontinent labored especially hard. Sikhs, particularly, had become the single most affluent ethnic community in Britain. Many of these wealthy Sikhs had started off as farmers in the Punjab.

It was in Britain that the Khalistan movement gathered steam. Men like Jagjit Singh Chauhan, who became unhappy with Indira Gandhi's stonewalling tactics concerning Sikh demands for greater autonomy in the Punjab, decided that the time was propitious to launch an agitation for not an autonomous state but an independent and theocratic nation—Khalistan. Khalistan means "Land of the Pure" (so does the word Pakistan; perhaps it is no coincidence that Islamic Pakistan, once part of Greater India, has secretly trained guerrillas involved with the Khalistan struggle). Chauhan raised millions of dollars for his cause from rich Sikhs all over the world. Khalistan cells were created in Canada and the United States, where there are significant Sikh enclaves. The Khalistan supporters issued their own fancy passports and their own currency, neither of which, of course, was legal anywhere but in Chauhan's home in London.

The Khalistanis feared that Sikhism was on the decline: Sikhs were freely intermarrying with Hindus; Sikh males were cutting off their long hair (their religion requires males never to cut their hair) and beards; some Sikhs were returning to the folds of Hinduism—Hindus viewed Sikhism as not a separate religion but as a variation of Hinduism, much as Hindus hundreds of years ago had initially tended to regard Buddhism as a branch of their own faith. (Eventually, Buddhism established itself as a major religion outside India; in India, the Hindus's priestly caste, the Brahmins, declared, in a theological *coup d'éclat,* a brilliant tactic as it were, that Buddhism's founder, Gautam Buddha, had actually been the ninth avatar, or reincarnation, of the god Vishnu. The Lord Vishnu, the priests would explain, periodically came down to Earth in the guise of a mortal so that he could offer salvation to sinning human beings. Centuries later, Hindu clergymen countered the growing influence of Christian missionaries in much the same way: they said that Jesus Christ was also a reincarnation of Vishnu.)

The Khalistanis' fears were exacerbated by reports that orthodox Hindu proselytizers in the Punjab were proclaiming that Sikhs were only Hindus by another name. The Khalistanis were aware of Hinduism's great modus operandi—triumph not by coercion but by cooption; Hinduism assimilated and absorbed, it did not convert by the sword as Islam did. Chauhan and his supporters felt that the purity of Sikhism could only be preserved in a totally independent Sikh nation. They began to solicit and receive the endorsement of many Sikh clergymen in the Punjab, who shared Chauhan's apprehension that unless something dramatic was done soon—like creating a new Sikh nation—Sikhism would be completely absorbed by Hinduism in the not-too-distant future. Supporting Chauhan, too, was Sant Jarnail Singh Bhindranwale, the fiery Sikh fundamentalist. Bhindranwale, once an ally of Mrs. Gandhi, holed up in Sikhism's holiest shrine, the Golden Temple in Amritsar. From there he directed a terrorist movement that would result in the deaths of hundreds of Hindus and moderate Sikhs in the Punjab who did not support him. Indian intelligence officials were convinced that Bhindranwale's terrorist activities were financed by Sikhs living abroad, including Jagjit Singh Chauhan. These officials also seem convinced that the Sikh separatists were somehow being helped by the American Central Intelligence Agency. (The widely held assumption among Mrs. Gandhi's aides was that the United States wanted to keep India—which was perceived as a Soviet ally—off balance; Indian officials noted that with the deepening military and economic ties between the Reagan administration and Pakistan, India was forced to buy more high-tech weapons from the Soviets.)

Indira Gandhi viewed the Khalistan "struggle" not only as a secessionist movement but also one that directly and immediately threatened the unity and integrity of India. If Sikhs were allowed to break away into their own nation, then would not the people of another strategic border state, Kashmir, also accelerate their simmering movement to gain independence from India? Mrs. Gandhi was aware that in the cases of both Punjab and Kashmir, neighboring Pakistan, India's bitter foe, was providing moral support, and maybe more. Sikhs were in the majority in the Punjab; Muslims enjoyed a majority in Kashmir. If the Punjab became Khalistan and Kashmir became independent—or was annexed by Pakistan, as was possible—then, as the Indian writer M. J. Akbar has said, the Indian capital of Delhi would "end up as a border city."

This Mrs. Gandhi could never allow.

So on this October morning in London, Chauhan and his friends were beside themselves with joy when they heard that Indira Gandhi had been murdered by two of her Sikh security guards.

"In June, when we said we would kill her, no one believed it," said a Sikh who identified himself as Baldev Singh. "We've done it. And we will continue until Khalistan is formed."

Later in the day, various television programs recapped Prime Minister Gandhi's turbulent career. The BBC ran snippets from one of her last television interviews.

Did she fear being killed by the Khalistanis who had vowed vengeance, an interviewer asked Mrs. Gandhi?

"I've lived with danger all my life," she replied, "and I've lived a pretty full life. And it makes no difference if I die in bed or die standing up."

Late in the evening of Wednesday, October 31, Rajiv Gandhi appeared on Doordarshan, India's government-run television network, to address the 800 million people whose prime minister he had so suddenly become. He spoke from One Safdarjung Road, with a garlanded portrait of his mother in the background. He spoke slowly, in English first, then in Hindi, and his face was composed. He did not even look tired, although his day had begun this Wednesday at four o'clock in the morning in the state of West Bengal, where he had been sent by Mrs. Gandhi on a political mission.

"Indira Gandhi, India's prime minister, has been assassinated," the new prime minister said. "She was mother not only to me but to the whole nation. She served the Indian people to the last drop of her blood. The country knows with what tireless dedication she toiled for the development of India.

"You all know how dear to her heart was the dream of a united, peaceful, and prosperous India. An India in which all Indians, irrespective of their religion, language, or political persuasion, live together as one big family in an atmosphere free from mutual rivalries and prejudices.

"By her untimely death, her work remains unfinished. It is for us to complete this task.

"This is a moment of profound grief. The foremost need now is to maintain our balance. We can and must face this tragic ordeal with fortitude, courage, and wisdom. We should remain calm and exercise the maximum restraint. We should not let our emotions get the better of us, because passion would cloud judgment.

"Nothing would hurt the soul of our beloved Indira Gandhi more than the occurrence of violence in any part of the country. It is of prime importance at this moment that every step we take is in the correct direction.

"Indira Gandhi is no more, but her soul lives. India lives. India is immortal. The spirit of India is immortal. I know that the nation will recognize its responsibilities.

"The nation has placed a great responsibility on me. I shall be able to fulfill it only with your support and cooperation. I shall value your guidance in upholding the unity, integrity and honor of the country."

If his speech seemed a bit disjointed, that was because at least half a dozen aides had contributed to it. One draft was written by H. Y. Sharada Prasad, Mrs. Gandhi's information advisor and chief speech-writer; other contributors included Rajiv Gandhi's closest friend, Arun Singh, a former corporate executive and scion of a royal family. Arun Nehru, Rajiv Gandhi's third cousin and his adviser on Congress Party affairs, also made some suggestions. Even Sonia Gandhi pitched in.

Even though the speech was broadcast close to midnight, some 400 million Indians—half the nation's population—were estimated to have watched Rajiv Gandhi on television.

He had been sworn in as prime minister barely five hours before the speech at a simple ceremony at Rashtrapati Bhavan, the residence of India's constitutional head of state, President Zail Singh. There, under a glittering chandelier in a vast chamber called the Ashoka Hall, Rajiv Gandhi had become India's seventh and youngest head of government. Zail Singh, an amiable Sikh who had been selected for the job by Indira Gandhi mostly because of his total loyalty to her, fawned over the new prime minister, who did not seem inclined toward much small talk. Members of the cabinet waited around.

Zail Singh had risen that day in Sanaa, the capital of the Yemen Arab Republic. Yemen was the second stop on a two-nation official tour that began in Mauritius. It was his secretary, A. C. Bandopadhyay, who told Singh the news of the shooting of Indira Gandhi. The president decided at once to abandon his tour and leave for India. He asked that the formal guard-of-honor ceremonies at the airport not be observed. His chartered Boeing 707 would ordinarily have flown from Sanaa to Bombay for a refueling stop, but Singh requested that the pilot fly directly, if possible, to New Delhi. The plane's crew was not happy with the request, but under the circumstances they said they would oblige. During the five-hour plane journey, Singh's aides—Bandopadhyay, Special Assistant I. S. Bindhra, and Ramesh Bhandari, a senior secretary in the external affairs ministry—kept in touch with Delhi by radio. Singh himself declined lunch and lay in his bed for more than three hours. He reflected on the years he had served Indira Gandhi. And on his own years as chief minister of the troubled Punjab—he was Mrs. Gandhi's emissary to Sikh leaders who agitated for greater autonomy for the state—and how he had failed to bring about any lasting solution to the Sikh crisis. And now Indira Gandhi was dead, killed by two Sikh guards.

Singh was met at Delhi's Palam International Airport by Vice President R. Venkataraman; Rajendra Kumar Dhawan, Mrs. Gandhi's closest aide; Balram Jakhar, the speaker of the Lok Sabha, the lower house of Parliament; Dr. P. C. Alexander, principal private secretary to Mrs. Gandhi; and Arun Nehru.

During the twenty-minute ride from the airport to the All-India Institute of Medical Sciences Arun Nehru raised the question of succession.

"The Congress parliamentary board has decided that Rajivji should become PM," Nehru, a giant of a man with a permanent scowl bolted to his face, said to Singh. Vice President Venkataraman said that it was the best choice for the country.

The board currently had just four members instead of the normal nine: Home Minister P. V. Narasimha Rao, Finance Minister Pranab Mukerjee, Maragatham Chandrasekhar, and senior Congress Party aide Kamlapati Tripathi. Mrs. Gandhi had been a member of this board, which served as the highest policy-making unit of the ruling Congress Party. When the assassination occurred, Narasimha Rao was politicking in his home constituency of Warangal, in Andhra Pradesh, and Mukerjee was accompanying Rajiv Gandhi in West Bengal, his own home state. Tripathy and Chandrasekhar were also out of Delhi. It did not, of course, matter that these men were out of station. Arun Nehru, who had muscled his way to preeminent power in the Congress Party, had already resolved that his cousin, Rajiv Gandhi, would become India's next prime minister. He was supported in this by Sitaram Kesari, treasurer of the Congress Party. Nehru and Kesari met with top Congress officials in a fifth-floor conference room at the All-India Institute of Medical Sciences and declared that the party had no other choice but to name Rajiv Gandhi to succeed his mother. Concurring with this were Chief Ministers Chandrasekhar Singh of Bihar, Janaki Ballav Patnaik of Orissa, Arjun Singh of Madhya Pradesh, and Shiv Charan Mathur of Rajasthan. The Nehru–Kesari decision was conveyed to other senior Congress Party officials all through the afternoon. A formal letter advising President Zail Singh of the Congress parliamentary board's "decision" was drafted by G. K. Moopanar, general secretary of the All-India Congress Committee. The letter also formally requested Singh to appoint Rajiv Gandhi as prime minister (under India's Constitution, it is the president who must name the prime minister).

Rajiv Gandhi and Zail Singh linked up with each other on the eighth floor of the All-India Institute of Medical Sciences. Singh hugged Gandhi. He plucked his trademark red rose from the buttonhole of his achkan, or long, fitted jacket, and gently placed it on Indira Gandhi's body. The red rose was her father's trademark, too—he always wore one in his lapel. He then asked Rajiv Gandhi to come to Rashtrapati Bhavan at 6:30 P.M.

When Gandhi turned up at the president's sprawling sandstone home—where Britain's viceroys had once resided and ruled—most of the Congress Party's top officials had already assembled in the Ashoka Hall. Gandhi wore a white kurta and tailored pyjama trousers. He had shaved. His eyes seemed slightly red, but otherwise he looked remarkably in self-control.

At 6:40 P.M., or nine hours after his mother was felled by a fusillade from assassins' guns, former pilot Rajiv Gandhi was sworn in as prime minister of India. He had never held a cabinet portfolio before; he had been a member of Parliament only since 1982; he had entered politics only reluctantly, under much emotional pressure from his mother after the death of her initial heir apparent and younger son, Sanjay. All Rajiv Gandhi had ever wanted to do was fly planes for Indian Airlines. Now he was a pilot in charge of 800 million Indians.

4

Aftermath

BY 2 P.M. on Wednesday, October 31, All-India Radio's hourly news bulletins started referring to the fact that Indira Gandhi had been shot in the garden of her home and that she was being treated at the All-India Institute of Medical Sciences in New Delhi. By four o'clock that afternoon, a large crowd had gathered in front of the Institute's main entrance.

Dev Dutt, a Delhi journalist, was in that crowd. This is his account of what happened that afternoon:

"There were slogans mostly in praise of Mrs. Gandhi, and a few slogans threatening revenge. But there was no tension. There were a number of Sikhs in the crowd. Their faces showed no fear or apprehension. We talked to some of them in order to gauge their state of mind. The Sikhs seemed to be supremely confident about the goodwill of their Hindu brethren. It seems they nursed no suspicions against the Hindus. They did not show any traces of nervousness of any kind. The non-Sikhs in the crowd did not seem even to notice the presence of Sikhs and took their presence as normal.

"While this crowd waited patiently, the flow of traffic and the normal business around nearby kiosks continued. I was standing near the street crossing in front of the institute when thirty or forty young men emerged out of the crowd and formed a neat column three or four men deep and ran toward the crossing near a traffic island. They caught hold of a scooter that was parked on the other side and set it on fire. Then these young men moved toward some nearby buses that had been slowing down on account of the fire. They began to pull Sikhs out of buses. They started to pull off their turbans and beat them relentlessly. I saw five turbans burning in a row on the road.

"There were no policemen in the area. The group had a free hand. After about twenty minutes, a group of khaki-clad men arrived and began to chase away the miscreants.

"It is difficult to explain the sudden eruption of violence in the institute area that afternoon. But the question is: Who were these people who came out of the crowd and went on a rampage?"

The incidents near the All-India Institute of Medical Sciences were the first in Delhi in which Sikhs were targeted and manhandled. By late evening, non-Sikh mobs were rampaging through Sikh neighborhoods elsewhere in the capital. Led by men identified by some of the victims as local Congress Party leaders and Delhi administrative officials, these mobs burned down houses, raped women, looted homes, and murdered Sikh males. A senior member of Mrs. Gandhi's party was seen directing some of the rioters.

Over the next four days, more than two thousand Sikhs died at the hands of these mobs in Delhi. Most died gruesome deaths: they were often burned alive, or were hacked to pieces while female members of their families were stripped and made to watch. Prepubescent boys were castrated by mobs. The carnage spread to neighboring states as well. In Uttar Pradesh, more than a thousand Sikhs were reported killed in cities such as Kanpur, Lucknow, and Ghaziabad. In Haryana, the death toll exceeded a hundred. In Bihar, the toll rose to three hundred. Sikhs were also slaughtered by well-armed mobs in Madhya Pradesh, West Bengal, Himachal Pradesh, and Maharashtra. Most of these states are governed by the Congress Party.

It is impossible to say with certainty how many Sikhs died in the five-day period following the murder of Indira Gandhi. But officials of the Delhi-based People's Union for Democratic Rights (PUDR) and the People's Union for Civil Liberties (PUCL)—who investigated many of the incidents in the capital and who produced a well-documented report—say that the national death toll probably exceeded three thousand. While the actual property loss may never be known, many estimates suggest that between October 31 and November 5, more than $250 million worth of property was destroyed in Delhi alone.

The organizations' report—which was largely written by Rajni Kothari, a respected political scientist—was titled "Who Are the Guilty?" It sold briskly. The report charged that the Delhi government had in effect encouraged Hindu and Sikh communalism to "feed upon each other" in the Punjab, and that the repercussions of the Punjab situation were being felt in Delhi. The Sikh community must be reassured in the aftermath of the holocaust in Delhi, the report said.

Investigators from the PUDR and the PUCL found that the attacks against Delhi's Sikh community were hardly spontaneous expressions of grief and anger over Mrs. Gandhi's assassination—as the Delhi authorities have asserted they were. The rampaging mobs were well led, well armed, and well informed about just where Sikh families lived. Congress Party leaders were seen turning up with lists of residents not only in poor localities such as Munirka, Mangalpuri, and Trilokpuri, but also in rich neighborhoods such as Friends Colony and Maharani Bagh. Thugs—or goondas, as they are commonly known in India—arrived in Delhi Transport Corporation (DTC) buses, or in vans and trucks and jeeps ordinarily used by local Congress Party workers.

The PUDR and PUCL investigators—whose report has not been contradicted by the government—found that there were two distinct phases to the violence against Delhi's Sikhs.

The first phase was marked by three rumors that were spread around the capital on the evening of October 31: (1) Sikhs were reported to be distributing mithai and lighting oil lamps to celebrate the demise of Mrs. Gandhi; (2) trainloads of hundreds of murdered Hindus were said to have arrived from the Punjab at the Old Delhi

Station; and (3) Delhi's water supply was said to have been poisoned by Sikhs.

Subsequent inquiries showed that no one had actually witnessed the sweetmeat distribution. There had been no trainloads of dead Hindus coming in from the Punjab—but Delhi policemen had been cruising in vans through certain neighborhoods and announcing by loudspeaker that such trains had indeed arrived at the Old Delhi Station. It was also the police who announced that Sikhs had poisoned the city's water supply.

The second phase, the PUDR/PUCL report said, "began with the arrival of groups of armed young people in vans, scooters, motorcycles or trucks from the night of October 31 and morning of November 1 at various places like Munirka, Saket, South Extention, Lajpat Nagar, Bhogal, Jangpura and Ashram in the south and southeast; the Connaught Circle shopping area in the center, and later the trans-Jamuna colonies and resettlement colonies in other areas in the north. With cans of petrol they went around these localities and systematically set fire to Sikh houses, shops, and gurdwaras [temples]. We were told by local eye-witnesses that well-known Congress leaders and workers led and directed the arsonists and that local cadres of the Congress Party identified the Sikh houses and shops. A senior police official pointed out to us: 'The shop signs are either in Hindi or English. How do you expect the illiterate arsonists to know whether these shops belonged to Hindus or Sikhs—unless they were identified to them by someone who is either educated or a local person?'

"In some areas, like Trilokpuri, Mangalpuri, and the trans-Jamuna colonies, the arsonists consisted of Gujjar or Jat farmers from neighboring villages, and were accompanied by local residents, some of whom again were Congress activists. In these areas, we were told, Congress followers of the Bhangi caste (those belonging to the Harijan, or 'untouchable' community) took part in the looting. In South Delhi, buses of the Delhi Transport Corporation (DTC) were used by the miscreants to move from place to place in their murderous journey. How could the DTC allow its buses to be used by criminals?

"The attacks in the resettlement colonies of Trilokpuri and Mangalpuri, where the maximum number of murders took place, again displayed the same pattern. The targets were primarily young Sikhs. They were dragged out, beaten up and then burnt alive. While old men, women and children were generally allowed to escape, their houses were set on fire after looting of valuables. Documents pertaining to their legal possession of the houses were also burnt. In some areas of Mangalpuri, we heard from survivors that even children were not spared. We also came across reports of gang-rape of women. The orgy of destruction embraced a variety of property ranging from shops, factories, houses to gurdwaras and schools belonging to Sikhs. In all the affected spots, a calculated attempt to terrorize the people was evident in the common tendency among the assailants to burn alive the Sikhs on public roads. Even five days after the incidents, on November 6, in the course of one of our regular visits to Mangalpuri we found that although the ashes had been cleared, the pavement in front of the Congress Party office was still blotched with burnt patches, which the local people had earlier pointed out to us as spots where four Sikhs were burnt alive."

Throughout the carnage, Delhi's policemen were either totally absent from the scene; or they stood by while mobs freely burnt Sikhs live; or they themselves participated in the orgy of violence against the Sikhs. But in Lajpat Nagar, on November 1, when a group of concerned citizens tried to organize a peace march in support of Hindu–Sikh amity, a police jeep blocked the way and police officials demanded to know if the marchers had official permission.

In areas such as Trilokpuri, policemen were seen supplying diesel oil and petrol to arsonists.

In Kotla Mubarakpur, several witnesses heard a police inspector say to a group of rioters: "We gave you thirty-six hours. Had we given the Sikhs that amount of time, they would have killed every Hindu."

A number of Hindu residents of areas such as Mangolpuri tried to hide their Sikh neighbors from the marauding mobs.

But when two Hindus, Dharam Raj Pawar and Rajvir Pawar, went to a police station at Ber Serai and asked for police protection for their Sikh friends, a policeman said to them: "You being Hindus should have killed those Sikhs. What are you doing here? Don't you know a train has arrived from Punjab carrying bodies of massacred Hindus?"

On the evening of October 31, Atal Behari Vajpayee, an opposition leader, called on Home Minister P. V. Narasimha Rao to express outrage over the mounting attacks against Sikhs.

"Everything will be brought under control within a couple of hours," Narasimha Rao told Vajpayee, a former foreign minister.

But Narasimha Rao did not impose a curfew until two days later, and he belatedly called the army in to restore law and order. But even then, the violence against the Sikhs continued, aided and abetted by those in power.

One eyewitness to the events of October 31–November 5 was Ashwini Ray, head of the department of political science at Delhi's Jawaharlal Nehru University. This is his account:

"There was a police vehicle with four policemen parked near Bhogal market. I came out of my house and saw smoke billowing out. I heard the sound of a tire bursting. Policemen were reading newspapers and drinking tea inside their car while arson was going on all around. I went to the police car to ask why they were not stopping the arson and was told to mind my own business. I then saw several looters carrying off radio and television sets from stores right in front of the parked police vehicles. Some of the policemen asked the people to hurry with the loot."

Few looters or rioters were arrested during the October 31– November 5 carnage. But the police did take into custody several Sikhs who defended themselves and their families with weapons. The Rajiv Gandhi government dragged its feet in providing relief money to Sikh victims, authorizing the equivalent of no more than $300 per family. Few of the victims have received this money.

The report prepared by the PUDR and the PUCL makes dramatic points in its conclusion:

"The social and political consequences of the government's stance during the carnage, its deliberate inaction and its callousness toward relief and rehabilitation are far reaching.

"It is curious that for several hours the government had between the time of Mrs. Gandhi's assassination and the official announcement of her death, no security arrangements were made for the victims.

"The riots were well organized and were of unprecedented brutality. Several very disturbing questions arise that must be answered:

"What were the government and the Delhi administration doing for several hours between the time of the assassination and the announcement of Mrs. Gandhi's death? Why did the government refuse to take cognizance of the reports of the looting and murders and call in troops even after the military had been 'alerted'? Why was there no joint control room set up and who was responsible for not giving clear and specific instructions to the army on curbing violence and imposing curfew?

"Who was responsible for the planned and deliberate police inaction and often active role in inciting the murders and the looting? Who was responsible for the planned and well-directed arson?

"Why were highly provocative slogans (such as 'Khoon ka baadla khoon' ['blood for blood']) allowed to be broadcast by Doordarshan during the televised transmissions depicting the mourning crowds at Teen Murti Bhavan, where Mrs. Gandhi's body was kept on display?

"Why has the Congress Party not set up an inquiry into the role of its members in the arson and looting?"

These were questions that Sikhs and decent men and women all over India kept asking long afterward.

In those hours and days of terror following the assassination of Mrs. Gandhi, there were Hindus who came to the assistance of besieged Sikhs. A number of young people got together in Delhi and formed an umbrella organization called the Nagarik Seva Manch— Citizens' Service Group. A brave Sikh named Tejeshwar Singh, a publishing executive who also anchors the government's evening

television newscast, defiantly led a procession of Hindus and Sikhs
through Delhi's streets. The participants urged Indians to shun violence and renew their commitment to communal harmony.

"Hindu-Sikh bhai bhai!" the marchers shouted. "Hindus and
Sikhs are brothers!"

But as the procession moved through low-income neighborhoods,
crowds sometimes heckled them. Stones were thrown at Tejeshwar
Singh. The marchers were threatened with bodily harm. Among
those who jeered at the marchers were men whom they identified as
prominent Delhi legislators and Congress Party officials.

During the holocaust, a number of Hindus offered shelter to their
Sikh friends. My brother-in-law, Ajai Lal, and his wife, Indu, went
across to the home of their Sikh neighbor, Anand Singh, and invited
the former army colonel to pack up and stay with them until the
trouble subsided. When Hindu friends found out that Khushwant
Singh, the well-known Sikh writer and historian, had sought refuge
in the Swedish Embassy, they implored him to come to their homes.

Scores of Sikh men in Delhi cut their long hair, threw away their
turbans, and shaved their beards so that they would not be singled
out as Sikhs. The barbershops in Delhi's luxury hotels did roaring
business.

Noni Chawla, a young executive with the ITC–Sheraton Hotel
group, moved to his employers' flagship hotel, the Maurya-Sheraton,
with his wife, Nilima, and their two children. The homes of a number
of Sikhs in the Chawlas' affluent neighborhood in the Vasant Vihar
section of Delhi had been attacked by mobs who came armed with
voter lists. Several Sikhs were dragged out of their houses, stripped
in the streets, beaten, then burnt alive.

"What kind of a country has this become?" asked Noni Chawla,
who refused to doff his turban or cut his hair.

"I've never felt discriminated against in India," Chawla said. "But
clearly times are changing. Among many young Sikh professionals I
now hear talk of emigrating to the West. We don't want our children
taunted in school. A lot of us feel a sense of alienation, of separation.
I think Sikhs will have an increasingly difficult time in India."

At ten o'clock on the morning of Wednesday, October 31, Payal Singh and several other Sikh friends and relatives boarded a train in the eastern metropolis of Calcutta. Singh, a writer, and her group were headed for Delhi to attend a wedding.

It was not until six o'clock that evening that the Sikhs heard the All-India Radio bulletin about Mrs. Gandhi's death—and about the fact that her assassins had been two Sikh security guards.

"Every passenger irrespective of his religion was in a state of shocked silence," Singh later recalled.

At eleven o'clock the next morning, the train reached Ghaziabad. Delhi was still many miles away.

"That was the beginning of two harrowing hours for us, when we were suspended between life and death," Payal Singh wrote in the *Illustrated Weekly of India*. This is what she said in her extraordinary account:

"A bloodthirsty mob, almost like a pack of hungry wolves hunting for prey, went from coach to coach in search of Sikhs.

"In a frenzy of madness, the mob, armed with iron rods and knives, brutally dragged out Sikhs, burnt their turbans, hacked the men to death and threw them across the tracks. Even the old and feeble were not spared. The barbaric mob, totally devoid of rationality, declared that women would be spared. But in what sense were they spared? After all, what can be more torturous for women than seeing male members of their family hacked to death in front of their eyes?

"The main doors of our coach were locked from inside. And we waited with bated breath. The mob, hell-bent on destruction, was not to be deterred.

"They pounded on the heavy metal door for over fifteen minutes. The incessant pounding was accompanied by threats to set the train on fire. One non-Sikh passenger shifted uncomfortably in his seat and said he felt all of them would lose their lives if the door was not opened. But he was sternly reprimanded by the others who declared that under no circumstances would the door be opened.

"The petrified screams of two women inside our compartment, our own pleas, and the persuasion of the other non-Sikh passengers finally seemed to convince the mob that there were no sardars inside. The mob retreated."

When Payal Singh's train reached Delhi at three o'clock that afternoon, its surviving Sikh males helped carry out corpses from compartments. By then other trains were also arriving in Delhi from northern Indian cities. Scores of Sikh males lay dead in them.

"The bodies had been battered," Payal Singh said later. "Those Sikhs were innocent people who had done nothing. Except for being Sikhs and traveling toward Delhi on that fateful day."

Late in the evening of Wednesday, October 31, I dined with Dilip and Nina Sardesai at the Cricket Club of India in Bombay. Nina Sardesai, a professor of sociology at St. Xavier's College, is a cousin of my wife, Jayanti; her husband, Dilip, is a businessman and a former cricketer who has played on the national team. We were joined by Nina's sister, Jaymala Bhandarkar, and her husband, Anil, who is Pan Am's marketing director in Bombay. The occasion was Nina's birthday. The Sardesais had insisted I eat with them.

Ramchandra Moray drove me to the club. Traffic was thin, and few people were out on the streets. It was as if the sidewalks of Bombay had been rolled up. Restaurants were shut. No shops seemed open. In this southern part of Bombay, I saw no policemen.

"Everybody is home watching television or listening to the radio, sahib," Moray said. "What a day this has been for India!"

At the club, dinner had been laid out on a veranda overlooking a vast cricket field. The cuisine was Chinese. No one, however, felt like eating much. The conversation at the table was about what would happen to India's Sikhs.

"I'm telling you—there's bound to be a massacre of the Sikhs," Dilip Sardesai said. "At times like these, good sense does not prevail in India."

"I hope Bombay is spared," Anil Bhandarkar said.

"Unlikely," his wife said.

"Too many goondas here who'd like nothing better than to bash some Sikh heads," Nina Sardesai said.

After dinner we retired to the club's lounge to watch Rajiv Gandhi address the nation. It was approaching midnight. Half a dozen Sikhs sat quietly in one corner. The non-Sikhs in the room looked furtively at them. I thought: here we go. The Sikhs are already aliens in their own country.

It was Anil Bhandarkar who suggested that I visit some Sikh neighborhoods the following morning to assess the mood. There are an estimated three hundred thousand Sikhs in this city of eight million people, which has long been known for tolerance among religious groups. Neighborhoods such as Sion, Koliwada, and North Dadar contain significant Sikh enclaves. Bombay may have a mottled history of strife between Hindus and Muslims, but Sikhs have traditionally lived in harmony with non-Sikhs here. Many Sikhs own automobile shops or work in the automobile spare parts business. Some operate restaurants; still others are carpenters or handymen. Some drive taxis. In this city of much unemployment and poverty, few Sikhs are jobless.

And so it was that I found myself the next morning in the Sion section of the city. I had been given the name of a man named Bhupinder Singh Chatwal, a dealer in automobile spare parts.

He lived in a three-room apartment not far from the Sion railway station. I had telephoned him to say I was coming. But when I rang the doorbell, he let me in only reluctantly.

I could hear his wife, Surinder Kaur, speaking to her four small children in the bedroom next to the living room.

"You are not to step out of this home," she said. "Under no circumstances are you to leave the safety of these four walls."

She joined her husband in the living room, and offered me tea.

"Have you bought the padlock yet?" she asked Bhupinder Singh. She had slept late this morning, but the previous night had requested her husband to make the purchase.

"No," Bhupinder Singh said.

"And why not?" Surinder Kaur said, her voice rising just a fraction.

"Because I didn't think it was safe to go out this morning."

I was aghast hearing this. I was brought up believing that Sikhs were the proudest, most courageous people of all Indians. They were tall, they walked with their heads in high heaven, and they were fearless. There were some 120,000 Sikhs in the Indian armed forces, and 22 percent of the officer corps was Sikh. Sikhs were brave in battle; and in civilian life they had for centuries been the traditional protectors of the Hindus.

And now Bhupinder Singh was saying he was afraid to go out of his home?

"We know we will be the victims," he said to me, his deep voice cracking a bit. "It is only a matter of time."

We were visited by his next-door neighbor, Mahinder Singh, who owned an electric goods store. He had just received a telephone call from relatives in Delhi apprising him about the mounting violence against Sikhs in the capital.

"Our fear is that we will be made scapegoats," Mahinder Singh said. Like Bhupinder Singh, he was in his late thirties. "And once any rioting or violence starts, then the antisocial elements take over soon. I dare not keep my shop open."

He paused to sip tea.

"Tell me," he said, his eyes welling with tears, "why should all Sikhs bear the responsibility for the horrible event in Delhi yesterday?"

What could I say to Mahinder Singh? That the weak will always prey on the strong when given a chance? That the "tolerance" of India's majority Hindus was a fiction? That the death of Indira Gandhi showed how fragile our secular structure was, how easily it could be shaken and abused?

I did not say any of this to him.

"Look," I said, "if there's any trouble here at all, please contact me. I'm staying at a friend's apartment. It's large enough to hold all of you. Please come there. I promise you complete safety."

As Ramchandra Moray drove me back to the Colaba apartment, I reflected on what I had just told the Sikhs. If indeed there was violence against them in Bombay, could I, a Hindu-born man, really protect them against a mob's blind fury?

Part Two

PASSAGE THROUGH INDIA

1

In The Punjab

I HAD never met Inder Mohan Khosla until this morning. He was distantly related to me by marriage, and I had learned that he had recently been posted by his bank to Amritsar, the site of Sikhism's holiest shrine, the Golden Temple. Arriving in Delhi from Bombay not long after the assassination of Mrs. Gandhi, I found out from relatives that Khosla was himself in the capital that day and was preparing to return to Amritsar. I telephoned him at the place where he was staying.

I wanted to visit the Punjab, I said, and he was my only contact. I told Khosla that I wanted to see for myself what everyday life was really like in that troubled border state, the home of Sikh fundamentalists who wanted to carve out from the Punjab a theocratic nation called Khalistan. I wanted to worship at the Golden Temple; I wanted to see if Sikhs still welcomed Hindus at their most treasured house of prayer. I wanted to understand just what was this "Punjab problem" that had spawned so much hate and bitterness and so much violence and that threatened the territorial integrity of India; that finally had resulted in the murder of the country's prime minister in her own garden by trusted security guards, both Sikhs.

"You're welcome to fly back with me," Khosla said. His voice was warm and hospitable. "And you're welcome to stay with us. If you don't mind an overfriendly dog, that is. Our dog simply has no manners."

We agreed to meet at Delhi's domestic airport. Khosla said he'd save a place for me in the line at the check-in counter.

"But how will I recognize you?" I said. "The place will be mobbed."

"You won't have any problem," Khosla said. "There will, of course, be a very long line of people going to Amritsar. But every one of them will be a Sikh. The Sikhs are rushing back to the Punjab, especially with these riots now in Delhi against their community. You'll spot me very easily. I'll be the only non-Sikh in the line."

Sikhs were everywhere at Delhi's disorganized domestic airport. Most of them carried so much baggage that I despaired our plane wouldn't be able to take off because of the weight. Some of these Sikhs seemed to have returned from the Gulf states, which over the last decade lured tens of thousands of plumbers and carpenters and artisans and mechanics from the Punjab with irresistible offers: these young men would not have hoped to make that kind of money had they stayed home. It was not uncommon for a Punjabi handyman with just a high school education and some experience under his turban to be earning $50,000 annually in the oil-rich states of the Arabian peninsula. This was a lot of money for anyone to be pulling in, but in Indian terms it was a grand fortune—five hundred thousand rupees, at the current exchange rate, or more than most Indians make in a lifetime. And for someone who had been a simple villager in the Punjab until his journey abroad, the amount was bewildering. So the Sikhs, unaccustomed to such large incomes, went berserk. They bought up entire stores.

On this morning, several dozen of them were returning to their home state, their purchases in tow. Strewn around the poorly lit check-in area were huge Sony television sets, refrigerators, sewing machines, dishwashers, stereo sets, bicycles, toys, chandeliers, portable cassette players, vacuum cleaners. Under a peculiar government rule—intended, I was told, to ensure that arms weren't smuggled in as unaccompanied baggage—these goods could be despatched to the Punjab by air freight only after the owner had first checked in at the airlines counter. The Sikh men who were returning home after their two or three years abroad had also acquired smartly cut suits and sweaters. The fragrance of strong colognes suffused the area. But for some reason nearly all wore scruffy shoes. There was little chatter or conversation among these men. Their faces were grim. Few argued with airlines officials when they added up the excess-baggage levies. The Sikhs did not seem to be happy to be going home again.

"Over here!" someone shouted. "Next to the TV and behind the dishwasher!"

It was Khosla. He was tall, barrel chested, and wore a woolen suit and a tie that featured airplanes. Even before we shook hands, Khosla said: "Ah, this tie. We do have a pilot who's our maximum leader now, you know!"

I took an immediate liking to Khosla. He laughed and joked through most of the hour we spent in the departure lounge, while the Indian Airlines Boeing 737 was being loaded. There were nearly two hundred passengers on the flight, and only four of us were non-Sikhs. I was uneasy. What lay ahead? Would the Punjab erupt? I overheard some fellow passengers discuss what was going on in Delhi. Entire Sikh neighborhoods were being set upon by mobs howling for revenge. There was now widespread concern that Sikhs in the Punjab would retaliate and murder minority Hindus in their state.

Khosla said he thought this unlikely. The Indian army was out in such force in Punjab, he said, that no violence would occur there. Maybe an isolated incident here and there—but nothing like what was happening in Delhi.

"Besides, I think Sikhs are well aware of the fact that there are Sikh enclaves all across India," Khosla said. "If they were to murder Hindus in the Punjab, they would at once invite retaliation in other parts of the country. There simply aren't enough Sikhs—just 14 million in a country of nearly 800 million. How does a minority like this retaliate effectively?"

Khosla paused, sensing my unease.

"Don't worry," he said, with a broad smile. "Nothing's going to happen to you. You'll be all right in the Punjab."

He became a little impatient when we wound up waiting inside the plane for another hour while security guards, accompanied by large Alsatian dogs, unloaded the baggage containers, no doubt to search for weapons and bombs. Officials have become very suspicious about Amritsar-bound flights since one was hijacked in mid-1984 and ordered flown by Sikh terrorists to neighboring Pakistan, India's long-standing foe whose government has been said to support the Sikh agitation for an independent nation. I recalled a conversation I had had with an aide to Prime Minister Rajiv Gandhi in which I pointed out that India's arming and financing of the guerrillas who fought to create Bangladesh out of the erstwhile East Pakistan more than a decade ago was interference, too, in the domestic affairs of another sovereign nation.

"That was different," the official said, not at all pleased that I had raised the business of Bangladesh. "India was asked for help by the Bangladesh freedom fighters."

"How do you know that Pakistan hasn't been asked for help by the Sikh separatists?" I said.

Our plane took off on its northwesterly flight. In less than forty-five minutes, just as I was polishing off a surprisingly savory cheese delicacy, the aircraft started its descent. Amritsar came into view. It was no more than a brown blotch on a carpet of green. Fields stretched out in all directions from the city; snow-white egrets rose in tufts in these paddies. The plane banked steeply, and I could see the Golden Temple. Its central shrine, the gold-sheathed Harimandir, glistened in the middle of a pond. My heart raced. This was my first glimpse of Sikhism's Mecca since childhood, when my parents had taken me on a journey across India to see shrines of all faiths. "The buildings may be different, their priests may be different," my father had said to me, "but the purpose of every religion is the same. It is to uplift mankind." I had often recalled his words, and I remembered them now: Sikhism had always prided itself on its tolerance; but in recent years, Sikh fundamentalists had started to complain about Hindu encroachment: Sikh terrorists had gunned down Hindus in the Punjab not over political differences but because they were Hindus. We landed at Raja Sansi Airport. The first persons to greet disembarking passengers on the tarmac were not airline officials but guntoting soldiers. There were also brown-uniformed Punjab policemen, green-uniformed Border Security Force troops, and olive-uniformed men of the Central Reserve Police Force. I saw bunkers where machine guns had been mounted. Plainclothesmen of the Central Bureau of Investigation scrutinized all arrivals, not bothering to be surreptitious: they would occasionally go up to a passenger and demand his documents. Inside the baggage-claim area, there were more policemen. A fat Sikh, whose badge identified him as Superintendent Nirmal Singh, moved through the crowd, chatting with those he knew and questioning those he didn't. Nirmal Singh saw me chatting with Khosla and his driver, and I was left alone. Since the Indian army's storming of the Golden Temple in June 1984 to flush out the terrorists who had taken sanctuary there, the Punjab authorities had banned all foreigners from entering their state—especially foreign journalists. I had kept my Indian passport handy in my jacket in the event someone asked me for identification: the Punjab police were not known for their gracious treatment of anyone they suspected of violating laws. The kiosk in the arrival lounge offered only Hindi film magazines and biscuits. The glass-fronted advertisements for local hotels were not lit. Khosla's driver gathered our baggage and we drove off toward the city, which was a good twenty kilometers from the airport.

We passed vast wheat fields, Sikhs on tractors, and small trucks laden with hay. The houses I saw were all made of brick and concrete —there are few mud huts in the Punjab, as there are in other Indian states. Television antennas sprouted from many of these homes. The 12 million people of the Punjab produce 60 percent of India's annual foodgrain production of 140 million metric tons; most Punjabi farmers earn a lot more each year than the national per capita income of $250. Because of a new canal system financed by the central government and high-yield seeds that were distributed by Delhi in the

1950s, crop production in the Punjab has risen by six times since 1951. Sixty percent of the state's population was engaged in agriculture, which accounted for more than 62 percent of the Punjab's annual income. The high-yield grain developed in the United States and at Ludhiana State University in India and tried out in the Punjab by Norman E. Borlaug, an American scientist, resulted in rice production increasing from 892 kilograms per hectare in 1950 to 3,000 kilograms by 1981; wheat production grew from 901 kilograms per hectare to 3,100 kilograms during the same period.

The "green revolution" that Borlaug generated in the Punjab had many spinoffs. The number of primary schools in the Punjab rose from 7,183 in 1967 to 12,400 by 1982; in 1967, there were just 700 high schools in the state, but by 1982 the figure had climbed beyond 2,200. In 1967, there were 71 colleges in the Punjab, and in less than two decades there were an additional hundred. There were no medical colleges in the state in 1967; by 1982, there were nine, including two around Amritsar. Educated Sikhs went abroad to work and sent back more than a billion dollars a year to their relatives in the Punjab. This money stimulated consumerism. You could now buy not only electronic goods but also fancy foodstuffs and textiles and home appliances and furniture almost anywhere in the state—not only in large cities such as Amritsar and Jullundur and Chandigarh. There were now few beggars in Punjab's villages and towns and cities. It was rare to see a hungry Punjabi, and rarer still to see a destitute one.

On the way to Khosla's home, we passed billboards advertising color TV sets, fashionable clothes, tape recorders and radios, and motorcycles. We passed several advertisements inviting Punjabis to travel to exotic locations abroad. "Visas guaranteed," one ad promised. "No waiting in line at embassies. But hurry! Or else you may have to wait in line at our office!" Plump children played near the tar road; some waved happily to us. We passed *dhabaas*, or typical north Indian roadside restaurants, their chimneys pushing out powerful aromas of tandoori chicken and spicy curries. Sikhs, many in loosely bound turbans, squatted outside grocery stores, munching apples and oragnes. Few women seemed to be outdoors.

The air was clear and cool. The greenness was dazzling.

There were few civilian cars on the road into Amritsar. But we passed dozens of military trucks and jeeps. We passed antipersonnel vehicles, each mounted with machine guns. Army patrols were everywhere.

I was in the Punjab.

Inder Mohan Khosla lived in a sprawling bungalow at the edge of the city. The house was typical of the homes in Amritsar's richer neighborhoods, and it had been acquired decades ago by Khosla's bank for its senior representative in the city. It was filled with Indian antiquities and art treasures. He and his wife, Anjali, were longtime collectors. Anjali was visiting her parents in Bombay, and the Khoslas' only daughter was away at boarding school. The family dog, a gargantuan golden retriever, was delighted to see his master again. The dog usually spent so much of his time chasing birds on the huge lawn surrounding the Khosla home, that for him to be let into the four-bedroom house was always a treat.

"All quiet here?" Khosla asked his servants. He had been away in Delhi for almost a week.

"Of course, sahib," said one of them. "What can happen in Amritsar?"

Khosla decided he would visit his office. It was Saturday afternoon, but the bank would be open until five o'clock. We drove into the heart of Amritsar. There were army patrols everywhere, but no signs of real tension. Shops were open. Garish movie posters were put up on the walls of many of the city's aging one- and two-story buildings. The narrow streets were jammed with bicyclists, both Sikh and non-Sikh. Couples with little children went about in auto-rickshaws, the tiny taxis that are pulled by scooters. There were several large billboards inviting patronage at sweetmeat stores: Amritsar is known for its marvelous desserts, and Amritsarites are legendary for their sweet tooth. It was getting a bit nippy, and I wished I had a sweater.

At the bank, Khosla introduced me to his employees. They were overwhelmingly Hindus; I could spot only three Sikhs in the cavernous main hall. Khosla's subordinates seemed happier to see me than their boss, whose temper and insistence on such un-Indian matters as punctuality had often resulted in more than one employee receiving a public dressing-down. I got around to talking with a man named V. M. Gupta, who seemed eager to put across a Hindu point of view concerning the assassination of Indira Gandhi and what was happening in the Punjab.

"The Sikhs here say that Indira was killed in retribution for the invasion of the Golden Temple," said Gupta, a thin, middle-aged man. "I don't think that ordinary Sikhs supported Sant Jarnail Singh Bhindranwale and his gang of thugs who went around killing Hindus and those Sikhs who didn't agree with them. But the feeling here was that the Golden Temple should have been spared. People were astonished at the amount of damage to the shrine. Sikhs held that anybody who invaded their temple wouldn't be spared."

How did people feel about Indira Gandhi's death?

"We Hindus are very sad," Gupta said. "We are very upset that a woman who did so much for the country was killed so brutally. Hindus of all political parties really believed that Mrs. Gandhi was the savior of all communities in the Punjab. Now that she's been killed, what hope is there left for peace here? But among the Sikhs there is celebration."

"What kind of celebration?" I asked.

"They lit up their gurdwaras, they distributed sweets on the day she died," Gupta said. "There even were fireworks."

"Did you witness any of this?"

"Not personally."

"Then how do you know all this?"

"Sir, it's common knowledge in the Hindu community that the Sikhs were joyous when Indiraji was killed," Gupta said, a trifle uncertainly. "Those Sikhs now all have sympathy for the idea of Khalistan. They don't think of themselves as Indians. They don't think there is security for Sikhs in a Hindu India."

Are the Hindus frightened that the Sikhs will get at them because of what's been happening in Delhi?

"The Hindus aren't afraid in Amritsar—where 60 percent of the city's million-strong population is Hindu," Gupta said. "But elsewhere in the state, the population ratio favors Sikhs by 52 percent to 48 percent. We are particularly concerned that the rural Jat Sikhs will hit the Hindus."

Gupta paused to sip tea that a peon had brought.

"There is a feeling taking hold among Hindus that you cannot trust the Sikh," Gupta said, presently. "There is a feeling that he's a betrayer. People's racial memories are long in the Punjab. Hindus remember still that during the 1857 Sepoy Mutiny against the British, the Sikhs betrayed the nationalists by helping the British to put down the rebellion. There is a feeling among many Hindus that the Sikhs have always thought of themselves before thinking about their country. There is a feeling that Sikhs are traitors.

"I can bet you, sir, that every Hindu in Amritsar feels that it is not a good thing that Sikhs are being killed at present in Delhi. But Sikhs have rejoiced when Hindus were killed in Punjab by Bhindranwale and his terrorists. You can safely say, sir, that we Hindus are very, very angry. The old harmony that used to be found here between Hindus and Sikhs is not there now—and it won't return."

Not far from the bank where Gupta and I spoke that afternoon was a Hindu temple, which Gupta suggested I visit. The temple honored the Hindu Lord Shiva, and its visitors traditionally included Sikhs—just as worshippers at the nearby Golden Temple always included Hindus. I noticed that a brick wall was being built around the Hindu temple's main shrine.

"Why this wall?" I asked the Brahman priest in attendance. He was a small, rotund man who wore a silk dhoti, or robe, and whose shaven head sprouted a neatly braided pigtail. He had a kindly countenance. "Are you expecting trouble from the Sikhs?"

"No trouble," the priest said. "It's just our way of saying that only Hindus are welcome here."

The Punjab's Hindus and Sikhs lived mostly in amity for four centuries.

There was periodic agitation since the 1930s for a separate Sikh nation—which at first was called Sikhistan, then Khalistan, or "Land of the Pure"—but a hardcore separatist movement did not get going until the late 1970s. By then, Sikh leaders had realized that the arithmetic of population in the Punjab, as elsewhere in India, increasingly favored the country's Hindu majority, which was breeding at the rate of nearly 3 percent a year, or twice the rate of the Sikhs. That translated into diminishing power for the Sikhs, these leaders said.

In a perceptive report prepared for the United States Congressional Research Service in August 1984, Richard P. Cronin said that the Sikh–Hindu crisis was rooted in a long-term assertion of a Sikh communal identity. Cronin, an expert on Asian affairs, said that in addition to this assertion, four specific developments helped exacerbate the "Punjab Problem": one, the return to power of Prime Minister Indira Gandhi's Congress Party in the January 1980 national parliamentary elections and her subsequent dismissal of the opposition Akali Dal and Janata coalition that had governed Punjab state since 1977; two, the victory of the Congress Party in the June 1980 state elections; three, growing economic discontent among Sikhs and other Punjabis over agricultural pricing and industrial licensing policies of the Gandhi Government; and finally, the emergence of Sant Jarnail Singh Bhindranwale, a militant Sikh fundamentalist, as a dominant force in the Sikh heartland.

Cronin, whose research resulted in a remarkably clear analysis of the Punjab situation, said that the accelerating tempo of the Sikh agitation for a homeland and the violence in the Punjab may be dated from the brief arrest of Bhindranwale in connection with the assassination of a Hindu Punjabi newspaper editor, Lala Jagat Narain, in September 1981. The government's ineffective attempts to deal with Bhindranwale led him from one political triumph after another until he met his death in the June 5–6 army attack on his headquarters in the Golden Temple in Amritsar, according to Cronin.

"Wherever blame may lie for the failure to find a peaceful settlement, an early end to the confrontation is unlikely," he said in his report, which was published two months before the murder of Mrs. Gandhi.

Cronin said: "It also remains to be seen what the long-term impact will be on the stability of this vital grain-producing state. Although Hindus predominate in the cities and towns, the Sikhs constitute a strong majority in most of the countryside. Punjabi Hindu traders and businessmen in rural villages are especially vulnerable to local Sikh majorities. Even before the Golden Temple incident, terror and communal killings had spread to border villages north and south of Amritsar, causing anxious Hindu Punjabis to flee. The Hindu majority in Punjab's cities and towns also resorted to violence. A continuation of this violent polarization would be a major setback for India and could presage a wider breakdown of civility between ethnic, religious and linguistic groups that live side-by-side in many parts of India."

Polarization. That is precisely what characterized Sikh–Hindu relations in the Punjab when I got there following the assassination of Indira Gandhi.

The genesis of the Sikh–Hindu polarization of the 1980s dates back to the last century, when India's British rulers successfully sowed the seeds of mutual suspicion among members of the two communities. It was quite an achievement, and one that was the harbinger of what would be repeated again and again: divide and rule. The British proved adept at pitting community against community, region against region, rajah against rajah—thereby giving themselves the opportunity to settle quarrels they themselves had spawned and thus consolidate their own position.

The differences the British generated among Sikhs and Hindus were especially noteworthy because Sikhism was born out of Hinduism in the sixteenth century; unlike Hinduism, which evolved over the centuries out of the hymns and naturalistic beliefs of the pastoral Aryans who came to India from Central Asia, Sikhism is a revealed religion. Its founder, Guru Nanak (1469–1539), claimed to have had mystic experiences. God appeared to him and said, according to

Nanak himself: "Nanak, I am with thee. Through thee will My Name be magnified. Go into the world and teach mankind how to pray. Be not sullied by the ways of the world. Let your life be one of praise of the word *(Naam)*, charity *(Daan)*, ablution *(Ishnaan)*, service *(Sewa)*, and prayer *(Simran)*." Nanak was a simple, gentle soul whose sensibilities were outraged by the mistreatment of the lower classes by upper-caste Hindus, and by the abuses perpetrated by the country's Muslim rulers of the time.

Khushwant Singh, the eminent Sikh historian and writer, says that it is still unclear whether Guru Nanak intended to reform Hinduism, or form a new sect, or bring Hindus and Moslems together. "It would appear that in his early career he tried to bring the two communities closer to each other," Singh says. "Being himself a Hindu he was at the same time equally concerned with reforming Hinduism. But as the years went by and his message caught on among the masses, he decided to give his teachings permanency through a sect of his own."

His disciples were called Sikhs—the word means "disciple." They did not chant Sanskrit hymns to stone idols, as Hindus did, but sang devotional songs that Nanak had composed himself in his native language, Punjabi. Sikhs also broke down existing caste barriers and encouraged communal dining in the guru's kitchen, a ceremony known as "Guru ka Langar." Nanak's chief disciple, Angad, devised a new script, Gurmukhi. Several decades later, Arjun, one of Sikhism's ten main gurus, built the Golden Temple in Amritsar. It was Arjun's son, Sikhism's sixth guru, Hargovind, who fashioned a militant role for the Sikhs. He urged his followers to arm themselves. He appointed himself both spiritual and temporal head of the Sikh community. The Sikhs were seen as the militant arm of Hinduism. In fact, says Khushwant Singh, Sikhism's ninth guru, Tegh Bahadur, appeared before the ruling Mogul court as a representative of the Hindus of northern India to resist forcible conversion to Islam. He was beheaded. Tegh Bahadur's son, the tenth and last guru, Gobind Singh, completed the transformation of the Sikhs into a martial community. He directed his male followers not to cut their hair and beards, to append the name "Singh"—which means "Lion"—to their first names, and to always carry a kirpan, or sword.

The Sikhs continued to be the defenders of India's Hindus against Muslim tyranny: they fought not only the Moguls but also Persian, Afghan, and Pathan invaders. Sikh kings like Ranjit Singh worshiped in Hindu temples and made the slaughter of the Hindus' sacred cow a criminal offense punishable with death. But the British had arrived on the scene by then; by 1849, they had annexed the Punjab, where Ranjit Singh had established his formidable empire. The Muslim rulers of India, the Moguls, had also by now been reduced to figureheads. It was the British who sowed the seeds of Hindu–Sikh separatism, according to Khushwant Singh. They rewarded loyal Sikh princes with land, they inducted Sikhs into the British Army in large numbers, and they used Sikh troops to keep rebellious Hindu chieftans under control.

While this was happening, a Hindu revivalist wave washed across northern India. Hindu leaders of the Arya Samaj proselytized against Sikhism and tried to bring Sikhs back into the Hindu fold. This raised the Sikhs' hackles. The Akali movement of the 1920s to wrest control of the Sikh gurdwaras, or temples, from the Hindu-influenced priests who managed them, also aggravated Hindu–Sikh relations. The Akali movement found expression in the creation of the Akali Dal, which was formed as the militant wing of the Shiromani Gurudwara Prabandhak Committee, the organization that eventually took over the supervision of Sikh temples. It was at a huge Sikh rally in Amritsar on August 20, 1944, that Master Tara Singh, a cagey old Sikh leader, first issued a formal call for a sovereign Sikh nation. His colleagues were amused.

By this time India's Muslims had started agitating for their own state, Pakistan (which, like Khalistan, also means "Land of the Pure"). Sikhs correctly saw the rising Muslim communalism as a threat to their own well-being, just as it was to that of the Hindus. When Partition came in 1947 and Pakistan was carved out of India, the Sikhs of the Punjab were the worst losers. The choicest farmland of the state was in its western region, which was given to Pakistan. Thirteen of the Punjab's twenty-nine districts went to India, and just

38 percent of the land area—mostly scrubland or meadows with poor topsoil—and very little of the vast irrigation network that the British had helped build. Two million Sikhs, terrified of being locked into the new Muslim state of Pakistan, migrated eastward to India, leaving behind their hereditary homes and possessions, and also one hundred fifty Sikh shrines.

Their migration, and that of another two million Hindus from Pakistan to India, coincided with a reverse flow of traffic of four million Muslims who left East Punjab and northern India to relocate to Pakistan. They clashed. A bloodbath ensued. Nearly 2.2 million men, women, and children died, many of them Sikhs. This tragedy perhaps explains why Sikhs—who form 10 percent of India's military forces of 1.2 million—fought especially ferociously in the three wars between India and Pakistan since independence in 1947. But considering the historical Sikh animosity toward Muslims, it is especially puzzling how proponents of Khalistan have proclaimed Pakistan as an ally in their "struggle" to set up a new nation in the Punjab. (The Pakistanis may well be unaware of it, but the Khalistan proposal also calls for the inclusion of a sizable chunk of the Pakistani portion of Punjab; the great city of Lahore will be part of Khalistan, as will virtually every district of the flourishing farmbelt that now feeds Pakistan.)

In the two decades after independence, Punjab's Sikhs worked especially hard to make their state India's success story. The central government in Delhi, under Prime Minister Jawaharlal Nehru, encouraged economic development and poured billions of rupees into projects for building canals and dams in the Punjab. Sikhs also prospered elsewhere in the country: they gained a virtual monopoly over the road transportation industry, for instance, and they obtained important positions in the government bureaucracy.

Khushwant Singh says that the notion of an autonomous Sikh state started taking shape with Nehru's announcement that new Indian states would be fashioned along linguistic lines. Nehru's decision was shaped by a lengthy and violent agitation in the Telangana region of south-central India—in the area that is now Andhra Pradesh state—

for a Telugu linguistic state. Thirteen of India's fifteen major languages would thus find a formal home within the boundaries of a new state. But Punjabi was the only language not thus represented. Sikhs resented this, and the Akali Dal launched a Punjabi Suba—or "linguistic state"—movement in April 1960. Punjab's Hindus suspected that in demanding a Punjabi-speaking state what the Sikhs were really after was a Sikh majority state. So when census commissioners came around, the Punjab's Hindus claimed their chief language was Hindi —not Punjabi, which was actually their prime lingua franca. "The battle over language in effect became a confrontation between Punjabi Hindus and Punjabi Sikhs," Khushwant Singh says.

That battle eventually led to the Indian government's decision in 1966 to split the Punjab (which soon after Independence in 1947 had been converted into two administrative units that were called the Patiala and East Punjab States Union, more popularly known by its acronym, PEPSU) into three states: Haryana, with 16,835 square miles and 7.5 million people, of whom barely 5 percent were Sikhs; Himachal Pradesh, with 10,215 square miles and 1.2 million people, barely 2 percent of them Sikhs; and Punjab, with 20,254 square miles and a population of 12 million people, about 52 percent of them Sikhs. The Sikhs got their Punjabi-speaking state, but its land area now covered just nine districts, not the Punjab's original thirteen. And the Punjab had to share its capital city of Chandigarh with neighboring Haryana, until such a time when Haryana built its own capital. (It still has not.) The prime minister at the time of the creation of Punjab State was Indira Gandhi.

The Punjab thrived economically, largely because of the "green revolution." As the state prospered, Sikhs started to look for new ventures in which to invest their wealth, for a better yield on their crops to pay for the rising costs of fertilizers and mechanization. Richard Cronin says in his congressional report: "Many Sikhs came to see the Indian government's policy of controlling all industrial licensing from New Delhi and steering investment to poorer but more populous and vote-rich provinces in the Hindi heartland as an obstacle to these aspirations. Some frequently quoted figures include the claim that 70 percent of the state's cotton and 60 percent of its molasses are 'exported' for processing to other states due to the refusal of New Delhi to approve licenses for plant construction. The Delhi government was also judged slow to create adequate price incentives for Punjabi wheat and rice."

Revolutions have a way of fizzling out, and the Punjab's "green revolution" and the economic progress associated with it reached a plateau in the early 1970s. Punjabi farmers found themselves not as well-off as they were a decade ago.

Around this time, Sikhism's elders discovered to their dismay that the religion's hold over the young was loosening as Western life-styles were imported into the state. Moreover, unemployment was now on the rise because other than agriculture there were no major industries in the state. As families grew bigger, land holdings became smaller. The annual influx of more than 200,000 low-caste Hindu workers from Uttar Pradesh and Bihar states who were hired to work on Punjab farms because of a local labor shortage also created some social tensions. Many of these migrant workers would stay on and enroll as voters—thus fattening the percentage of Hindus in the state. Sikh clergymen felt that their religion was under siege. More specifically, they felt that Sikhs and the Punjab were being Hindu-ized.

Even as the proportion of Sikhs in the Punjab was declining, Mrs. Gandhi's ruling Congress Party in Delhi accelerated its interference in socioreligious politics in the state. Mrs. Gandhi seemed determined to prevent the political ascendancy of the main Sikh party, the Akali Dal. The Akalis stepped up their demands for the readjustment of state boundaries to include in the Punjab the Punjabi-speaking areas of neighboring Haryana, Rajasthan, and Himachal Pradesh; the Akalis also wanted Chandigarh to be the exclusive capital of the Punjab; they demanded a fairer allocation to the Punjab of the waters of the Ravi, Sutlej, and Beas rivers. On October 16, 1973, the Akali Dal approved a document, known as the Anandpur Sahib Resolution, that not only included these demands but also referred in vague language to a "separate Sikh nation." Actually, the word used in the resolution was "quam," which in Punjabi meant anything from a community to a nation. That resolution was interpreted by Mrs. Gandhi and her advisers as a call for a separate state.

The Anandpur Sahib resolution was passed at a meeting the Akali Dal held in the historic Punjab town of Anandpur, where the head of the ninth Sikh guru, Tegh Bahadur—who was decapitated by the Mogul emperor Aurangzeb on November 11, 1675—was cremated by his son and successor, Guru Gobind Singh. Anandpur is the site of one of Sikhism's five major gurdwaras (the other four are the Golden Temple in Amritsar; Dam Dama Sahib in Ropar; Patna Sahib in Bihar; and Hazoor Sahib in Maharashtra's Nanded district). The Akalis said in their resolution that the central government in Delhi should restrict its functions in the Punjab to defense, foreign affairs, communications, and currency. The resolution advanced the proposition that the Sikh religion was "not safe without sovereignty." The historian Khushwant Singh has said that this could be interpreted "as leading to Khalistan."

A separate state was never formally called for by the Akalis—but Punjab's Sikh fundamentalists thought it to be a terrific idea. The purity of Sikhism, they said, could only be preserved in an independent Sikh nation. Their fervor was fueled and financed by wealthy Sikhs living abroad. One of these Sikhs was a London physician named Jagjit Singh Chauhan, a former secretary-general of the Akali Dal and a finance minister in the Punjab, who proclaimed himself "president" of Khalistan and even produced Khalistan passports, postage stamps, and currency.

The fundamentalists rallied around a fiery leader, Sant Jarnail Singh Bhindranwale. He had helped Mrs. Gandhi and her Congress Party to undercut and embarrass the Akalis. But Bhindranwale soon convinced himself that he was capable of dispensing with Mrs. Gandhi's patronage and that he could blaze a new career as an advocate for Khalistan. He recruited men who shared his firebrand fundamentalism, soon launched a terrorist campaign to murder Punjab's Hindus and moderate Sikhs, and drew national attention.

It is disputable whether it was Bhindranwale's status as a media star rivalling Mrs. Gandhi or his role as a terrorist leader that roused the prime minister's choler. After dithering for months over whether she should send her troops to flush Bhindranwale out of his sanctuary in the Golden Temple, Mrs. Gandhi finally authorized the military operation for June 5–6. Bhindranwale was killed during that operation, and so were hundreds of men, women, and children who had come as pilgrims to Sikhism's holiest shrine. Sikhs around the world were outraged. Some swore vengeance.

For almost three years prior to her death, Mrs. Gandhi had been negotiating with the Sikhs. The Akalis had submitted a list of forty-five demands to the Delhi government in September 1981. These demands—which were virtually identical to the ones enumerated in the Anandpur Sahib Resolution—were grouped into religious, political and economic categories.

I met with a man named Manmohan Singh, who was among those involved in the negotiations. Singh, a pleasant man of about sixty, is chairman of Frick India, a flourishing engineering company. A Sikh, he has headed various chambers of commerce. The talks started in October 1981, Manmohan Singh told me, but they progressed only fitfully, floundering often over the issues of Chandigarh—the capital that the Punjab shared with neighboring Haryana and which the Akalis wanted turned over to their state immediately—and the sharing of river waters. In mid-February 1983, Mrs. Gandhi announced the partial acceptance of some Sikh religious demands: instead of the original Akali demand for a radio station, for example, she agreed to allow the broadcast of religious services from the Golden Temple on the government's network, All-India Radio. The government also agreed to the Akali demand that Sikhs be allowed to carry the kirpan —the traditional knife that all Sikhs are asked by the religion to carry always—on all internal flights of Indian Airlines: the specification was that the kirpan not be longer than six inches.

But the Akalis dismissed these concessions as being fraudulent. They stepped up their agitation against Mrs. Gandhi. Manmohan Singh was one of those who urged everyone to cool down. But the prime minister was in no mood to listen to anyone. Singh recalled to me a conversation he had had with Mrs. Gandhi's principal private secretary and her key adviser on the Punjab.

"The PM never listens—either she demands an explanation, or she gives you a lecture," Singh quoted the official as saying. In fact, Mrs. Gandhi declined to meet personally with the Akalis, passing on the task instead to top aides such as Dr. P. C. Alexander. Her son and heir apparent, Rajiv Gandhi, also occasionally met with the Sikhs. Manmohan Singh told me that the Akali Dal's president, Harchand Singh Longowal, expressed to him his dismay over Mrs. Gandhi's refusal to meet with him or the rest of the Akali leadership.

"She's said to oppose the Anandpur Sahib resolution," Longowal said to Manmohan Singh. "But why don't you tell her for me that she can delete anything from it she wants—and we will agree!"

Singh said that when he relayed Longowal's request to Dr. Alexander, the latter said: "The Anandpur Sahib resolution is not even an issue in all this."

The Akalis and others familiar with the on-again off-again negotiations suspected that Mrs. Gandhi was being recalcitrant because she had an ulterior motive. She let the Punjab crisis drag on, they suspected, in order to rally the state's Hindus behind her and in order to unify the Hindu majority of the north Indian states, all of whom were concerned about the growing shrillness of the Sikhs's agitation. The Hindus wanted the Delhi government to deal more forcefully with the Sikhs. By stonewalling the Sikhs, Mrs. Gandhi was consolidating her position with the Hindu majority of North India, whose support she deemed especially critical in the national elections that were to be held by January 1985.

As the Akalis' dealings with Mrs. Gandhi faltered, the strength of the Bhindranwale extremists rose. More than five hundred Hindus and moderate Sikhs were killed by the terrorists. On April 25, 1984, a senior Punjab police official, a Sikh named A. S. Atwal, was shot to death at the entrance of the Golden Temple. The assailants were seen running into the temple, and the widespread assumption was that they were Bhindranwale's men.

But Bhindranwale told Manmohan Singh that his group had nothing to do with the Atwal murder, an assertion that now seems suspect.

"I can prove to you that it was the Indira Congress people in Punjab who killed Atwal," the thirty-seven-year-old preacher told Singh. "Why do the government accuse me of being a murderer? In my whole life I haven't even killed a sparrow."

But Bhindranwale's sentiments to Manmohan Singh ran counter to his other pronouncements. His homilies were always fiery and filled with threats against Hindus. He promised that if the Sikhs did not get their own nation, "rivers of blood will flow" in the Punjab. He drew crowds the like of which had never been seen before in the Golden Temple.

Manmohan Singh told me that the mobs that attacked Sikh homes in Delhi after the murder of Indira Gandhi often shouted the name of Bhindranwale—they were taking revenge for the murders Bhindranwale and his men committed.

He himself had to flee his home in Friends Colony, hidden in his car.

"Even in the darkest days of the Partition, I walked upright across the border from Pakistan," Manmohan Singh said to me. "Even then I didn't have to hide. At my age, I cannot forget this humiliation. It will never be the same for me again."

His twenty-two-year-old son, Gurmohan Singh, had said to him: "Dad, at your age isn't it simply better to stay at home and fight the mobs with your gun—rather than hide like this in your car?"

And Manmohan Singh had replied: "No, at my age, discretion is the better part of valor."

As he was being driven away from his home, Manmohan Singh thought of how, only a few weeks ago he had led a delegation of Indian businessmen to the United States. He had told Americans in speech after speech how proud he was to be an Indian.

"I would never have dreamed that in my own country I would have to run away from a mob like this," Manmohan Singh said to me, tears in his eyes.

I was taken by Inder Mohan Khosla, my host in Amritsar, to the home of Karuna and Satish Chander Mahajan. Mahajans had lived in this city for several generations, and had prospered in business. Both Satish and Karuna, an elegant middle-aged Hindu couple, seemed pained at the chasm that now separated Amritsar's Sikhs and Hindus.

"There's a total divide between Sikhs and Hindus," Karuna Mahajan said, in her book-lined living room. "They no longer come to our homes, and we are seldom invited to theirs."

How long had it been since the Mahajans visited the Golden Temple?

"The temple doesn't have any longer the aura the Vatican does," Mrs. Mahajan said, with surprising acidity in her voice. "It's become the hotbed of Sikh politics. Sikhs and Hindus are being increasingly separated—but the separation of the Sikh religion and Sikh politics is no longer there."

I was tempted to walk into the Golden Temple by myself. After all, Hindus had been visiting it for hundreds of years. But Inder Singh Monga, a Sikh I met at Khosla's bank, suggested that I wait a bit.

"There's a meeting on at the temple," said Monga, who worships daily at the temple. "All the high priests are there today. They're deciding what to do about the killing of Sikhs that is going on in Delhi. You might want to wait until tomorrow."

The five high priests of Sikhism ordinarily met at the Akal Takht, Sikhism's Vatican. It is an impressive three-story building with marble walls, domes with gold leaves, and balconies that offer an unimpeded view of the Harimandir, the main Golden Temple, which sits in the middle of a pond that Sikhs consider sacred. It is from the Akal Takht that the high priests periodically issue hukamnamas, or encyclicals, and tankhaiyas, or formal condemnations of irreligious conduct. The priests usually met without fanfare and worked quietly. Few of India's 14 million Sikhs had heard of these five men, fewer still knew their names.

"Most of us Sikhs don't even know who these five men are," Noni

Chawla, a young man who is the marketing director of the ITC–Sheraton hotel chain, had told me in Delhi. "Sikhism is a religion that doesn't demand too much attention to its hierarchy."

But Mrs. Gandhi had jailed the political leaders of the Sikh community. Officials of the Akali Dal and the Shiromani Gurudwara Prabandhak Committee—the 129-member organization that oversees most of India's Sikh temples, with an annual budget of $10 million raised mainly from individual donations—had been incarcerated since October 1983, when the Punjab was put by Mrs. Gandhi under direct control of the Delhi government. Bhindranwale, who had become a de facto leader of the Sikhs, was dead. A political vacuum now existed among Sikhs. So the five head priests of the Akal Takht found themselves in an unaccustomed and uneasy role as high-visibility Sikh spokesmen. This role required them to span the long-standing divide between their religion and politics.

And the head priests had quickly made a mess of things.

Their spokesman, Giani Kirpal Singh, issued a condolence statement following the murder of Mrs. Gandhi. Within a day, he withdrew it.

"We are neither happy with her death nor do we condemn it," Kirpal Singh was quoted as saying.

The remarks did not please Amritsar's Hindus.

The day I turned up in Sikhism's holiest city, the head priests were reported to have urged Sikh members of Mrs. Gandhi's ruling Congress Party to immediately resign. The following day, they rescinded that directive.

In Hindu homes, and even among some Sikhs I met in Amritsar, the five priests were coming under increasing criticism for not issuing a strong call for religious harmony and asking Sikhs not to retaliate for the attacks against them in Delhi and northern India. Their silence was construed as suggesting timidity or as an implied threat that left open the possibility of a Sikh counterassault.

Some weeks before the Gandhi assassination, the high priests had written a note to President Zail Singh, a Sikh and a former chief

minister of the Punjab. The government, the priests said, was court-
ing trouble. Zail Singh, who was widely and correctly perceived
as a stooge of Mrs. Gandhi—who had selected him to be India's
Constitutional president, a position of much pomp and no power—visited the Golden Temple on September 26, 1984, not long
after the Delhi government had repaired some of the damage to
the Golden Temple incurred during the military assault in June.
Giani Kirpal Singh, the first among equals of the five head priests,
hectored him publicly.

"If the government continues its anti-Sikh attitude and treats us
like second-class citizens, it will not only endanger the unity of the
country, but also cause communal disharmony," Kirpal Singh said.
He then listed the things the high priests wanted done immediately:

• The revocation of the Delhi government's ban on the All-India
  Sikh Students Federation. Many members of this organization had
  been imprisoned on charges of terrorism.

• The unconditional release from prison of all Akali Dal leaders as
  well as activists of the Sikh Students Federation. These leaders,
  and also top officials of the Shiromani Gurudwara Prabandhak
  Committee, had been locked up to prevent them from further
  agitation.

• Adequate compensation to the families of the people who were
  killed or injured during the army's assault on the Golden Temple.
  The government had not released the names of the terrorists who
  were killed during the army operation, nor the names of pilgrims
  who were trapped in the Golden Temple and died in the cross fire
  between the troops and the terrorists.

• An end to the random arrests of Sikh youths in the Punjab. The
  authorities periodically rounded up youths suspected of sympathizing with terrorists.

The hectoring and scolding were deliberate. The high priests had earlier excommunicated Zail Singh by issuing a tankaiya against him: he was accused of religious misconduct. Why such a strong step? Because the president of India is technically the commander in chief of the country's armed forces, and since the military had assaulted the Golden Temple the president should be held accountable for the action.

Zail Singh was almost reverentially subdued when he visited the high priests in Amritsar.

"I ask for sincere forgiveness from the gurus for the unfortunate incidents," he said.

That was at once interpreted by the priests as an apology from the Gandhi government for the military assault. The tankaiya against Zail Singh was lifted. He was a Sikh again.

I was introduced to a man named Bhagwant Singh Ahuja, a tall, stocky Sikh who ran a profitable trading business, with shops in the Punjab, Delhi, and Bombay. Ahuja said he would take me to the Golden Temple—but only after the priests' meeting had ended. Implicit in what he said was the caution that perhaps it would be inflammatory for a non-Sikh such as myself to be seen in the precincts of the temple while a religious-political meeting was going on. That meeting would last through much of the night.

"This is a very dangerous time," Ahuja said. "People's emotions are very raw. We now more than ever need to get across the message that Sikhs and Hindus are brothers, that we have such great common links. But what's happening in Delhi now, this slaughter of innocent Sikhs—this is wrecking people's faith here in amity. The feeling among Sikhs is that a minority community is being held ransom because of the actions of two misguided madmen."

We were having dinner at Ahuja's home, a large bungalow with a glass wall that overlooked a neat lawn. The house itself nestled under mango and eucalyptus trees. On the mantel over a fireplace were porcelain figures and bronzes of various Hindu gods. There was a stone Buddha, and there was an exquisite wooden cross with the crucified Jesus.

"We need the healing touch," Ahuja said.

There was a murmur of agreement from around the mahogany dining table. With us were Ahuja's wife, his daughter, and two sons. Also present were a local judge named Gurdial Singh and his wife, and a couple of other Sikhs from the neighborhood. The round table easily accommodated a dozen diners. In the middle of the table were enormous dishes of tandoori chicken, curried lamb, parathas, or roasted bread, and spicy eggplant and potatoes. There was also a mound of saffron rice.

"Bhindranwale was spitting poison, he was propagating things that were not normal for the people of the Punjab," Ahuja continued. "The whole atmosphere was polluted here. People had lost faith in the Akali leaders as well. And Mrs. Gandhi was not applying the healing touch. So what were we left with? Bitterness, anger, sorrow. The joy of life, our hopes, these were all being darkened."

"Nothing justifies the atrocities in Delhi," Gurdial Singh, the judge, said. "I really question the allegations that Sikhs were distributing sweets to celebrate Mrs. Gandhi's death."

"I want to show you something," Ahuja said, getting up suddenly.

He returned shortly with a newspaper clipping and started reading extracts.

It was an article by Dharma Kumar, a well-known economic historian in Delhi. It appeared on the editorial page of the *Times of India,* and Mrs. Kumar, a Hindu, had said:

"If all the sweets in India had been distributed, that would not have justified the burning alive of one single Sikh. If burning alive were the punishment for vulgarity and folly, there would be few people left in India.

"Why should every Sikh be responsible for the doings of all other Sikhs?"

Earlier that evening, Ahuja and his friends had met with some Hindu neighbors. They had decided to form citizens' groups to patrol neighborhoods in the event of trouble. They also agreed to telephone and visit as many Sikh and Hindu families as they could to urge everyone to remain calm.

The bazaars near the Golden Temple were packed with people this Sunday morning. We parked outside one of the four main gates, in what seemed to me to be an extension of a bazaar: Ahuja's station wagon had to be squeezed between a vendor of oranges and a man who had set up a stall of spicy savories. Ahuja's wife and mother went in separately. He and I checked in our shoes at a booth near the entrance, and Ahuja rented for me a patka, or a sort of cap to cover my head—everyone's head must be covered when inside the Golden Temple. We washed our feet in a small basin and then walked down a flight of marble steps into the courtyard of the temple.

The Harimandir sparkled in the brilliant sunshine. The sacred pool in which it sat was lightly ruffled by a cool breeze. I looked around. I was the only non-Sikh male in the vast courtyard. The temple's public address system was broadcasting hymns in the Punjabi language that were being sung inside the Harimandir by granthis, or acolytes. Ahuja and I walked on the marble-floored perimeter, known as the parikrama. We occasionally weaved through columns and under doorways. Ahuja kept very close to me physically. I thought: this is a gesture of protection, this Sikh wants to make sure that his Hindu companion comes to no harm. If I was being bold turning up inside Sikhism's holiest shrine even as Sikhs were being butchered not far away in Delhi by non-Sikhs, then Bhagwant Singh Ahuja was even more courageous in escorting a Hindu to the temple. Several Sikhs stared at us as we walked by. Ahuja sometimes would stop at a ghat, or steps that led into the sacred pool, and sip holy water: I replicated his motions. The water was cool, even sweet.

We bought a tray of flowers from a vendor who had parked himself not far from the Harimandir.

"The very fact that you are here must tell you how tolerant Sikhism is," Ahuja said, as we walked on. "You are my brother. That is why you and I are here together. Even if you were my political enemy,

I would still bring you here. Why not? The temple is one place where we must all leave our politics and social differences outside."

He paused to bow before an ancient tree in whose shadow a Sikh saint, long dead, once lived and preached.

"But there are people who brought their politics and weapons into this temple," Ahuja said. "Look around you. Look carefully."

I was startled by what I saw. Abutting the parikrama were mounds of rubble. Marble flooring had caved in. Bullet holes pocked many buildings. The sunburst of shells marked several structures. Even the Akal Takht, which had been restored by the Indian Government at the cost of $40 million since the June storming of the Golden Temple by the Indian Army, somehow looked hastily patched up.

Heavy tanks had been brought in during that military operation to counter Bhindranwale and his terrorists. More than a thousand people died, although the Delhi government insists to this day that the figure was no more than four hundred. The man in operational charge of the military assault was himself a Sikh—Lieutenant General Ranjit Singh Dayal, chief of staff of the army's prestigious Western Command. General Dayal's main adversary was not Sant Jarnail Singh Bhindranwale, who had no formal military training, but another highly decorated war hero like Dayal himself, Major General Shahbeg Singh. Singh had been among those who trained the Mukti Bahini guerrillas who fought to establish the state of Bangladesh in what was then East Pakistan. But he was later cashiered from the Indian Army on corruption charges. Singh was subsequently recruited by Bhindranwale to train his growing band of terrorists. It was Shahbeg Singh who had planned the fortification of the Golden Temple. It was he who had trained Bhindranwale's motley band of militants in the use of highly sophisticated weapons such as antitank cannon. Those weapons were fired by the terrorists with deadly accuracy on June 5 and 6. Scores of brave Indian soldiers died. Officials in Delhi said that the army had been surprised to confront sophisticated weaponry in the Golden Temple. Obviously, the government's intelligence system had let it down.

Looking at the temple on this lovely November morning, it seemed inconceivable to me that anyone had dared to defile its serenity and sanctity—whether it be Bhindranwale or Shahbeg Singh or the Indian army. Temples are our last sanctuaries for peace and reflection. Punjab's Sikh terrorists had infiltrated not only the Golden Temple, but also forty-two other gurdwaras across the state. Why hadn't the priests of the temples protested? The lines between the spiritual and the temporal in the Punjab had blurred.

I wept.

Inside the Harimandir, the prayers were for peace and brotherhood this morning, as they are every day of the week. Granthis played on harmoniums. Priests chanted hymns in front of the holy Granth Sahib—the collection of sayings and songs of Guru Nanak—which lay covered by a burgundy silk shawl. The gold-sheathed walls glistened. There was a powerful fragrance of incense. I followed Ahuja in circumambulating the inner shrine, then I knelt in front of the Granth Sahib, and applied my forehead to the floor. A hand touched my head. I looked up. It was a Sikh priest, and he was blessing me. I rose, and he handed me some marigolds. He was an old man, and there was a gentle smile on his face.

Ahuja and I walked up to the balcony of the Harimandir. I looked out at the Golden Temple's courtyard, and beyond it toward an entire residential block that had been razed during the June military operation. So much history here, I thought, so much violence, and now what? Will Sikhs and Hindus ever again worship here without mutual suspicion? Will they intermarry with the same zest and enthusiasm? Will the Punjabi Hindu families, those who had traditionally converted their eldest sons to Sikhism continue the practice? Or will Sikhs now be a besieged minority in a country for which so many had shed their blood and perished in battle over the years? Ahuja and I looked at each other, as if the same thoughts rushed through our minds, but we said nothing to each other. What was there to say?

We started toward the parikrama again. On the way, Ahuja lingered near a blackboard on which was written in chalk the daily quotation from the Granth Sahib, which serves as Sikhism's bible. The script was Gurumukhi, which had been devised by Guru Nanak's successor, Guru Angad. It was one of the very first steps toward establishing a separate Sikh identity.

"This world is a transitory place," the quotation read. "Some of our compatriots have already gone, and someday the rest of us also have to go. This world is only a temporary abode."

It was an astonishing quotation to have put up at a time of such crisis, I thought. It was freighted with humility and fatalism. I wished I could have broadcast it to those Hindus in Delhi: the quotation would have put them to shame.

We climbed the stairs that led away from the parikrama. A fresh hymn was being broadcast now, sung in Punjabi by a granthi. He sang softly at first, then his voice rose clear and sharp.

"If God is with me," came the granthi's words, "what do we have to fear?—Nothing."

I returned to the Punjab in December, more than a month after my first trip, to see for myself what changes had taken place in the state. The assassination of Indira Gandhi was no longer the main item for discussion in most people's homes. One of her assassins, Beant Singh, was killed within an hour of the shooting; Satwant Singh, the surviving assassin, was now being questioned by the authorities. All sorts of theories were being advanced about conspiracies. The American Central Intelligence Agency—always a convenient scapegoat in most of the Third World, but particularly in India —was said to be behind the assassination of Mrs. Gandhi, whose political alignment with the Soviet Union had long been resented by Washington. Pakistan, which was said to support the separatists who wanted to establish Khalistan, was also believed to have been behind the plot. Relatives of Beant and Satwant were arrested in their Punjab villages, then freed, then re-arrested, and let go again. The investigators appeared to be making little progress.

Many Indians were coming around to the view that rather than being a major international conspiracy, the murder of Indira Gandhi had been a case of vengeance by a handful of Sikhs who were maddened by the invasion of the Golden Temple in Amritsar. Beant and

Satwant were reported to have taken vows of revenge at the Bangla Sahib Gurdwara in New Delhi. By mid-December, few Indians I encountered bothered to speculate much about conspiracies and the motives of the killers. Their attention, instead, seemed focused on the political future of India.

A national election campaign was in full swing in India—but the Punjab had been excluded from the parliamentary poll because of the political instability here. The army was still out in force around the state, but places like Amritsar were no longer under curfew. Rajiv Gandhi, the new prime minister, was going around the country saying that Sikhs would have no reason to fear for their safety under his administration; but few Sikhs had been compensated for the frightful loss to their property during the riots after Mrs. Gandhi's assassination. And not one rioter had been brought to justice.

The Hindus and Sikhs of the Punjab continued their dangerous drift away from one another. Few civic leaders in this troubled state dared to openly call for rapprochement. No one issued calls for national unity: there already were two countries within this one state. More than 8,000 men and women, suspected of being terrorists or of sympathizing with Sikh terrorists, were in the Punjab's jails; few of them had been allowed to see lawyers. Among those behind bars were said to be boys and girls under eleven years of age.

"It is very difficult now to go to the Punjab and talk to the masses about any reconciliation," Manmohan Singh, one of India's most respected Sikh industrialists, said to me. "There are thousands of Sikh students now in jail on what are at best vague charges. Their parents won't even hear of reconcilation.

"So what does one do? You bide your time."

I found that Hindus were even more angry that Sikhs had not, as a community, formally condemned the assassination of Indira Gandhi. And Sikhs were bitter that few of those who had murdered their brethren across north India and looted their homes had been arrested or punished.

"This is justice?" asked Mickey Singh, Bhagwant Singh Ahuja's son. "You call this a free, civilized society?"

He was echoing outrage that was being expressed around the country by people who were shocked at the breakdown of law and order in the wake of the Gandhi assassination. I asked Mickey, a tall, sturdy Sikh who is only twenty-three but who appears much older, what he thought Mrs. Gandhi's legacy was for the Punjab.

"Legacy?" Mickey Singh said. "You ask about legacy? Just look around you. Look at the army, and the unhappiness. You want to find out about her legacy?"

In the weeks since my first visit to Amritsar, the arithmetic of population in the Punjab had started to change.

More than 75,000 Sikhs emigrated to the state from other parts of India. They came here from Himachal Pradesh and Uttar Pradesh and Haryana, even as far away as Bihar and Orissa. They fled their homes to escape further harassment. Many of the emigres are widows and orphaned children. There are still some seven million Sikhs spread across states other than the Punjab—but the 75,000 men, women, and children who poured into this already troubled state brought with them tales of horror.

These tales were narrated every day, and the narrations exacerbated tensions.

One evening near Amritsar, I listened to Amrik Singh, a young carpenter who had transplanted himself from his home in Delhi. He spoke before a small gathering of friends and relatives in a dhaaba, a roadside restaurant. People squatted on the floor, huddled in blankets to keep out the December cold. Singh was a tall, thin man, with a mustache and narrow eyes that looked at you with pain. His voice was so low that the slightest rustling of someone's blanket would smother a sentence. But everyone's attention was riveted on him.

He said he lost his father, five brothers, and two sons during the riots following Indira Gandhi's assassination. They were hacked to death, he said. His wife was gang-raped while he was made to watch; his seven-year-old daughter was molested. He himself was repeatedly stabbed, almost castrated, and left for dead. Now he and his wife must start all over again in the Punjab.

His audience seemed stunned as he spoke. It is not often that a Sikh male will volunteer information that his wife's honor was violated. Women started weeping. Men began to shout in anger.

I thought: these tales will be told and retold until they become part of the Punjab's mythology. How many young men like Amrik Singh will swear revenge? How can Sikhs ever forgive Hindus? How will the bitterness and anguish ever disappear from this land? We need the healing touch, Bhagwant Singh Ahuja had said to me that November evening not long after the murder of Mrs. Gandhi. But who will bring a healing hand to these proud and wounded people of the Punjab?

Rajiv Gandhi? Will he be able to forget—and forgive—the fact that his mother was murdered by two Sikhs? His December election campaign was not especially heroic: his ruling Congress Party appealed shamelessly to the sentiments of India's overwhelming Hindu majority by charging that the Sikh leadership had balked at resolving the Punjab problem. He charged that opposition leaders were in collusion with antinational elements in the Punjab. A "foreign hand" was working actively to destabilize the Punjab, Gandhi said. He did not elaborate. This was not the sort of rhetoric that would reassure Punjab's Sikhs. But then, the Punjab was not voting in the 1984 election.

In Delhi I came across posters put up by Congress Party candidates that said: "Would you trust a taxi driver from another state? For better security, vote Congress." Since a large number of Delhi's taxi drivers were Sikh, the message was clear.

Even clearer, and more sickening, were billboards commissioned by Congress candidates in states like Andhra Pradesh and Kerala. These depicted a slain Indira Gandhi, blood gushing from her body, being held by her son Rajiv. Two Sikhs crouched at one side, their guns smoking. Indians rewarded Rajiv Gandhi's Congress Party with 401 out of 508 seats contested for the national Parliament.

Healing hand?

During my travels around India, I was astonished how many non-Sikhs, particularly educated and affluent Indians, voiced the view that the Sikhs "had it coming" to them.

One very cold January evening in Delhi, I sat in the drawing room of my brother-in-law, Ajai Lal, a successful producer of audio visuals and television commercials. The mood in Lal's home was one of general jubilation over Rajiv Gandhi's unprecedented victory in the December national elections. Gandhi and some of his top aides, such as Arun Singh, had studied at the exclusive Doon School in north India—and most of the males present this evening also were Doon graduates (they called themselves Doscoes). In fact, thirty-two newly elected parliamentarians had attended the Doon School in Dehra Dun.

One particular guest did not, however, dwell too much on the Old-Boy angle. He was a young local businessman, and he consumed several glasses of whiskey and kept up a harangue about the Punjab. He himself was a Punjabi Hindu.

"We will fix them now," he said. "They thought they were God's gift to India, eh? They thought they were the only strong, virile ones around, eh? Well, they sure showed themselves to be cowards recently, didn't they? How many faced the mobs with courage, eh?"

"Would you have faced a mob like that?" I asked.

The businessman shrugged. He helped himself to another whiskey.

"Those bastards," he said, presently, "those Sikh bastards. If I had my way, I would rip their bowels out. I would slaughter every last one of them. I would decimate them. Those arrogant, filthy bastards. Who do they think they are? They have destroyed India."

I shivered, and it was not because of the cold.

Few people expected that the Punjab problem would be easily resolved by Rajiv Gandhi, but fewer still believed that Sikh terrorism would again escalate; the army and various security agencies were thought to be in control of the situation in the Punjab, and Gandhi was emboldened to release several top Akali leaders from jail. He even offered to initiate talks with them. But in May, Sikh extremists moved on to fronts: they set off bombs in New Delhi and several other northern Indian cities. The bombs were skillfully hidden in transitor radios. Nearly a hundred people, some of them children, were killed. Earlier, a Congress party functionary was murdered in the Punjab, as were some police officers.

And the extremists, led by Sant Jarnail Singh Bhindrawnwale's eighty-five-year-old father, Joginder Singh, dramatically seized control of the decision-making echelon of the Akali Dal. To the consternation of Harchand Singh Lonowal, the Akali president who had managed a delicate balancing act between hardliners and moderates in the party, Joginder Singh announced on May 1 the formation of a special committee whose members included several hardliners and supporters of the Khailistan movement. Among these members were three government officials who had resigned from service last year in protest against the army invasion of the Golden Temple. The ascendancy of the extremists was seen as further evidence that the Khalistan movement had not been snuffed out following Sant Bhindranwale's death during the army assault on the temple. Moreover, there was now a growing feeling that with the hardliners dominating the Akali Dal leadership and with Longowal sidelined, the prospects for meaningful negotiations with the Gandhi government had dimmed.

After I heard about these developments, I got in touch with my friend Rahul Singh in Chandigarh. Rahul, a Sikh and the son of the writer Khuswant Singh, had been posted in the Punjab as editor of the Chandigarh edition of the *Indian Express,* the country's largest English-language newspaper. It had not been an easy assignment for him, for not only did he have to contend with ubiquitous censors but also with anonymous callers who sometimes issued threats against his life. On the day I called Rahul Singh, all India was reverberating with the news that the Federal Bureau of Investigation had foiled a plot by Sikh terrorists to assassinate Rajiv Gandhi during his scheduled official visit to the United States in June 1985. The FBI had arrested five suspects in New Orleans, who had reportedly sworn vengeance against the Gandhi family. According to the FBI, the suspects had also plotted to kill Bhajan Lal, chief minister of Haryana State, who had visited the Louisiana State University Eye Center for treatment. Law enforcement officials said that the Sikh terrorists planned to launch guerrilla-type activities against Indian diplomats and against Indian facilities in India and elswhere.

I found Rahul Singh uncharacteristically gloomy.

"Everything is so confusing," he said. "No one knows how things are going work out. Sanity and rationality are increasingly slipping away from us."

2

Kashmir—Trouble in Paradise

THE trips to the Punjab had depressed me. It was a state under siege, and it would stay that way for a long time. Indira Gandhi had bequeathed to her son and successor, Rajiv, an explosive situation that demanded extraordinary and enlightened leadership. But as I followed Rajiv Gandhi's election campaign in December, it struck me that he was sounding the same themes as his mother: national unity was in danger because the opposition was working to destabilize areas such as the Punjab; there were threats—which Rajiv did not specify—from Pakistan and China; a "foreign hand" was undermining the very notion of Indian nationhood.

The forty-year-old Cambridge-educated prime minister loftily called for national integration at scores of rallies where his listeners numbered in the hundreds of thousands; he crisscrossed India in air force jets and in government helicopters, speaking in Bombay in the morning and in Kerala at lunchtime and in Calcutta in the late afternoon, hugging babies in Bihar villages and promising peasants that a new era was upon this ancient land. He made television speeches and radio broadcasts. But not once did Rajiv Gandhi speak out against the holocaust that had been unleashed against the Sikhs of northern India, not once did he promise that wrongdoers would

be brought to justice. Sikhs had urged that the Akali Dal leadership
—which had been generally moderate—be released from jail and that
the new prime minister also initiate an investigation into the riots
against Sikhs in north India following the assassination of Mrs.
Gandhi.

It seemed to me that the rhetoric Rajiv was mouthing during his
election campaign would only make the business of national reconciliation that much more difficult for him later. Did he fully realize
this, or did he, in anticipation of his widely predicted electoral victory
(although few predicted that his ruling Congress Party would win by
a landslide) feel that ordinary Indians would soon forget campaign
broadsides and rally behind him to solve India's myriad ethnic and
communal problems? Did Rajiv really believe that he could, however
implicitly, pack venom against the Sikhs in his election exhortations
and then expect to pacify the Punjab at some later date?

On the way back to Delhi from Amritsar, I looked at a map of
India. What an immense country! As large as all of Europe, two
thirds the size of the continental United States, 1.26 million square
miles, with a population of almost 800 million people, or a fifth of
all humanity. India stretched 2,000 miles from the Himalayan
heights of Kashmir in the north to the beaches of Kerala in the south,
and 1,700 miles from the tea gardens and oil fields of Assam in the
east to the scorched plains of Gujarat in the west. India's coast was
more than 3,500 miles long; its borders with Pakistan, Nepal, China,
the Soviet Union, Burma, and Bangladesh ramble over 8,300 miles
of deserts, mountains, and tropical forests. Within those boundaries
were Hindus and Muslims and Parsis and Buddhists and Jains and
Christians and animists and "untouchables"—who together spoke 15
major languages and some 874 dialects.

As my Indian Airlines jetliner rose into the clear blue winter sky,
it struck me that the election campaign that was going on in the
country was an extraordinary exercise in democracy, the biggest the
world had ever known: of India's 800 million people, 390 million were
registered voters—more than the entire population of the United
States and Britain combined. India—the world's eighth biggest in-

dustrial nation; India—possessing the world's biggest group of scientists and engineers after the United States and the Soviet Union; India—having the world's largest military establishment after the Soviet Union, the United States, and China; India—exploder of nuclear devices, exponent of nonalignment, explorer of the Antarctic, exporter of topflight doctors and technicians and top-quality textiles; India—maker of more movies per year than any other country; India —launcher of satellite rockets, producer of computers, miner of the deep seas. Ancient culture, modern nation.

And yet, I thought, what a troubled country! No region was without its own special travails. Everywhere I looked at my map, I saw fires: Punjab in the northwest, where Sikhs fought for greater autonomy, and some for Khalistan; Kashmir in the north, another strategic border state, where local Muslims were believed to be "soft" on Pakistan and desirous of independence from India; Assam in the east, where local tribes massacred Muslim refugees; Andhra Pradesh in the south, where a regional ethnic party was clamoring for greater state rights; and Maharashtra in the west, where Hindus and Muslims had murdered one another. And there was Madhya Pradesh, in central India, where poisonous gas from a Union Carbide plant in Bhopal had resulted in the deaths of more than 2,000 men, women, and children and in the permanent blinding of thousands more. Was modern India afflicted by some ancient curse?

I recalled something that a distinguished Indian once said: "India today presents a very mixed picture of hope and anguish, of remarkable advances and at the same time of inertia, of a new spirit and also the dead hand of the past and of privilege, of an overall and growing unity and many disruptive tendencies. Withal there is a great vitality and a ferment in people's minds and activities. Perhaps we who live in the middle of this ever-changing scene do not always realize the full significance of all that is happening. What will emerge from the labor and the tumults of the present generation?"

The author of these words was Jawaharlal Nehru, and he said them in 1959, a year of much communal strife. As I recalled Nehru's words, it seemed to me that they were so appropriate to the India of late

1984, for this was as dark a time, if not darker.

In the seat next to me on the plane was a young Sikh woman who was heading back to Delhi to rejoin her Hindu husband. She had been to Amritsar, she said, to reassure her parents that all was well with her in Delhi and that the post-assassination riots had not touched her family. Many of her Sikh friends, however, had been hounded and harassed by mobs, although there had been no casualties among them.

On top of a heap of magazines she carried was a book of poems by Rabindranath Tagore, the Bengali literary giant who was awarded the Nobel Prize for Literature. I saw that a particular page had been flagged by a silk marker. I asked to see the book, whose title was *Gitanjali.*

The poem this young Sikh woman had marked read as follows:

> *Where the mind is without fear and the head is*
> *held high;*
> *Where knowledge is free;*
> *Where the world has not been broken up into*
> *fragments by narrow domestic walls;*
> *Where words come out from the depth of truth;*
> *Where tireless striving stretches its arms towards*
> *perfection;*
> *Where the clear stream of reason has not lost its*
> *way into the dreary desert sand of dead habit;*
> *Where the mind is led forward by Thee into*
> *ever-widening thought and action—*
> *Into that heaven of freedom, my Father, let my*
> *country awake.*

When I was very young, I had been made to memorize that poem in school. All children in Indian schools learn it by heart. I'd forgotten it over the years, but as I reread Tagore now I realized how splendid a prayer he had written for India.

And I wondered if Rajiv Gandhi still remembered it from his school days, and if he had reread Tagore since.

After my visit to the Punjab, I went to see a man named Romesh Thapar in Delhi. He is a tall, silver-maned man, with a rich, resonant voice and the assured ease of an aristocrat. Thapar is one of India's best political analysts. He and his wife, Raj, publish a magazine called *Seminar,* which for nearly three decades has been the country's most important intellectual monthly. Along with their friend, Professor Rajni Kothari of the Center for the Study of Developing Societies, the Thapars have become sought-after sources for local writers and visiting journalists. They are very congenial, and a seeker of insight has yet to be turned away by them, no matter what the hour or the visitor's ideology. Because they rarely refrained from questioning Mrs. Gandhi's policies, the Thapars and Professor Kothari had not endeared themselves to the prime minister's aides and associates. Romesh Thapar received me in his art-filled house on Kautilya Marg, just a mile or so from Rajiv Gandhi's residence, and Raj Thapar promptly offered tea and toast. The collation warmed me up; the Delhi winter had frozen my insides.

Romesh Thapar had once been one of Indira Gandhi's key advisers, but subsequently had a falling out with the prime minister. By the time they parted company, more than a decade ago, Thapar had become thoroughly disillusioned with the prime minister's style and policies, including what he perceived as Mrs. Gandhi's efforts to undermine the judiciary by appointing political supporters to the bench, and her frequent attacks on critics in the media. Thapar vigorously opposed the "Emergency"—and as a result, his magazine was shut down by the authorities for several months. Thapar feels that Mrs. Gandhi deliberately allowed the Punjab situation to deteriorate so that she could exploit it politically. He feels that under Mrs. Gandhi an unprecedented crisis of political and economic management had set in.

"When Indira died, she left nothing behind—she left nothing behind of any redeeming value," Romesh Thapar said.

Thapar also feels that as more and more Indian states were alienated, the Congress base was restricted to the Hindi-speaking heartland in the north. Thus, Rajiv Gandhi and his Congress Party had to mobilize Hindu opinion in order to ensure victory in the December 1984 parliamentary elections. They did so "shamelessly," Thapar said, and with the not inconsiderable help of nearly $300 million that was reportedly spent on slick, cynical advertising and electioneering. (One indication of the alienation of Indian states was the fact that in the March 1985 state assembly elections, the Congress was unable to make inroads in Andhra Pradesh and Karnataka, southern states controlled by opposition parties; the Telugu Desam Party in Andhra, and the Janata Party in Karnataka, in fact, won more seats in the March elections than they had in previous elections. In the western industrial state of Maharashtra, long a Congress stronghold, Rajiv Gandhi's party had a pretty close shave—it won 161 out of 288 state assembly seats, a dozen less than in the last election.)

"The question now is, will the trauma of 1984 continue into 1985?" Thapar said. "How will Rajiv Gandhi manage relations between the center and the states? If there is to be a new social order, it will have to spring at the level of our states. The corrective measures in our subcontinent have to come from the states—because it is in the states that you implement policy and affect the everyday life of people. Any alternatives to the current national political mess, any new social order, must come at the state level. So if you are traveling through India's states, I wish you Godspeed!"

Later that cold evening in Delhi, I reflected on India's remarkable history and political development. What was this India that I was about to traverse and rediscover, this land of my birth and breeding?

The entity that is India today consists of twenty-two states and nine "Union" territories, or areas directly controlled by the Delhi government, which everyone calls The Center; some states, like Madhya Pradesh, are larger than France. When the British left in 1947 after ruling the Indian subcontinent for 150 years, there were 565 princely states in the territory that was then partitioned into India and Pakistan. These states were given the option of joining either India or Pakistan; virtually all chose to be part of India, whose leaders vowed at the very outset to establish a secular state (as opposed to

Pakistan, which was set up as an Islamic nation).

The departure of the British in 1947 was the culmination of a long and sometimes turbulent "freedom struggle" during which leaders such as Mahatma Gandhi, Jawaharlal Nehru, and Nehru's daughter, Indira Gandhi, were frequently arrested and jailed by their colonial rulers. It was during this freedom movement that Mahatma Gandhi fashioned his philosophy of "ahimsa," or nonviolence. He urged his followers to counter the brute strength of the British Empire with passive resistance. It was a philosophy that decades later would influence the Reverend Martin Luther King, Jr., who adopted it for his civil rights struggle in the deep South of the United States.

Independence brought India into the modern comity of nations, but Indian civilization had been around continuously since at least 2900 B.C. Inhabitants of the Indus River valley developed an urban culture based mostly on commerce and trade. Around 1500 B.C., Aryan tribes rode in from central Asia and drove the Indus inhabitants—known as the Dravidians—southward. During the next several centuries, various indigenous Hindu and Buddhist kingdoms flourished in India; the land also attracted waves of invaders from Persia and Muslim Asia, marauders whose greed was stirred by accounts by such travelers as Marco Polo and Vasco da Gama of fabulous wealth in India's temples and royal courts.

Most of these invaders foraged, pillaged, raped, and then left. But some stayed on, the most prominent of these being the Moguls. They established a dynasty that ruled most of India until the British conquered the subcontinent in the nineteenth century. It was the Moguls who accelerated the conversion of millions of Indians to Islam, which was often accompanied by great cruelty toward those who resisted conversion. But the Moguls also left behind extraordinary architectural achievements—the Taj Mahal in Agra, the Shalimar Garden in Kashmir, the sandstone city of Fatehpur Sikri, the Red Fort in Delhi. And it was the Moguls who established ateliers where miniature paintings were produced—paintings that survive to this day and which can command hundreds of thousands of dollars at international auctions.

The British did not enter India as the Moguls did, which is to say that they did not come with swords unsheathed and war cries on their lips. They came instead as traders and established a warehouse in Surat in 1619. They came under the auspices of the East India Company, which had been formed in London to promote trade in spices. Various native rulers, flattered by gifts given to them by the foreigners and perhaps intrigued by the sight of white skins, offered the traders "protection." Christian missionaries arrived in force, too, to introduce British-style education and to "convert the heathens." The traders steadily expanded their influence sometimes by subterfuge and sometimes by outright conquest. Local kingdoms, already beset with internecine succession problems and family squabbles, fell like kingpins. By the 1850s, the British East India Company controlled most of the land area that today covers India, Pakistan, and Bangladesh.

But in 1857, much of northern India revolted against the British. The revolt, known as the Great Mutiny, was largely the work of Indian foot soldiers, or sepoys. Most of them were Hindus who revered the cow, or Muslims who abhorred pork, and they were angered by the fact that animal fat was used to grease cartridges which had to be bitten open when loading the new Enfield rifle. Their mutiny sparked riots in cities such as Lucknow, Meerut, and Cawnpore, and there was considerable savagery against Britons. But in the end there were simply too many poorly led and disorganized groups in too many places, and the mutiny was put down by the better-equipped British troops, who were ably assisted by Sikh regiments.

The Great Mutiny resulted in the formal takeover of Indian territories by the British Crown. India was now part of Britain's empire.

The Welsh writer James Morris has a particularly eloquent passage in *Heaven's Command*, which forms part of his trilogy on the British Empire: "Swept away with the carnage of the Indian Mutiny were the last dilettante deposits of England's eighteenth-century empire. There had been a pagan, or at least agnostic charm to that old sovereignty—short on convictions, rich in gusto and a sense of fun —but there would be little that was airy or entertaining to the new empire emerging from the shambles of Lucknow and Cawnpore.

"It knew its values now, stern, efficient and improving, and it recognized as its principal duty the imposition of British standards upon the black, brown and yellow peoples. The Mutiny had demonstrated indeed that not all the colored peoples were capable of spiritual redemption, as had earlier been supposed, but at worst the British could always concentrate on material regeneration—the enforcement of law and order, the distribution of scientic progress and the lubrication of trade."

That is exactly what Queen Victoria's minions proceeded to do. They fashioned regional police forces; they whipped into shape an impressive national army; they introduced telegraph communications; they built more than 25,000 miles of railway tracks; they established a nationwide postal service; they raised schools and churches; they constructed roads through thick jungles and tall mountain ranges; they started the elite Indian Civil Service to which educated Indians eventually began to be admitted.

But the British also bled India dry. India's fine cotton fed the looms of Lancashire; the indigenous textile industry was crushed by the import of British fabrics fashioned from Indian cotton and silk. Indian iron ore went to Britain's steel mills, only to reappear in India in the form of locomotives and vehicles and machinery. The British barred industrial development in India because it would compete with their own factories and furnaces. Poverty widened in India. Joblessness increased.

In 1885, an Englishman named Allan Octavian Hume started an organization he called the Indian National Congress. Hume was a liberal-minded man who had served in India for many years as a British bureaucrat, and it was his feeling that the country's colonial rulers were dangerously out of touch with everyday people's feelings. Hume was keen that his new organization should serve as a vehicle of communication between the rulers and the ruled. Unlike the overwhelming majority of Britons of his time, Hume did not subscribe to the theory that India's white rulers were racially superior to its brown masses.

The Indian National Congress quickly became a forum not only for ideas concerning relations between the British and their subjects but also a platform from which India's struggle for independence was launched. Starting in 1920, Mohandas Karamchand Gandhi—later to be known as the Mahatma, or "saintly soul"—transformed the Congress into a mass movement. He used it to mount a popular campaign against the British.

The British finally left in 1947, but not before they had carved out from Greater India a homeland for many of the subcontinent's Muslims. The division of India into India and Pakistan was known as The Partition, which to this day evokes memories among many Hindus, Sikhs, and Muslims of widespread bloodshed and rioting. Although India became independent in 1947, it did not formally become a sovereign republic until January 26, 1950, when its constitution was promulgated. Jawaharlal Nehru, who had become prime minister in 1947, continued in that post until his death by natural causes in 1964. The Nehru years saw India make important progress in industrialization. Those were also the years when the country was divided up into linguistic states. Nehru was succeeded by Lal Bahadur Shastri, a veteran of the freedom struggle. Shastri died in January 1966, soon after India had defeated Pakistan in the second of three wars between the two states since Independence. Shastri's successor as prime minister was Indira Gandhi. She was to serve in that office almost exactly as long as her father had.

"Nehru, Shastri, Indira—there evolved over the years a gradual suspicion among everyday people about the Indian state itself. During the latter part of Indira's reign, the state dropped all notions of benevolence. And people's suspicion about the state, which kept accumulating wide-ranging police powers, was coupled with the disgust people felt over the growing corruption and criminalization in public life. Then you had situations like Punjab and Kashmir, where she constantly employed cost-calculating approaches instead of instituting measures that would lead to lasting solutions of thorny problems. She let thorny problems become thornier."

The speaker was Ashis Nandy, an associate of Delhi's Center for the Study of Developing Societies. Professor Nandy and I were talking in his musty, book-filled, and generally untidy office at the center's building on Rajpur Road in Old Delhi. Squirrels played on the well-kept lawn outside his office. Bougainvillea and magnolia trees added plentiful color to the scene. Nandy, a prolific writer and academician, was urging me to start my fresh round of travels in Kashmir. By the time I met Nandy, I had already been to the Punjab where I saw for myself the impact of Indira Gandhi's handling of a sensitive communal issue in a strategic border state. Now I was eager to go to Kashmir, where Mrs. Gandhi had won the last political battle of her life: she had conspired to topple the legitimately elected government of an opposition party and replace it with a government that supported her.

I found it useful to meet with people like Romesh Thapar and Rajni Kothari and Ashis Nandy. They gave me their valuable time, asking nothing in exchange except my attention. Without unduly imposing their own assumptions and opinions, they helped me make the connections between what I saw and heard and felt and the broader currents that are coursing through India.

As I flew to Kashmir, I thought about what Ashis Nandy had said about Indira Gandhi's "cost-calculating" approach to the management of power. She had, in fact, gone home again to Kashmir to whip it into line.

For Mrs. Gandhi was a Kashmiri brahman, a descendant of the scholarly, shrewd, and sturdy Hindus who flourished in a mountainous state that was overwhelmingly Muslim. The Nehrus—her father's family—had, of course, left Kashmir long before her birth to settle in Allahabad, a city on the banks of the River Ganges. Still, in Indira Gandhi's heart home was always Kashmir. The few people she was close to in her adult life were almost all Kashmiris. (Of course, she married a Parsi, of whom her father had not especially approved; the marriage failed. Nehru once wondered to a friend whether Indira would have been happier had she married a Kashmiri.)

I looked out of the window of the Indian Airlines airbus—and I gasped at the view. The plane was cruising over the snow-helmeted Pir Panjal Range. The crenellated peaks shimmered in the clear winter sunlight. To the west were the rich, alluvial plains of Pakistan; to the east lay the mountainous wastelands of Tibet, and beyond Tibet, China. Soon we were over the mighty Banihal Pass, through which invaders over the centuries had entered Kashmir. It was ironic, I thought, that the most recent invader had been a hometown girl.

Kashmir. The Switzerland of India, with 85,000 square miles of choice real estate, over which India and Pakistan fought three costly wars to establish proprietorship. Kashmir, more than 80 percent Muslim, but ruled traditionally by a Hindu clan whose scions squandered their fortune on sex and soft living, while their subjects starved. Jawaharlal Nehru once said about this state: "Kashmir, even more than the rest of India, is a land of contrasts. In this land, overladen with natural beauty and rich nature's gifts, stark poverty reigns and humanity is continually struggling for the barest of subsistences. The men and women of Kashmir are good to look at and pleasant to talk to. They are intelligent and clever with their hands. They have a rich and lovely country to live in. Why then should they be so terribly poor?"

Poverty in the midst of great natural beauty is a characteristic of many Third World countries. The beauty of Kashmir is especially breathtaking, with the green and fertile valley surrounded on all sides by tall sentinels of snow—which is why the scenes of deprivation are so dismaying. On the road from the airport, I passed massive camouflaged military bunkers in the shadow of which nestled knots of wooden houses. At first sight, they resembled those marvelous toy homes one comes across in the Swiss countryside, with A-shaped roofs and long beams supporting the ceilings. But instead of neat gardens and well-turfed yards, there were open sewers and dusty spaces in front of these houses. Men and women walked forlornly, with kangris, or charcoal stoves, under their robes; the kangris made everyone look heavily pregnant, men and women, but in a state where subzero temperatures are not unusual during the winter and where there is no such thing as central heating, the kangris serve as portable

heaters—just as hand-carried air conditioners cool American as-
tronauts' spacesuits as they walk from bunker to spacecraft before the
launch. During political rallies, kangris serve as deadly weapons: the
very day I arrived in Kashmir, more than thirty people had been hurt
in a kangri free-for-all that erupted at a rally sponsored by Rajiv
Gandhi's Congress Party.

The road from the airport was edged with poplar, walnut, and
chinar trees. I passed apple and cherry orchards and saffron fields.
The road rolled over many culverts and streams; handsome children
frolicked by these streams, but their clothes were frayed and often
torn. There was a rundown appearance to these houses, an impression
that was sustained all along into Srinagar. There was nothing beckon-
ing, or even welcoming, about this capital city of two million people.

I checked in at the Hotel Broadway, a modern Scandinavian-type
building with comfortable rooms and a polite staff. In the lobby were
several electric stoves. Large men wearing thick sweaters and peaked
wool caps lounged on sofas, consuming liquor. I was immediately
beset by carpet salesmen and purveyors of shawls. To decline such
offers was to offend, and the salesmen sulked away. But I wanted to
read up on tourist literature, which I had picked up at Srinagar's
airport. I was also waiting for my friend Rahul Singh, who was driving
up to Srinagar from the state's winter capital of Jammu, which lay
south of the massif I flew over on the way to Kashmir's elevated
valley. Rahul Singh was editor of the Chandigarh edition of the
Indian Express, and he was coming to Kashmir to get a reading on
the election campaign that was on in full fury here. We'd agreed to
link up in Srinagar, a place neither of us had visited for years.

The tourist brochures were shabby. The photographs were poorly
reproduced. Kashmir did not seem inviting in this literature. And,
indeed, tourism—the mainstay of the state's economy—was falling
off. I had been told in Delhi that in the first eleven months of 1984,
Kashmir attracted 275,000 domestic tourists and about 45,000 foreigners; the previous year, the figures had been 400,000 Indians and
44,000 foreigners; and in 1982, more than 600,000 Indian tourists
and 50,000 foreigners were estimated by the authorities to have

skiied, toured, trekked, played golf and tennis, fished, hiked, camped or climbed moutains in Kashmir. State officials attributed the decline in tourism to poor publicity about Kashmir, and the poor publicity to the fact that since 1983 the state had been experiencing a political upheaval. Moreover, tourists who traveled by land seemed deterred by the fact that virtually all major roads into Kashmir led up from a troubled neighboring state, the Punjab.

Tourists were also deterred by reports of growing unemployment in Kashmir. This, to be sure, was a classical case of the chicken-or-egg theory, because with fewer tourists coming to Kashmir, the state's tourism industries and such tourist-predicated businesses as carpet manufacturing and shawl making slid into the doldrums. About 75 percent of Kashmir's six million people lived in the Srinagar Valley, the rest in Jammu. In the valley alone, there were said to be more than 200,000 unemployed adults by December 1984. (Those who do visit Kashmir wind up with unexpected bonanzas: I was able to buy an intricately knotted and designed Kashmiri silk carpet at Ali Shah's shop outside Srinagar for the equivalent of $600—or at a 50 percent discount; in New York I was subsequently offered six times the amount for my new acquisition!)

Kashmiris have long felt that the Delhi government has neglected their economic development, despite the strategic importance of the state, which has borders with Pakistan and China. This sentiment was highlighted by Sonam Gyalsan, a lean, compact lawyer from the remote Kashmiri province of Ladakh. I was introduced to Gyalsan by a jolly local character named C. B. Kaul, who is Srinagar correspondent for the *Indian Express*. Kaul had brought Gyalsan to my hotel so that he could meet Rahul Singh, but since Singh was late in getting here from Jammu I served as a stand-in. Gyalsan, whose family members in Ladakh are still pastoral tribesmen, is a member of the Kashmir state assembly, and he invited Singh and me for breakfast the next morning. He cooked a Ladakhi breakfast for us in his small suite in Srinagar's hostel for legislators.

There was no heat in the suite, nor gas, nor electricity. Gyalsan lit up a kerosene stove and swiftly concocted a thick soup called snamthuk. In it were chunks of mutton, bits of goat's cheese, barley, flour, ginger, and rich local butter. The snamthuk was very filling, yet it was followed by boiled eggs, outsize apricots that Gyalsan had brought from Leh—Ladakh's capital—boiled cauliflower, and milky tea that was so sweet that my teeth vibrated as I consumed it. The meal made me drowsy, but I perked up when Gyalsan started to talk.

"We are at the brink of extinction in Ladakh," he said, in crisp English.

Extinction?

"Absolutely," Gyalsan said. "We tribesmen are the modern-day 'untouchables' of Kashmir. There are still 140,000 of us in Ladakh's two districts, Leh and Khargol. But look how we are forced to live —in caravans, in shacks made out of sheepskin, in degrading poverty. I have tried to impress on the powers-that-be in Delhi and in Srinagar that Ladakh should be developed in the national interest. After all, we, more than any other Indians, directly face two enemies—Pakistan and China. We are in the front line. Ours is the first blood to be shed whenever there are wars, or even minor skirmishes. And what do we get in return? Nothing. No jobs, little investment in economic development. Even the Indian Army people are sometimes arrogant in their dealings with us. Indira Gandhi said she cared for all of India's border peoples. Not much evidence of her caring in our area. I hope Rajiv Gandhi is more attentive."

Sonam Gyalsan's life story is a sort of Indian Horatio Alger tale. He was born forty-four years ago in a caravan near Nurla Village in Ladakh, the youngest of five brothers and a sister. His parents were nomadic traders in wool, and they frequently wandered into neighboring Tibet. Gyalsan traveled with them as they traversed mountain roads that rose as high as 18,000 feet. Winters were harsh, but at these heights it was bitterly cold even during the summers. His parents would stop at tiny hamlets to bargain for Shartush shawls, made out of the fine hair that grows under the necks of the spiral-horned wild mountain goats known as tsos. (These shawls now can cost the equivalent of $7,000.) When he was sixteen years old, his parents arranged his marriage to Tsering Dolkar, a fourteen-year-old girl. (They now have four children.) As Gyalsan learned to read and write in his parents' caravan, it struck him that there weren't too many people he encountered who enjoyed literacy. And the people of Ladakh, whose native language was Tibetan, simply could not communicate with traders and visiting politicians from the Kashmir Valley; the outsiders spoke Kashmiri and Hindi and Urdu, but seldom Tibetan.

"As a child I was inspired by biographies of Nehru and Mahatma Gandhi," Gyalsan said. "These books instilled in me a strong drive to uplift myself. I studied very hard and obtained admission to a high school in Srinagar, and then won a scholarship to Ram Jas College in Delhi. It was on a visit home one day that I learned there wasn't a single lawyer in Leh. Feuds and disputes were still being settled the old-fashioned way—with fists, or knives, or abusive language! I decided to become a lawyer."

He received a law degree from Delhi University and returned home to Ladakh to set up his practice. He started civic organizations to inculcate in Ladakhis notions of hygiene; he coaxed friends in Delhi to underwrite visits by physicians to attend to Ladakhi children's illnesses—the infant mortality rate in this remote northeast province of Kashmir was well over 300 per every live 1,000 births; he persuaded the Srinagar administration to build several primary schools; Gyalsan even founded a chapter of the Lion's Club in Leh —at 12,000 feet above sea level, the Leh chapter is believed to be the highest Lion's Club in the world.

It was only a matter of time before he entered politics. Gyalsan headed several delegations that went to Delhi to ask Mrs. Gandhi to formally declare Ladakh a backward area so that it could receive special development funds from the central government. The prime minister wasn't especially receptive. No special funds were allocated for the development of Ladakh, although vacation bungalows for government officials were erected near Leh. A hydroelectric project called Stakna was delayed so much by the government that the initial budget of $5 million now ballooned to five times that, with Delhi giving the money only grudgingly. The mostly Muslim Kashmir state officials in Srinagar didn't seem particularly inclined to assist the 140,000 people of Ladakh, most of whom were Buddhists.

So Sonam Gyalsan ran for the state assembly elections and won a seat. In the legislature, he has been vocal and insistent about obtaining a better deal for Ladakh.

"I see myself as a link between my backward society and the rapidly progressing modern-day India," Gyalsan said to me. "I'm a Buddhist —and Buddhism asks each of us to go outside of ourselves and look for the larger good. I don't especially subscribe to political rhetoric. I say to the big shots in Delhi: 'Don't just tell us how much Ladakh means for the security of the nation—show us.' Delhi has been allowed by people like us to get away with neglect and inattention. Well, our time has come. We won't stay silent any longer. We want everything that other Indians want—better schools, better homes, better health care, more jobs, cheaper food, good roads. We want to be part of the Indian dream, and not just dream that dream."

Sonam Gyalsan was exceptionally articulate about his objectives for the people of Ladakh, a people who have not profited by their association with India. But they are not alone. In states like West Bengal, Bihar, Orissa, Andhra Pradesh, Maharashtra, you can still come across backward tribes whose life has not improved in the thirty-eight years since independence. Such tribal communities as the adivasis and bhils still live in primitive conditions, foraging through forests for food, occasionally slaughtering a goat, sometimes raiding farms in the stealth of the night. At least Gyalsan's Ladakhis are represented in a legislature, at least Sonam Gyalsan can relay their yearnings and longings to a wider audience. The aborigines of most of India have little such representation, few special allowances.

Gyalsan had spoken about his people's dreams. Different people dream different things. The mostly Buddhist people of Ladakh are, after all, a minority community in a state whose population is overwhelmingly Muslim. Indira Gandhi had long suspected—as did a few of her father's key advisers—that some of these Muslims did not want to continue to be a part of India, that they either preferred to join Pakistan, which was an Islamic state, or that they wanted their own separate nation.

That suspicion continues, and it lies at the heart of India's "Kashmir Crisis."

To understand the crisis, one must go back to the nineteenth century. Kashmir until then had been ruled by a succession of Muslim rulers, mostly descendants of the Moguls or of various invaders who came from Afghanistan and central Asia. In the early part of the last century, Kashmir was absorbed into the empire of Ranjit Singh, the Sikh maharaja who had braved the British and built a kingdom whose power was unchallenged at the time. One of his ablest generals was a man named Gulab Singh Dogra, a Hindu of the western Indian Rajput clan. Gulab Singh had performed well in battle, and Ranjit Singh rewarded him with suzerainty over Jammu, a territory that was situated south of Kashmir. Ranjit Singh died on June 27, 1839, and almost immediately the British began freshly plotting to seize the Sikh empire.

They began secret negotiations with Gulab Singh Dogra. He gave British troops safe passage through Jammu on their way to fight the First Afghan War in 1841. They were trounced in that war's critical battle, at the Khyber Pass in January 1842, but Gulab Singh was seen as a friend because of his assistance. Four years later, Gulab Singh displayed his friendship again, this time by refusing to assist his patrons, the Sikhs, in the First Anglo–Sikh War of February 10, 1846. The Sikhs lost that war, and Gulab Singh was widely accused of being a traitor. But he came out ahead. A month after the Anglo–Sikh War, the British "allowed" him to buy from them the territories of Jammu and Kashmir, which they had seized as a result of their victory over the Sikhs. Gulab Singh Dogra paid a nominal sum of seventy five lakh rupees, or the equivalent of $75,000.

Gulab Singh and his heirs were forever indebted to the British after the "purchase" of Kashmir. They showed gratitude by sending Kashmiri troops to help the British further defeat the Sikhs, then sent troops again to overwhelm the Afghan tribes, and helped in British military campaigns in the two great wars of this century. The Dogras were not benevolent rulers of their mostly Muslim subjects. They were profligate, they were corrupt, they were depraved. Maharaja Hari Singh, who was Kashmir's ruler when India became independent in 1947, paid a heavy price for his licentiousness: blackmailers took photographs of him in the nude with a British prostitute in a London hotel room, and Hari Singh was made to cough up $6 million.

At the time of independence, the rulers of the 565 princely territories of India were given the choice of joining India or Pakistan. Pakistan's leaders cast covetous eyes on Kashmir. The understanding was that states with heavily Muslim populations would associate themselves with the new Islamic nation of Pakistan, particularly if they were contiguous to it. Kashmir met both criteria. But Hari Singh dithered. And local Muslims, led by the spectacularly popular Sheikh Mohammed Abdullah—widely known as Sher-E-Kashmir, or "The Lion of Kashmir"—did not seem especially thrilled with the idea of being part of Pakistan. Sheikh Abdullah, who had started a political party known as the National Conference, was a great secularist and was influenced in his beliefs by his close friend, Jawaharlal Nehru. Abdullah insisted that Hari Singh had no right to make any decision concerning the status of Kashmir—only the people could decide this, Abdullah said at rally after rally across the state, and not some degenerate feudal ruler.

The degenerate maharaja finally did accede his state to India. But only after Pakistani-sponsored tribesmen had launched an attack on Kashmir. Sheikh Abdullah and other Muslim leaders sought India's military help. Nehru, who had become prime minister of independent India, wanted to make sure that he could legally send his troops to counter the Pakistani-inspired attack on Kashmir. He first wanted Hari Singh to agree to let Kashmir join India. But Hari Singh had packed up his jewels, Persian rugs, and paintings, gathered his family and his concubines, and fled to Jammu. He was traced there by Nehru's trusted aide, V. P. Menon, who got the maharaja to sign a document of accession. Kashmir was now formally part of India.

Accession to India was thus done under pressure, even though there was no opposition to it at the time from Kashmir's leading politicians, such as Sheikh Abdullah. Nehru pledged that the accession would be validated by a popular referendum under international auspices, perhaps the United Nations. Sheikh Abdullah himself said: "Kashmir has linked itself to India, not because it has been lured by any material gain but because it is at one with her in the Gandhian ideals of justice, equality, and humanity. A progressive state could join hands only with another progressive one and not with a feudal state like Pakistan. Our decision to accede to India is based on the fact that our program and policy are akin to those followed by India. New Kashmir and Pakistan can never meet. Pakistan is a haven of exploiters. India is pledged to the principle of secular democracy in her policy and we are in pursuit of the same objective."

The Lion of Kashmir became the state's chief executive. Throughout his life and until his death on September 8, 1982, he always publicly swore allegiance to India. But some of Nehru's key aides in Delhi whispered in his ears that the sheikh was secretly "soft" on Pakistan or that, worse, he wished to break away from India. The sheikh early on insisted that India should hold a referendum, as indeed Nehru had promised; there was little doubt in the years immediately after independence that Kashmiris would have voted overwhelmingly to stay with India.

But Sheikh Abdullah and Jawaharlal Nehru had a falling out over the referendum issue—which Nehru aides saw as a code for Kashmiri secession from India—and over the next twenty years the sheikh spent more time inside Indian jails than outside them. No referendum was ever held in Kashmir. India and Pakistan went to war three times. Countless debates were held at the United Nations over Kashmir. Pakistan continued holding on to a bite-sized bit of Kashmiri territory in the northwest of the state, and in the northeast China illegally held on to a sliver of mountainous wasteland.

Even though Sheikh Abdullah was incarcerated for a long time by the Indian government under the National Security Act, his supporters continued to agitate for a referendum, or a "plebiscite." It was only on February 24, 1975, that the sheikh and his supporters agreed to disband their movement for a plebiscite. Their agreement was formalized in the six-point "Kashmir Accord," which was sculpted by Prime Minister Indira Gandhi's trusted foreign policy advisor, G. Parthasarathy.

The accord resulted not only in the abandonment of the plebiscite movement; it pledged Sheikh Abdullah to honor Article 370 of the Indian Constitution, which gave Kashmir special status within the Indian union. And the accord specifically emphasized that Kashmir was a constituent unit of India. The accord cleared the way for a triumphant return to power by the sheikh, who was duly made Kashmir's chief minister on February 25, 1975. He was to serve in that office until his death of a heart attack seven years later, at the age of seventy-seven. Whatever his political appeal, the sheikh's administrative helmsmanship had not been especially distinguished: corruption rocketed under the sheikh, the state's development plans went astray, and the budget ran amok.

Dynastic politics is perhaps a special characteristic of Kashmiris. Jawaharlal Nehru was followed as India's prime minister by his daughter, Indira Gandhi (after the two-year interregnum of Lal Bahadur Shastri, of course). And now Sheikh Mohammed Abdullah's annointed heir apparent, his flamboyant son Farooq, was sworn in as Kashmir's chief minister.

Farooq Abdullah had trained to be a physician and, indeed, had practiced medicine for several years in Britain. He married an Irishwoman. He loved fast cars and motorbikes. He was so fond of Mrs. Gandhi that he called her "Mummy."

But "Mummy" was less than appreciative of two things: one, the fact that however supportive Farooq Abdullah was of her as a national leader, Kashmir still was governed not by her Congress Party but by the National Conference, which was technically at least an opposition party. And second, the fact that Farooq Abdullah had joined with chief ministers of other opposition-ruled states in starting a forum to reform center–state relations. Mrs. Gandhi felt that implicit in the formation of this forum was the hope that India's squabbling opposition parties would fashion a common front against her ruling Congress Party in the next parliamentary elections, which were widely expected to be held by January 1985.

Farooq Abdullah, perhaps out of political naiveté and inexperience, may not have realized that his very presence on a public platform with opposition politicians would be viewed dimly indeed by Indira Gandhi. "Mummy" set into motion a plan to unseat him, initiating first a sinister whispering campaign against the physician-turned-politician. Suggestions were floated that Farooq Abdullah was sympathetic toward Sikh separatists. Then a rumor circulated in Delhi that Abdullah had made a secret deal with Pakistan's military dictator, Mohammed Zia ul-Haq, under which the National Conference would act as a fifth column in India on behalf of Pakistan. Some Gandhi associates openly joked about Abdullah's sexual preferences and questioned his loyalty to his wife.

In *India: The Siege Within,* M. J. Akbar makes the following assessment of this period in Farooq Abdullah's star-crossed tenure as Kashmir's chief minister:

"The Abdullahs were always conscious that, no matter how many times they protested otherwise, they would forever be vulnerable to the charge of being 'soft' toward Pakistan, and in quiet league with secessionists. They knew that each time Delhi wanted them to kneel, it would always resurrect this allegation and, if necessary, even use such an excuse to dismiss the government. Sheikh Abdullah had spent his life listening to accusations of treachery; his only answer lay in his personal faith and self-confidence, and in the end he was vindicated. Farooq Abdullah now knew that it was only a matter of time before the many hostile forces started such a smear campaign against him."

"He decided to meet the problem head-on," Akbar writes. "One of the mistakes which the Sheikh had made, in his son's view, was that he had kept himself confined, by and large, to his own state. Farooq Abdullah decided that he would build personal and political bridges across the country. He would convince India, and not just Mrs. Gandhi, about his commitment to the country. If he could clear the minds of the people and the political parties in the rest of the country, he would be much less dependent on the goodwill of just one party, the Congress. If, therefore, he was ever called secessionist, he hoped that there would be more than one powerful voice in India saying that the accusation was a partisan fraud designed to cover up an unethical power game."

The game was much more unethical than Farooq Abdullah had bargained for. Mrs. Gandhi coaxed his brother-in-law, G. M. Shah, to form a cabinet with the help of "defectors" from Abdullah's National Conference. The men and women who now affiliated themselves with Shah were all promised—and subsequently given—cabinet positions. Farooq Abdullah seemed unaware that these moves were being plotted in his own backyard. On the afternoon of the evening he was deposed, the tall, handsome chief minister was reported to be gamboling with Shabana Azmi, the film actress, who was in Kashmir to shoot a Hindi movie.

Srinagar's masses rioted when they heard the news of Abdullah's overthrow. Mrs. Gandhi sent in troops to restore law and order. Opposition leaders around the country roared their disapproval.

No amount of protests helped. Farooq Abdullah was out, G. M. Shah was there to stay, and Indira Gandhi had won what would be her last political victory.

Indira Gandhi may have succeeded in dethroning Farooq Abdullah in July 1984, but by the end of the year he had humiliated her Congress Party in the Kashmir Valley.

Not long after the assassination of the prime minister, it was announced by her son and successor, Rajiv Gandhi, that national parliamentary elections would be held across India on December 24 and 27. Astrologers consulted by Congress Party chieftans said that those were the most auspicious dates for a poll, and so it was decided that the election would be held in some states on the first date and in the rest of the country on the latter date.

In the event, Rajiv Gandhi's Congress won an unprecedented 401 out of 508 seats contested in all of India's states except Assam and

Punjab (where the poll was postponed on account of unstable political conditions). The 107 seats the Congress did not win included all three in Kashmir. Farooq Abdullah's National Conference steamrollered candidates put up by Abdullah's brother-in-law, Chief Minister G. M. Shah. The losers, who were backed by the Gandhi Congress, included Shah's own son. The winners included Farooq's mother, Begum Akbar Jehan Abdullah.

But the election was some days away when Rahul Singh and I arrived at Farooq Abdullah's National Conference campaign office. It occupied a basement of the modern Nawa-I-Subh Building near a Srinagar landmark, the Zero Bridge. Party workers scurried about, carrying posters that featured Farooq Abdullah's smiling face. The party's flags—red, with a plow in the center—were being distributed, as were banners that carried slogans criticizing G. M. Shah and the Congress Party. C. B. Kaul, the local correspondent of the *Indian Express,* was our escort, and he seemed to know everybody. We lost him at one stage in a knot of people, and when I went looking for Kaul I traced him not visually but through his high-pitched laugh.

"Good fellow, this Kaul," someone said to me. "Has a sense of humor. Now why can't all press chaps be like that?"

I had hoped to meet Farooq Abdullah, but he was out of Kashmir. There were a number of similarities between him and Rajiv Gandhi, and I thought that some day these two men would surely collide in the political arena—it was probably written in the stars. Each was of Kashmiri extraction; each had a foreign-born wife—Abdullah's wife was Irish, Gandhi's wife was Italian—and each had met his wife in Britain; each had two children; each was tall and handsome and personable; each loved machines—Farooq, motorcycles and fast cars, Rajiv, planes; each was a scion of an illustrious family; each had been brought up in a politically active family; and each had a powerful, even overbearing mother.

It was Farooq Abdullah's mother, the formidable Begum Akbar Jehan, whom we got to see this morning. Her husband, the late sheikh, was notorious for his roving eye, but the Abdullahs enjoyed a mostly solid married life for forty-nine years. She bore the sheikh five children: the eldest, a daughter named Khalida, who married G. M. Shah; Farooq; another son, Tariq; another daughter, Suraiya; and Mustafa Kamal, a son. Begum Abdullah—"begum" is a honorific given to women of stature in the Muslim culture—herself came from a wealthy family: her father, Harry Nedou, was a Christian who converted to Islam; he owned Nedou's Hotel in Srinagar. Akbar Jehan was not brought up behind the purdah, nor was she kept behind it by her husband—as so many Muslim women still are in Kashmir. The sheikh sought her assistance in his political party, the National Conference, and she quickly gained a wide following in her own right. There were people who even thought her to be the best politician in the family.

On this morning, the begum was at the local television station. She was taping an appeal for votes that would be broadcast that evening; it was not a paid political broadcast but a free one, given to her party under a national agreement by which all major political parties received some free time on India's government-managed airwaves to take their case directly to the people. Television had come to India with a vengeance, I thought: this single broadcast alone would be heard by more people than the begum had addressed in all her fifty years in politics. Rajiv Gandhi's television speech to the nation on the night his mother was murdered was estimated to have been seen by more than 450 million people, or nearly twice the population of the United States!

The begum was herself a candidate for Parliament in the Anantnag constituency outside Srinagar. (She would win handily.) We waited more than two hours for her. Various National Conference functionaries kept pouring hot coffee for us; we were fed with tales of alleged improprieties on the part of G. M. Shah's henchmen. A pink-faced man named Wali Mohammed Itoo parked himself next to me. His elegant Kashmiri silk shawl had been sprayed with cologne.

"Shah's men have murdered democracy in Kashmir," he said. "And Indira Gandhi put them up to it. Now we are concerned that they will commit massive fraud to win Kashmir's three parliamentary seats." (His fears did not materialize: Abdullah's party captured all three seats in the election.)

Itoo had been speaker of the 76-member State Assembly when Farooq Abdullah was Kashmir's chief minister. When Abdullah was toppled, his friend Itoo was unceremoniously pulled out of the speaker's gilded chair and pushed out of the assembly chamber by Shah's musclemen. Now Itoo is suing Shah in the state's high court.

An elderly Sikh named Sant Singh Teg came up to us. He gripped both my hands.

"You must tell this to the world: Farooq Abdullah is a protector of the Sikhs," he said, in Hindi. "There are two hundred thousand of us in Kashmir. Only Farooq stands between us and the blood-thirsty people down in Jammu who want to kill us. Tell this to the world." (Sant Singh Teg was alluding to Hindu militants who had burned Sikh homes and shops in Uddampur, a town not far from Jammu, a few days before I got to Kashmir. Only the intervention of the Indian army prevented what would undoubtedly have been a massacre of the small Sikh community there.)

I remembered that Indira Gandhi had insinuated that Farooq Abdullah had given shelter and succor to Sikh terrorists in Kashmir. I mentioned this to Sant Singh Teg, who is leader of Kashmir's Sikh community.

"Do I look like a terrorist to you?" he said. "The Congress has spread vicious rumors just to discredit Farooq. We have nothing to do with the Khalistan people. We are Indians first and foremost. Sheikhsahib had said that thousands of times, Farooqsahib says it all the time. What has Farooqsahib done that shows otherwise? Tell the world that."

There was a flurry of activity in the hallway outside. Begum Abdullah had arrived. Everyone stood up. She was very short—from her photographs I had expected her to be much taller; her face was unlined, although she must have been pushing seventy (Kashmiri women are known for their great beauty, which many manage to preserve—as the begum obviously had done—well past their chronological youth). She wore a brown kaftan, and her head was covered with the same silk-woolen material: Kashmiris call the outfit fheran. She inquired after our welfare and offered us more coffee. I thought she seemed a bit agitated, and I said so.

"You are correct," the begum said. "These policemen and soldiers here bother me. Do you know that after my son was unconstitutionally overthrown back in July, Indira sent more than 30,000 paramilitary troops into Kashmir. What did they come here for? To give protection to the undemocratic government that Indira had installed. These troops are still here."

But wasn't Kashmir always heavily guarded by federal security forces? Wasn't the threat of a raid by Pakistan-sponsored marauders always present?

"But these new forces here are meant to squash public protests against Shah's illegal regime," Begum Abdullah said.

Had Chief Minister Shah and his wife, Khalida—who was the begum's eldest daughter—met with Mrs. Abdullah recently?

The begum sighed and looked at her manicured hands.

"My son-in-law has parted ways with us and has taken to the Congress," she said, softly. "We count him as a traitor. He is a traitor to the Kashmiri people, to the country, to our party, and to the democratic ways we have always adopted. He has created chaos, he has done a lot of harm. I haven't been in touch with my daughter Khalida. It's a great sacrifice for a mother when she sees that her own child has parted ways with her in order to head toward the camp of enemies."

But hadn't Rajiv Gandhi praised Shah for having reinstituted law and order in Kashmir?

"What law and order? Now you find killings, injustice. Nobody seems to feel secure. With Rajiv's ascendancy we had hoped for the better. But he has kept a lot of his mother's advisers, which is a sad reflection on him. Those very advisers, like Alexander, gave Indira so much wrong advice, which made her take so many wrong steps."

(The adviser Begum Abdullah named was Dr. P. C. Alexander, who served as principal private secretary to both Indira Gandhi and Rajiv

Gandhi. Dr. Alexander resigned in late January 1985 after disclosures that several of his staff members allegedly spied for American and French intelligence agencies.)

"The problem with Indira Gandhi was that she could never trust the states—particularly if those states were administered by parties other than the Congress," the Begum said. "So power was increasingly concentrated in Delhi. State chief ministers had to go begging to Delhi for permission each time they wanted to sneeze. How can you run a huge federal system like India this way? Her style brought India to the edge of the precipice. What a legacy for Rajiv to overcome!"

What about her son's alleged association with Punjab's Sikh separatists?

"It was absolutely baseless that Farooq had anything to do with people like Bhindranwale," the begum said. "Farooq in fact had warned Indira that she needed to solve the Punjab's problems the soonest. He told her that the Sikhs did not feel that they were being treated as equals. He told her that the Punjab was Kashmir's lifeline because of the road traffic that transports grain to us and that takes our fruit produce to be sold elsewhere in India. Farooq told her that the situation in Punjab, if allowed to deteriorate, would affect the wellbeing of Kashmir. And that has now happened. Our tourism revenues used to be a hundred crore rupees a year [the equivalent of $100 million], with a multiplier effect of three times. Now what are we left with? Barely a fraction of those revenues.

"Farooq told Indira that it was in the national interest that she solve amicably the Punjab problem. But Indira said that she didn't feel it was time for her to talk with the Punjab's leaders. Then she accused Farooq of being an extremist. I wouldn't like to say anything more that would hurt her departed soul—but she has left us all in quite a mess."

Begum Abdullah asked for another cup of coffee.

"Anyway, we hope for the better," she said. "We hope good sense prevails."

She got up to leave for a rally in Anantnag. We accompanied her to her car. Just before she drove off in a procession of jeeps and trucks whose speakers blared out slogans and other campaign propaganda, Akbar Jehan Abdullah leaned out of her window and said:

"Tell me, haven't Kashmiris got the right to live with dignity? That's what we've always fought for. That's what we are still fighting for."

It is not only Kashmir's indigenous politicians, such as the Abdullahs, who have long been suspected by Delhi of harboring secessionist, or pro-Pakistan, sentiments. The Abdullahs have had to prove themselves as being more "kosher," more "Indian" than political leaders in other Indian states. But even ordinary Kashmiris are generally perceived by ordinary Indians elsewhere as not quite emotionally "with" India. The feeling among many top government officials in Delhi is that the Kashmiri Muslim has yet to completely reconcile his state's formal affiliation with India, and that among these Muslims India is still viewed as an alien country. These officials point to surveys that have showed that the most popular radio and television programs in the Kashmir Valley are not those broadcast by India's government networks but by those of Pakistan. (That may well be because Pakistan's broadcasts, although heavily religious in nature, are generally much better produced than the Indian ones.)

What Kashmiris call "Delhi's handiwork" has involved a continuing effort to discredit the state's political leaders, especially those not belonging to the Congress Party. For example, Mrs. Gandhi's henchmen have spread the word that Farooq Abdullah accumulated a personal fortune of $50 million during his twenty-two months as Kashmir's chief minister, and that among other things he maintained a fleet of twenty expensive foreign cars. His father, Sheikh Mohammed Abdullah, amassed even greater wealth, according to the propaganda spread by the Abdullahs's opponents. But whenever Farooq Abdullah referred to reports that some of Indira Gandhi's factotums were charging million of rupees in fees just to provide access to her or to ensure that a valued industrial license was approved, he was at once accused of being unpatriotic, or of lying.

The whispering campaign concerning Kashmiris' "Patriotism" had been also extended to the state's muslim religious leaders and organizations.

Here the critics and questioners have probably been on firmer ground—for the theological leaders of this overwhelmingly Muslim state have frequently flip-flopped over their allegiance. The Jamaat-E-Islami, a religious organization with considerable support among peasants, had been openly pro-Pakistan. It was only when neighboring Pakistan's military dictatorship started establishing a cruel, intolerant theocracy that the popularity of the Jamaat-E-Islami began to wane in Kashmir. The Muslims of Kashmir may be religious, but they have never been known as Hindu-haters or Hindu-baiters; and Kashmiri Muslims like the idea of free speech and their leaders have seldom advocated clamping down on political or even theological dissent. I think General Zia ul-Haq has done India a great service: he has shown Kashmiri Muslims how intolerant and intolerable life can be in his Islamic state—and this in turn seems to have convinced many Kashmiri Muslims that they would be guaranteed far more liberties under Delhi's continued Raj than under Islamabad's iron rule.

For many years, the chief religious priest of Kashmir, a man named Maulana Yusouf Shah, advocated affiliation between Kashmir and Pakistan. Shah's heir, Moulvi Mohammed Farooq, endorsed his predecessor's position concerning Kashmir; but Moulvi Farooq then suddenly abandoned his pro-Pakistan stand and declared himself a supporter of Farooq Abdullah, who frequently advertised his own pro-India position. There are those who suggest that much money changed hands before Moulvi Farooq altered his political views; certainly, the moulvi's backing of Abdullah was a major political plus for the son of Sheikh Mohammed Abdullah, who had been bitterly opposed for decades by the moulvi's predecessor, Maulana Yusouf Shah.

I wanted to meet Moulvi Farooq. C. B. Kaul, the *Indian Express* correspondent, arranged an appointment for Rahul Singh and myself. There was nothing that Kaul did not seem to be able to do: he had extensive contacts; he spoke the local language because he himself was a Kashmiri; he knew wonderful restaurants where Srinagar's political gadflies gathered for hearty repasts and hectic repartee; he knew shops where Rahul Singh and I could buy choice but cheap walnuts, almonds, and dried apricots; he took us to boutiques where we purchased silk scarves. We set off for the moulvi's home, which was several miles north of Srinagar. ("Moulvi" means head priest, as does "mirwaiz," another honorific used for Mohammed Farooq.) Srinagar seemed gray and bleak; thick clouds hid the serrated mountain wall beyond the city. The roads were rutted. We drove by the Hari Parbat, a hillock crowned by a fort built in the sixteenth century by the Mogul Emperor Akbar. At the foot of the fort were Muslim, Hindu, and Sikh shrines—a lasting tribute to Akbar, who was a champion of secularism. We passed several lakes on which were berthed Kashmir's famous houseboats. These serve as hotels during the tourist season, and guests are transported to their quarters from the shore by gondola-like canoes. Debris and excrement floated on the lakes of Srinagar. This was India's star tourist attraction?

Moulvi Farooq lived in a heavily guarded house made of red brick, glass, and concrete. Chinar trees—whose leaves are almost heart-shaped—graced the front and back yards. The doors were made of solid teak, as were the window frames; the furniture was walnut wood. The curtains were of thick wool, with chinar-leaf patterns embroidered on them. We were requested to remove our shoes, as is the custom in orthodox Sunni Muslim homes. We were first taken through an inner courtyard to a waiting room, and the floor in this unheated area was so cold that shivers scrambled up my spine. There were three video machines in the waiting room, where the moulvi often shows religious documentaries to his visitors.

We were spared these films. The moulvi was prepared to see us immediately. We trekked through the cold courtyard again, and we were shown into a bedroom-cum-office. The moulvi rose to greet us.

He was tall, hirsute, fit-looking. He wore pink-tinted glasses, a typical Kashmiri lambswool peaked cap, and a sherwani, or long jacket that was buttoned up from knees to neck; sherwanis ordinarily are tightly fitted, but the moulvi wore one that looked like a loose smock: it was made of white wool, and there were intricate green patterns on the sleeves and collar.

The moulvi sat down in a high-backed chair, behind which was a picture window. He then signaled us to sit on the floor in front of him, on a thick Kashmir rug. An old manual typewriter rested in a corner of the room; the bedstead was covered by a magnificent silk spread. One wall held bookshelves. The moulvi's aides brought blankets and covered our crossed legs. They also placed kangris, or coal stoves, in front of us. It was so comfortable that I felt like taking a nap.

But refreshments arrived. Hot coffee was served, then pastries and biscuits. The moulvi consumed nothing, although his aides feasted. Outside, the sun had broken through the clouds, and now the moulvi's head was framed by a halo. It occurred to me that his seating arrangement was deliberate. It was difficult for us, huddled on the floor, to gaze up at him and make out his facial expressions, for we were staring directly toward the window and the dazzling sunlight outside. It was almost as if the moulvi were in a pulpit instead of a chair, looking down at his audience. This was theater.

And the moulvi was theatrical in his speech and gestures. He spoke in cadence-filled Urdu and Kashmiri—which Kaul translated for us —and sometimes he employed English phrases.

"I am a simple man who preaches a simple message," the moulvi, who was born in 1944, began. "I believe in democracy, and I desire that morality should be practiced in politics."

He rose from his chair and raised his hands toward the heavens.

"There should be nation building," he roared. "Nation building is important to build people's character. In Kashmir, I want all the rights that are guaranteed under the Indian Constitution. I want Kashmir to be an ideal democratic and secular model-state. There should be no religious or communal or political intolerance. There should be room for all in India, and a modern secular state must respect the fact that a province can be heavily Muslim by faith and yet totally secular in practice. I want bonds of the heart, not chains that are held in place by the police and the army. I want silken threads, not iron chains."

Had he not recently called for a merger of Kashmir with Pakistan, I asked?

The moulvi sat down.

"There is a campaign against me because I preach tolerance and Indo-Pakistani amity," he said, in a less strident tone. "The campaign is on because I head a certain religion whose followers are in a minority in India. But because I am a religious leader doesn't mean that I cannot be secular-minded. The feeling in Delhi seems to be that if I'm not a member of the Congress, then I must be antinationalistic. Delhi is pushing people here up against the wall. Temperamentally, I am a democratic person: I value India's democratic efforts, its rich cultural traditions. I see Kashmir belonging to this tradition. Kashmir hasn't acceded to the Congress Party but to an India of certain principles, democratic principles. But when I say that I'm a Kashmiri, that doesn't mean I'm anti-India."

I thought that last sentence was significant. Successive leaders in Delhi have interpreted Kashmiri aspirations for greater autonomy as being coded calls for establishing a separate state, or for politically linking up with Islamic Pakistan. Instead of encouraging genuinely popular Kashmiri leaders like Farooq Abdullah who were in a position to consolidate pro-Indian sentiments in the state, Congress officials in Delhi worked hard to overthrow them because these leaders did not belong to the Congress Party. Delhi repeatedly neglected to take into account a fundamental fact of life in ethnically varied India— that every state occasionally needs to assert its special regional identity. Whatever his theatrics, I believed the moulvi when he said that his being a Kashmiri did not mean he was anti-India.

The moulvi has succeeded in combining his spiritual duties with temporal functions, something that few religious leaders in India have been able to do. He has succeeded because there is no competition for him in Kashmir—the moulvi, or mirwaiz, is traditionally the Sunni Muslims' undisputed leader. Moulvi Mohammed Farooq has shrewdly fashioned an able cadre of workers who not only proselytize at the hundreds of mosques around the state but also work with officials of political parties, which themselves are heavily Muslim in composition.

"I don't see a contradiction between religion and politics," Moulvi Farooq said. "While I don't support demagoguery, I feel it is the responsibility of theological leaders to pay attention to the political health of their community. My pulpit is my platform."

From his pulpit he has called for a new political dialogue between India and Pakistan, something that Prime Minister Rajiv Gandhi is said to want as well. He has called for a fresh reassessment of center–state relations, which Rajiv Gandhi may be more reluctant to undertake. And the Moulvi has called for a complete revision of Delhi's attitudes toward Kashmir; he wants new guarantees of autonomy, of political noninterference, of new infusions of federal funds for economic development. This Rajiv Gandhi is least likely to do, particularly in these halcyon days of his national political triumph.

And yet I found something vaguely disturbing in the moulvi's combining of the spiritual and the temporal. It challenged the very essence of India's secular system, I thought—no matter that Moulvi Farooq had protested his own commitment to secularism. He seemed to have mobilized the support and sentiments of many of Kashmir's Muslims, who apparently thought it quite all right that a spiritual leader should dabble in politics as well; moreover, the moulvi was wooed by Kashmir's political establishment—Farooq Abdullah had thought it important enough to seek the Moulvi's endorsement.

I thought: what if the moulvi expanded his influence to the rest of India's eighty million Muslims? What if these masses were politicized in the manner approved by the moulvi? How impressionable would they be to theological rhetoric? How would India's Hindu majority, already suspicious that the country's Muslim represented a fifth column on behalf of Pakistan, react and retaliate? There was no comparable Hindu religiopolitical leader in India. And a chilling question: if, at some later date, a Muslim preacher emerged who called for a new commitment by India's Muslims to Pakistan, or who called for a new Islamic state within India (India's Muslim population, after all, was close to that of Pakistan), would there be a blood-bath reminiscent of the 1947 Partition?

These questions eddied through my mind as I flew from Kashmir to the south-central state of Andhra Pradesh.

It was in Andhra that the seeds of India's linguistic states were sown nearly three decades ago, and it was in Andhra, too, that some very bloody riots between Hindus and Muslims had taken place in recent months. And it was in Andhra that the new regional assertiveness of the country was to be seen. The leaders of Andhra were saying that India's states must be allowed greater political autonomy, that the time had come for the central government to allow the floodgates of grassroots creativity to be opened more fully.

With Indira Gandhi now gone, these states had a better opportunity than ever to get what they wanted.

3

The Andhra Factor

THE capital of Andhra Pradesh is a four-hundred-year-old city called Hyderabad. It has one of the most modern airports in India, and one that works remarkably well in spite of the heavy traffic. The city is situated some 1,800 feet above sea level on what is called the Deccan plateau. Hyderabad and its twin city, the much younger Secunderabad, together have a population of nearly six million. Hyderabad, with its crumbling forts, its ancient monuments, the Char Minar, its silver bazaars, and its filigree markets, has long been a tourist attraction. The climate is agreeable through most of the year. A number of the nation's top military officials have built retirement homes in the area; Hyderabad and Secunderabad have large cantonments, and retired military personnel find the atmosphere congenial.

Hyderabad used to be the seat of the old Deccani Muslim nawabs, or noblemen, and also of the nizam of Hyderabad state, once believed to be the wealthiest man in the world. (One nizam, in fact, was so rich that whenever he hosted huge banquets, which was almost every evening, he would bury gold nuggets in mounds of steaming rice he served to his guests: those who found these nuggets could keep them!) The noblemen of Hyderabad developed a highly literate and sophisticated culture. The "old world" manners and graciousness of the nawabs still survive in some measure in Hyderabad. Old Hyderabadi families still serve up heavenly meals in high style. But the grand old palaces and mansions of Hyderabad are being torn down at an alarming rate, to make way for modern high-rise apartment blocks or commercial buildings. Progress has come to Hyderabad in a big way. The old farmsteads around the city have been gobbled up by electronic factories and textile mills and glass industries. The air here, once considered the most salubrious of all of India's medium-sized cities, is steadily becoming sour. The plane trees are dying, and the meadows get browner every year.

In his highly readable *A New History of India,* Stanley Wolpert notes that at the time of independence, the nizam of Hyderabad dithered over joining India—even though his state had a majority Hindu population. The nizam wanted nationhood for Hyderabad; he was said to have hired Pakistani fighter planes to "attack" India in order to achieve his goal. But the nizam was tamed by the strong-willed Sardar Vallabhbhai Patel, then India's home minister: Patel dispatched two divisions of the army's Southern Command to "convince" the nizam that joining India was in his best interests. Hyderabad acceded to India.

Within a few years, this region was again in the news.

"The first vigorous agitation for a 'linguistic province' emerged in the Telugu-speaking region of northern Madras, which wanted a state of its own, to be called Andhra, after the ancient Deccan Empire," Professor Wolpert says. "Nehru was less supportive of the linguistic provinces movement than Gandhi had been, and he succumbed to its popular pressure only after Potti Sriramalu, the saintly father of the Andhra movement, fasted to death in December 1952, leading to the creation of Andhra on October 1, 1953." The princely state of Hyderabad was integrated into the new Andhra, as were the Telangana region that was part of the Madras Presidency, a section of the Bombay Presidency, and parts of a state called Madhya Pradesh.

The moment it was announced that a new state was being created along linguistic lines, scores of provincial leaders all across India began clamoring for states that would reflect their own language and ethnicity. Riots broke out. Property damage was in the hundreds of millions of dollars. Prime Minister Nehru did what heads of government do when they don't want to make a snap decision—he appointed a commission to study the nationwide agitation for linguistic states. That body was called the States Reorganization Commission, and it included three highly respected Indians: Saiyid Fazl Ali, H. N. Kunzru, and K. M. Panikkar. The commission members spent two years reviewing mountains of memoranda, interviewing thousands of individuals all over India, and reflecting on the possible repercussions of slicing up India into linguistic units. They were not at all sure that such linguistic division would be good for the country. But pressures for linguistic states were building up dramatically, and in December 1955 the commission made the recommendations on which India's twenty-two states eventually came into being.

The basis for creating linguistic states was not just the demand for establishing formally the supremacy of various languages in their respective regions. The creation of these states was also an acknowledgement of a basic fact of life in an ethnically diverse democracy: that politics in such a state are always the politics of the majority. Thus, the Telugu-speaking minority in the old Madras Presidency— where Tamil was the language of the majority community—felt it was being left out of the political process and therefore out of economic progress. When Kerala state was created in 1956, to cite another example, the Malabar region—which was part of the Madras Presidency as well—was grouped together with the princely territories of Travancore and Cochin because, like them, it too was heavily Malayalam-speaking. Regional culture in India is strongly linked to language: indeed, language, more than ideology or religion or even caste, is the main unifying factor in the country.

Whether the creation of linguistic states was good or not is a topic still under discussion in India. (The Indian press occasionally likes to raise the question of "fissiparousness" of these states. There was, in fact, a government-appointed study group some years ago called "The

Commission on Fissiparous Tendencies." No one I met in India could remember what happened to this body). And people remember how Nehru mollifed various state renegades. The chief example always cited in such discussions is that of Madras. In that southern region, well-organized Tamils had banded together in a political party called the Dravida Munnetra Kazhagam, widely known as the DMK. The DMK was overtly secessionist, much more so than any Sikh political group in the Punjab has been in recent years. Its leaders, such as C. N. Annadurai, asserted that the Tamils of the south needed their own nation to fully realize their potential; the message was that the Tamils resented efforts by the Delhi government to impose Hindi—a language spoken by 42 percent of the country's population, but mainly in the northern states—all across the country.

The DMK, because it was secessionist, was barred from contesting state elections in Madras—not because Nehru said so, but because Article 19 of the Indian Constitution prohibited any secessionist party from participating in an election. In 1962, while the Tamils' agitation was in full swing, Chinese armies invaded northeast India. The DMK's leadership, although in jail then, issued public statements supporting the Indian military's resistance to Chinese claims to barren, mountainous wastelands. After the cease-fire, Prime Minister Nehru did not forget the DMK's gesture. He quietly authorized his law minister to present in Parliament an amendment that eased the strictures of Article 19. The DMK could now contest state elections in Madras. It did so and won big. As the ruling party, it could hardly now agitate for secession. In more than two decades of DMK-dominated rule in Madras (whose name was changed to Tamil Nadu, or Land of the Tamils), no call to secession has been heard.

Nehru could have been obstinate, he could have kept the DMK leaders in jail, and he could have kept Madras state indefinitely under army rule. But he was convinced in his bones that when regional leaders called for secession, they did not necessarily mean it—it was often an expression of regional frustrations, a desire to assert their local cultural identity. Nehru increasingly felt that the extraordinary ethnic and cultural diversity of India's regions must be allowed to bloom and blossom. He was aware that few regions in India—including the Punjab—could survive as independent countries; few Indian states were totally self-reliant in food and industrial requirements. In short, hardly any region could break away from the Indian Union and expect to thrive economically. Nehru knew that a concession here and there might be construed as a giveaway on his part, but that interpretation would be far outweighed by the good his action did in the longer term for the country. Indira Gandhi never learned from her father such worthy lessons in political accommodation. One wonders how the Punjab situation might have turned out had she studied her father's methods more closely.

In the three decades since Potti Sriramalu fasted to death, Andhra Pradesh had become a key Congress Party stronghold in southern India. Its politicians prospered, its bureaucrats became corrupt. Indira Gandhi would decide in Delhi who served as Andhra's chief minister, and ministerial selections appeared to be based solely on one criterion: loyalty to the prime minister. She picked a succession of clowns to head Andhra's state administration. None of these men was likely to pose a challenge to Mrs. Gandhi, regionally or nationally. The state's economy languished. Law and order broke down. Even the police would riot for raises. But the Congress flourished because no opposition party could raise the money needed to develop a strong grassroots organization in this overwhelmingly rural state of 60 million people. Salvation, as it were, came in the form of a wealthy movie star who specialized in roles depicting mythological Hindu gods.

The actor's name was Nandamuri Taraka Rama Rao—known popularly as NTR—and he decided to switch from the world of make-believe to make-belief. He had starred in 300 films over thirty-five years in the business and had become the most popular star in the history of Telugu movies. Now NTR wanted to shape the political beliefs of his people. He formed a new party, called the Telugu Desam, or the Telugu State Party.

His ambition was simple: to gain power. But few leaders can afford an open declaration of such ambition. So NTR made the corrupt local Congress chieftans his main targets. More importantly, he said that regional creativity and aspirations were being stifled because Andhra was being ruled not from Hyderabad but from Delhi. He touched a raw nerve among the people, whose living conditions had been daily deteriorating. He capitalized on his stardom by appearing at public rallies in saffron robes, which recalled the roles of mythological gods and holy men that he often played in Telugu movies. The simple rural folk on the countryside showered him with rose petals; the city folk lavished rupees on the Telugu Desam party.

When the January 1983 election results were announced, NTR had won power. His Telugu Desam obtained nearly 150 seats in the 295-member Andhra Pradesh Assembly, with about 30 independently elected legislators pledging support to the party. As chief minister, the former film star moved quickly to establish his style. Road signs and bulletins in government offices now were required to be not only in English but also in Telugu. NTR made virtually all his public addresses in Telugu, too. He started a free midday meal-program in state schools. He authorized state subsidies for rice, an Andhra staple. The government's Anti-Corruption Bureau doubled its annual investigations to two thousand during NTR's first year in office. Shrewd leaders make use of their popularity by sometimes ramming through unpopular measures while they can—and NTR trimmed the state government's bloated bureaucracy of 30,000 employees by lowering the retirement age from 58 to 55 years. The state budget was streamlined, but more money was channeled into promoting cultural activities such as the Kuchipuri dance native to Andhra, the theater, and to assisting local poets, essayists, and novelists.

Back in Delhi, Indira Gandhi was alarmed. NTR had become a media star: foreign journalists and television crews started paying him a great deal of attention. Her aides warned Mrs. Gandhi that he would soon export his political and cultural revolution to other parts of the country. And if he became a national figure, NTR would be a direct threat to Mrs. Gandhi, whose own nationwide popularity was declining.

So Prime Minister Indira Gandhi set into motion a plan to get rid of Nandamuri Taraka Rama Rao. Rajiv Gandhi, who by now had been made a general secretary of the Congress Party, was persuaded to join in the plot. (Of course, all top Congress officials, including Mrs. Gandhi, later denied any complicity.) The Gandhis were still heady from the recent "victories" in Kashmir, where Chief Minister Farooq Abdullah had been toppled in July 1984, and in the border state of Sikkim, where a majority opposition government had been peremptorily dismissed.

In Andhra, as in Kashmir and Sikkim, the instrument of Mrs. Gandhi's machinations was the Delhi-appointed state governor. The Andhra governor was a man named Ram Lal, a former chief minister of Himachal Pradesh, against whom were still pending charges of misuse of power in that northern state. He suddenly announced that NTR had lost his majority. (In India, governors are appointed by the president upon the recommendation of the prime minister. Governorships are very comfortable sinecures; governors do exactly as they are told by Delhi.)

NTR had only been back a day from the United States when the governor's announcement was made. He had just undergone triple coronary bypass surgery in America. He learned that he was being replaced by a man he had named to his own Telugu Desam cabinet, Nadendla Bhaskara Rao. Governor Lal had dispensed with normal procedures in announcing the new government: ordinarily, no chief minister can be dismissed and someone else asked to form a new government unless there is a show of strength on the floor of the state legislature. Bhaskara Rao was not required to prove that he now commanded a majority in the assembly through defections that he had engineered from NTR's party.

NTR was appalled. So were most Andhra-ites. So was the nation. NTR claimed that he had documented evidence of the allegiance of 161 of the assembly's 295 members—enough to ensure a comfortable majority. He now did something so dramatic that the media were beside themselves with joy because of the opportunity that NTR's actions afforded them for a strong, continuing story: NTR rented a train and escorted the 161 legislators to meet President Zail Singh in Delhi.

There was simply no question that NTR had ever lost his majority. The 161 legislators happily posed for photographs on the steps of Rashtrapati Bhavan, the Indian president's sandstone palace. They waved affidavits of allegiance to NTR. Accompanied by NTR—who was so weak he had to be propped up in a wheelchair—the legislators spoke at rallies in Delhi. But even then Bhaskara Rao continued in office in Hyderabad. NTR now sequestered his legislators in hotel rooms in two neighboring states to make certain that none of them was bribed into defecting to Bhaskara Rao's party. Legislators were being offered the equivalent of $300,000 each to leave NTR's fold. Popular protests against Mrs. Gandhi mounted all over Andhra. There was violence. Finally, in a face-saving gesture, she removed Ram Lal as governor (Congress Party officials quietly spread the word that it was all Ram Lal's fault, that the governor and not Mrs. Gandhi had illegally deposed NTR!) and replaced him with Shankar Dayal Sharma, another Congress Party hack.

Sharma's arithmetic was better than that of his predecessor. He could count how many Andhra legislators supported Nandamuri Taraka Rama Rao. NTR was eventually reinstated. He was now more popular than ever before. Indira Gandhi had fought what was to be the last political battle of her life, and she had lost.

I had wanted to meet NTR, but I was told by his aides that the chief minister was terribly busy. I had arrived in Hyderabad with two London friends, Tim Llewelyn of the BBC and Leslie Plummer, a writer for Canadian newspapers. Like me, they had wanted to get a sense of India after Indira Gandhi. It was my father-in-law, Anand Mohan Lal of Secunderabad—no relation to ex-Governor Ram Lal —who suggested to us that the way to an important man's door was usually via his friends.

And so it was that we went to meet a man named Ramoji Rao.

Rao was the owner and editor of Andhra's biggest and richest Telugu-language newspaper, *Eenadu*. He was also founder of another daily newspaper, the English-language *Newstime*. Rao received us in his office. I was accustomed to editors' offices being busy and messy.

Ramoji Rao's office was clean, quiet, and mostly bare. The furniture consisted of a red vinyl couch and some wooden chairs. There weren't even copies of his own newspapers. The newsroom outside was deserted; it was lunch time.

Rao was a plump man who smiled easily and seemed keen to talk about the prospects for an India without Indira Gandhi.

"She was, of course, ruinous for India," he said. "But let's look at the son, Rajiv. Now just because he wears the kurta-pyjama and the Gandhian cap, does that qualify him to become a politician? Just because he was his mother's son, does that entitle him to become prime minister of India? Let's see what the young man is going to do. He'll soon find, though, that the sympathy 'wave' over his mother's death will ebb—and then he'll be on his own."

Ramoji Rao had vigorously opposed Mrs. Gandhi's intrigues in Andhra Pradesh. During the short time that Bhaskara Rao was chief minister, efforts were made to shut down both *Eenadu* and *Newstime.* Tax officials raided the homes of Ramoji Rao and his top executives. Every time Ramoji Rao drove his car, he was given a traffic ticket. Finally he decided to move into the newspaper's office.

"Under Indira Gandhi this country came very, very close to becoming a fascist Raj," Ramoji Rao said, with sudden passion. "She showed us all that with money and muscle you could control the country. Well, NTR showed her that we would not go under without a fight.

"I don't know why these people in Delhi keep raising the bogey of regionalism," he continued. "They know very well that Indian states cannot afford to secede. In Andhra, we don't want to be a separate country. We want to be an everlasting part of the Indian Union. The feeling of Mrs. Gandhi's people that if you let regional parties assert themselves then the country will one day break up— this feeling is totally erroneous. I think the Congress bosses used 'regionalism' as an excuse to help Indira centralize power in Delhi. NTR has shown that regional parties can be very good for their regions: they're in touch with the grass roots, they care about ordinary people."

The publisher rang a bell and ordered coffee for us. It came within seconds, as if Rao's peons had only been awaiting his summons.

"You really must meet NTR," Ramoji Rao said.

Tim Llewelyn, Leslie Plummer, Anand Lal, and I exchanged conspiratorial smiles.

"Could you arrange an appointment for us?" I said. "We'd be very grateful."

Ramoji Rao dialed a number. He spoke quickly and quietly in Telugu. I suspected that he had reached the chief minister on a private line.

"He's waiting for you," the publisher said. "My driver will take you to the chief minister's home. Let me know if there's anything else I can do for you. Consider this building your home always."

Ramoji Rao's driver took us through the densest sections of Hyderabad. There were more bicycles than pedestrians in the streets and the tinkling of their bells was an unsettling soundtrack to our journey; we couldn't even hear one another in Rao's car. Hundreds of cycle-rickshaws squeezed past us: I recalled that soon after he was reinstated, NTR made available more than a million dollars in low-or-no-interest loans to poor people wishing to buy these rickshaws. As a result, public transportation was amply available in this city, although the traffic had thickened intolerably. But the rickshaw owners would surely not abandon NTR when it was time to vote again.

I reflected on NTR's popularity. He had convinced the masses that he truly cared for the common man. But perhaps as importantly, he'd shown that a state leader could confront the national political establishment in modern-day India and could win if he was in the right. All along, NTR maintained that nearly three decades of centralized planning and decision making had not benefited India's states but instead had only widened regional disparities. NTR held that the main excuse for concentrating power and resources at the center had been the existence of mass poverty. NTR said that it was not enough for the Delhi government to encourage village councils and to sponsor provincial elections. The state governments themselves had to be endowed with sufficient power and resources.

We arrived at NTR's home. He did not live in the chief minister's official residence, a huge bungalow with long, rolling lawns and a view of a lake. NTR preferred his family's house, which was a three-story structure in the heart of the city. Tall steel gates and a high wall shielded the house from the view of passers-by, and several sentries had been posted at the entrance. Ramoji Rao's car was allowed in without any questions; obviously, both car and driver had been to this place many times.

Aides greeted us with smiles. We were led up a flight of steep stairs. I wondered how NTR, a heart patient, climbed these stairs; no elevator was in sight. Maybe he was carried up in the time-honored palanquin. We were led into a second-floor waiting area, which was the size of a ballroom. Chairs were placed against the walls; a floral-pattern rug stretched from end to end. Stacks of files were atop desks that sat in front of some chairs. No sooner had we entered this area than the aides beckoned us. We were taken to another room.

I was hit by an overpowering blast of incense. The room was small and smoky. There were more mountains of files on desks. Two bulbs on the ceiling spread weak light.

"Come in, come in," a deep voice said. "Do come right in."

In one corner of this room, clad in a saffron robe, with holy ash smeared across his forehead and a wooden cane in his hand, sat Nandamuri Taraka Rama Rao.

The voice had sounded friendly. But NTR seemed grim, even in pain. Behind him, high on a green wall, was a black-and-white framed photograph showing him receiving a large glittering trophy at some function. The person who was handing out the award was Indira Gandhi. NTR looked much younger in that picture, as did Mrs. Gandhi, so it must have ben taken many years ago when NTR was in the movie business. Still, it seemed an odd picture to put up in his own home, considering the bad blood between the two.

"One national leader is gone, and now we look to see what the next one will do," NTR began.

"Mrs. Gandhi tried very hard to do you in," I said. "But she lost, and you won. Now she is dead. Do you forgive her?"

"In our Hindu tradition, we think only of the goodness of the departed one's soul," NTR said, vaguely waving his hands. The thin light from the ceiling bulbs bounced off his rings, heavily studded with diamonds and emeralds.

"But my policies concerning the Congress will remain unchanged," he continued. "I will make clear my opposition to the Congress."

He spoke in English. He did not look sixty-six years old—the age attributed to him—much less a man who had been through major heart surgery a few months ago. The combination of his saffron robes and the weak lighting in the room could, of course, have created the illusion of youth. And why not? This man had been an accomplished illusionist all his life.

"Why do you wear saffron robes?" Tim Llewelyn asked. "For the effect?"

"Because they are comfortable," NTR replied, with a smile, not seeming to mind the lack of credulity in Llewelyn's tone.

The chief minister wanted to talk about his campaign to develop federalism in India.

"Federalism is not a new concept," he said. "Our Constitution clearly intended India to be a federal union, with a strong state system. You see, once you accept the linguistic principle as the basis for creating states, then states must be given the freedom to develop themselves within their own cultural framework. The states should not be made beggars, beggars who are made to wait with outstretched hands at Delhi's durbar."

NTR had met with Prime Minister Rajiv Gandhi quite recently. He had requested that the Delhi government make available an additional $40 million to the $350 million it had already approved for drought relief in Andhra Pradesh. From the way NTR said this, it seemed to me that Gandhi's answer had been in the negative. NTR had also raised with the new prime minister the question of increased participation by states in policies concerning the growth of industries, trade and commerce, and production. At present, more than 95 percent of all industrial output in India is directly controlled and monitored by the central government—even small items like razor blades, gum, matchsticks, soap, zippers, and home appliances cannot be produced without formal clearance from Delhi.

"My message to the people in Delhi is this: if the limbs are strong, then the body will be strong," NTR said. "So let the limbs get strong."

He would be broadcasting this message not only from Hyderabad, NTR said. Each one of India's twenty-two states was an appropriate platform from where to address Delhi.

I recalled a conversation I had had in Bombay with Nani A. Palkhivala, one of India's leading constitutional lawyers and a former ambassador to the United States. "The day is bound to come when India's states will repudiate the wrongful subjection by the Union and will awaken to claim their legitimate status under the Constitution," Palkhivala said. "A national consensus should clearly remind the center that it has not inherited the viceroy's mantel of paramountcy. What is needed at the center today is not an authoritarian government but the moral authority to govern. And the center would have no moral authority to govern unless it displays a sense of constitutional morality—particularly a sense of justice and fairness toward the states.

"We do need a strong union," Palkhivala had said. "But a strong union is in no way inconsistent with strong states. On the contrary, by definition a strong union can only be a union of strong states."

Not long after my meeting with NTR, his Telugu Desam Party won 28 seats in Andhra in the late-December parliament elections. In the previous Lok Sabha, or lower house of the national Parliament, the party had only two seats. Now Telugu Desam had become the biggest opposition party, followed by the Communist Party of India (Marxist Wing) with 22 seats. Rajiv Gandhi's ruling Congress Party won 401 seats out of the 508 seats contested nationwide. NTR announced that he was creating a nationwide umbrella organization called the Bharat Desam.

"It has been thrust upon us to play the role of the opposition at the national level," he said.

The gods had given yet another role for Nandamuri Taraka Rama Rao. All India, not merely Andhra Pradesh, was his film set now: NTR was now making a movie not just for Andhra-ites but for all Indians. The question in my mind was: Will it play in Patna? Or Banaras? Or Jaipur? Or Kanpur?

That evening I went to meet an old friend, Lessel H. David. He and his wife, Pramila, were both physicians; both had done acclaimed research in family planning, and Mrs. David operated a facility in Hyderabad where poor people were given low-cost health care and also vocational training. Lessel David no longer practiced medicine; he taught social medicine and organized seminars on development strategies at the Administrative Staff College in Hyderabad, where top corporate executives from all over India enroll for refresher courses.

The Davids had invited me to their new rented home, a spacious house perched atop Jubilee Hills, the city's newest residential neighborhood. It was dusk when I reached their place, and the lights of Hyderabad were spread out on all sides of Jubilee Hills, like diamonds and sapphires strewn on a jeweler's tray. It was cool up here. Pramila David offered me thick, milky tea, which had been flavored with elaichi, or cardamom; it was delicious. I told the Davids about my visit with Nandamuri Taraka Rama Rao.

"The movement for greater decentralization and for more autonomy for India's states will gather steam," Lessel David said, settling his large frame on an ottoman. "It will gather steam not because NTR is spearheading it—but because there is a deeply felt demand in villages and small towns. This business of referring to Delhi for every little thing is absurd."

He cited one absurdity. The curriculum for training midwives all over the country is fashioned by the Ministry of Health in Delhi. If any health facility wants to make changes in this curriculum, or adapt

it to suit local conditions, clearance must be obtained from Delhi—
a process that can take months.

Another example: the United States Agency for International Development had allocated $16 million for nongovernmental organizations involved in promoting family planning activies in states such as Andhra Pradesh, Bihar, and Uttar Pradesh where the birthrate was particularly high. But the Delhi government, which controls the disbursement of all foreign aid, had channeled only a million dollars to the states. Why? Because of bureaucratic delays and red tape. One would think, David said, that with India's population growth still alarmingly rapid—there will be a billion people in India by the end of the century, if not earlier—the central government would act more expeditiously to ensure that foreign aid is distributed where it is needed the most

"The center's hold over the states is very considerable," Lessel David said. "It has to be loosened in order to make things work better at the grassroots. If power doesn't devolve, then you'll have more Assams and Punjabs."

I asked him how he thought NTR might be received in other parts of India.

"Very well, I should think," Lessel David said. "Indians don't hate one another that much, you know. The class struggle in India is between the haves and the have-nots—not between the states. Besides, think of how spread-out the country's religious shrines are. Banaras, Hinduism's holy city, is in the north. The great Hindu temple of Tirupathi is in the south. Another great Hindu temple, Somnath, is in the west. Muslims from all over the country go to pray at the Jama Masjid in Delhi. Christians go to shrines in Goa and Malabar. In other words, Indians travel more than we suppose. There is a built-in network for tolerance. NTR can turn up in Bombay or Calcutta, and he won't be seen as a stranger. A novelty, perhaps, but not a stranger."

4

Ethnic Strains, Rural Stress

HYDERABAD is one of India's leading centers of Muslim culture. Of the area's six million people, about 600,000 are Muslims. The percentage of Muslims, in fact, is about the same as the national figure: there are an estimated eighty million Muslims in India today, or 10 percent of the country's overall population.

The Muslims of Hyderabad, with a few exceptions, are not a happy people. Here too, their sentiments mirror the national scene. Muslims are a troubled, unhappy minority in India. Trevor Fishlock, formerly the *London Times*'s Delhi correspondent, not long ago wrote an insightful book titled *India File* in which he characterized the country's Muslims as follows: "They are the rather unhappy remnant of a once powerful and conquering people whose forts, mosques, and domes dot the landscape and remain among the most distinctive of Indian images." Historical animosities between Muslims and Hindus have survived in the country, but particularly here in Hyderabad. No less a person than Chief Minister Nandamuri Taraka Rama Rao told me: "We have to have special protection for our Muslim minorities here." Some protection. Each year, majority Hindus start riots against Muslims here. Shops are burned and property is looted.

Sikhs may have become the latest villains for many Hindus because of the murder of Indira Gandhi by two of her Sikh security guards and because of the continuing tensions in the Punjab between the two communities. But for an overwhelming number of India's majority Hindus, Muslims remain the ancient enemy. There is little forgiveness toward Muslims, much less trust and tolerance, because of real or perceived historical wrongs.

If all this sounds too dramatic, consider the following: of the 4,000 officers of the elite Indian Administrative Service, only 120 are Muslims. In the 2,000-member Indian Police Service, there are only 50 Muslims. India has about 5,000 judges, but only 300 of them are Muslims. There are nearly 120,000 officers in the country's 14 nationalized banks, but only 2,500 of them are Muslims. M. J. Akbar, in his *India: The Siege Within*, refers to a survey done of some of India's top private sector companies. The survey found, for example, that in Pond's India Limited, only one of the corporation's 115 senior executives was a Muslim; at DCM, the figure was 2 out of 987; at Brooke Bond, 14 out of 673; at ITC, 17 out of 966; at J. K. Synthetics, 5 out of 536; at Sarabhai, only 5 out of 628 executives were Muslims.

When I visited Aligarh, once a flourishing city for Islamic culture and still the seat of the Aligarh Muslim University, I was told that the city's renowned locksmith industry had collapsed. Once the products of individual locksmiths from this Uttar Pradesh city used to be exported to the Middle East and to Europe. But these Muslim locksmiths could not overcome competition from the big lock factories that mushroomed in the 1950s and 1960s. Now there are few independent locksmiths left in Aligarh. And the government has made no efforts to assist those whose businesses collapsed when the machine age arrived: few of the old locksmiths were hired by the new factories.

"The ordinary Muslim has been left out of India's economic and political mainstream," George Fernandes, one of India's leading labor leaders and a former member of the cabinet, told me. "And he faces a bleak future. Muslims don't get ordinary jobs so easily. The Muslim is not wanted in the armed forces because he is always suspect—whether we want to admit it or not, most Indians consider Muslims as a fifth column for Pakistan. The private sector distrusts him. A situation has been created in which the Muslim, for all practical purposes, is India's new untouchable."

The economic plight of India's Muslims has been dramatically exacerbated since Independence, but it did not begin when British rule ended in 1947. Jawaharlal Nehru, in his *The Discovery of India,* said that historical causes blocked up avenues of development and prevented the release of talent. He identified these causes as the delay in the development of a new industrial middle class, and the "excessively feudal background" of the Muslims. Indeed, it can be argued that the Muslim ethos in India started shredding when the Mogul Empire collapsed in the late eighteenth century.

I met people in India who contended that the country's "Muslim question" would never be resolved until the "Pakistan question" was settled once and for all. Since independence in 1947, India's relationship with Pakistan has been disturbed and distrusting. Pakistan, after all, was an invented country, carved out of India's body because of the insistence of Hindu-haters like Mohammed Ali Jinnah. Jinnah was a British-educated lawyer who felt that Muslims would never enjoy first-class citizenship in a Hindu-dominated independent India. Some Indian Muslims will say that he was proven right—even though two of India's constitutional presidents have been Muslims, and Muslims have served in the national cabinet. A number of national organizations, but particularly the Hindu-based Rashtriya Swayamsevak Sangh (which is more popularly known by its acronym, RSS) have engaged in Muslim-baiting over the years. Their virulent propaganda: the Muslim may be an Indian citizen, but his sympathies lie with Pakistan.

When India was divided up in 1947, there was murderous rioting between Hindus and Muslims. Hundreds of thousands of people were killed. Some historians believe that if Mahatma Gandhi's will had prevailed and India had remained undivided, the subcontinent would have enjoyed more peace. India and Pakistan went to war over the disputed territory of Kashmir in 1947 and 1965. And in 1971, the two countries again fought a war—which resulted in the transformaton of East Pakistan into the independent nation of Bangladesh. Many Pakistanis still hold a grudge against India for having encouraged and supported the guerrilla movement that helped create Bangladesh.

These military conflicts—all of which were won by India—have resulted in a situation where India and Pakistan pump huge sums of money into defense: Pakistan spends nearly $2 billion a year on defense (its gross national product is roughly $31 billion); India, whose GNP is nearly $180 billion, is estimated by the London-based International Institute for Strategic Studies to spend $6.3 billion on defense. Neither country can afford such expenditures. Two thirds of Pakistan's 500,000-man military is positioned along the border with India. India has stationed several crack divisions of its 1.2 million-strong armed forces on its side of the border.

Since 1958, Pakistan has been almost continuously under military rule. An elected democratic administration was brutally squashed in 1977 by General Mohammed Zia ul-Haq, who took over as head of government. General Zia did not block the "trial" and subsequent execution of his civilian predecessor, Zulfikar Ali Bhutto. Not that Bhutto was ever a friend of India, but it was generally felt by India policy makers that a civilian leader in Pakistan was more likely to arrive at a political accommodation with India than a military figure. Indian leaders, to be sure, like to portray Pakistan as the continuing villain in the great drama of the subcontinent. But it might be recalled that when the then military dictator Marshal Ayub Khan proposed a no-war pact with India in the late 1950s, Nehru's aides ridiculed Ayub. Similarly, when Zia brought up the subject again during Mrs. Gandhi's last years, the Pakistanis were also ridiculed.

Indian leaders point to the current rearmament of Pakistan by its main Western ally, the United States. Washington is reported to give Islamabad more than a billion dollars of arms each year, allegedly to strengthen Pakistan against expansionism by the Soviet Union, which has already gobbled up Afghanistan, Pakistan's northwestern neighbor. But policy makers in Delhi have no doubts that these arms will be eventually used by Pakistan against India; American weapons were used by Pakistan in previous conflicts with India. India, for its part, is also accelerating the arms race by buying more weapons not only from its traditional supplier, the Soviet Union, but also from France, West Germany, and Britain.

Both India and Pakistan are developing nuclear weapons as well, although the leaders of both countries strenuously deny this.

"The fact remains that militarily Pakistan is no match for India," George Fernandes, the Indian labor leader, told me. "But Pakistan serves as a convenient scapegoat, an excuse for more arms deals which produce massive commissions for Congress Party agents who negotiate the deals with foreign suppliers."

George Fernandes's words echoed in my mind when I went to meet Mehboob Khan, a scion of an old-line nawabi family. His ancestors were Muslim noblemen who were given property and prominence by Hyderabad's early nizams some three hundred years ago. Khan's father, Shah Alam Khan, owned a large tobacco company. The family, consisting of Khan's parents, and his six brothers and their wives and children, along with his own spouse and five children, lived in a sprawling mansion. The house and its lawns were an oasis of sorts, for outside the high walls was one of the most congested sections of Hyderabad.

Khan had invited me for what Indians call "high tea." Laid out on a long mahogany table was a spread so immense that I could have feasted for a week. There were a dozen varieties of sandwiches; there were kababs, or grilled rolls of minced lamb; there were mutton chops; there were fried turnovers filled with curried shrimp; there were custard pastries; there were assorted biscuits; there were mangoes, oranges, grapes, apples, and bananas. And there was tea—rich, aromatic, sweet, milky tea. It was, Mehboob Khan said, only an ordinary high tea, and could I please forgive him.

For a moment I thought Khan was joking. But he was being perfectly serious. The exquisite rituals of hospitality among Hyderabad's Muslim nobility require such apologies. I had been introduced to Khan by my father-in-law, Anand Mohan Lal, who had cautioned me to be patient with such rituals. Khan explained how each item on his table was prepared. And he did not eat anything until I had finished. I thanked him profusely for the wonderful meal.

"It was nothing," Khan said, softly, "it was nothing at all."

He was a huge man, so huge that when he stood up he had to be careful not to bang his head against the chandelier that was fixed to the high ceiling of his living room. I had come to see him because of his connections in Hyderabad's Muslim community. Soon after I'd finished the high tea, a group of men walked in. Each wore a long sherwani, a gold-brocaded jacket that reached to the knees, and the typically Muslim peaked cap of lambswool. Each man also wore white pantaloons. They bowed to Khan, then quietly sat down.

Mehboob Khan had invited them to tell me about how Hyderabad's Muslims felt about their condition in modern-day India. Hyderabad, Khan told me, was an ethnic microcosm. What I would hear and learn here would be mirrored elsewhere in India, too.

His guests were apprehensive about what might happen to Muslims after the death of Indira Gandhi. They were alarmed at the riots against the Sikhs in northern India, where Hindu mobs marshaled by Congress Party chieftans had attacked Sikh homes, shops, and houses of worship. (There were no such attacks against Sikhs in southern India, whose states were controlled by opposition parties.)

"We are apprehensive because when one minority is subjected to this kind of brutality, how can other minority communities feel safe?" said Sulaiman Sikander, a local Muslim civic leader. "We thought for a long time that the Congress was a protector of the minorities. But in recent years we became disillusioned. And this episode concerning the Sikhs does not reassure us at all."

"Such riots aren't communal," Mehboob Khan said. "They are political. That's what is so troubling. Minorities are being made a hostage for political considerations—to get votes from the majority."

A man named Abdul Aziz spoke about the September 1984 Hindu–Muslim riots in Hyderabad. More than 150 Muslims died, he said, and dozens of shops owned by Muslims along Abid Road were

burned down. Mrs. Gandhi flew to Hyderabad for a political function, but she did not visit the affected areas. Despite an estimated
property loss of more than $10 million, the Delhi government sanc-
tioned only $10,000 in damage reparation payments.

"And worse, no one was arrested, no one was punished for the
attacks against us Muslims," Aziz said, in Urdu. "How can you create
confidence among minorities with a situation like this? There have
been riots against Muslims in Ahmedabad, Meerut, Assam, and
Muradabad—and no arrests there either, and very little by way of
compensation to those who lost so much."

It occurred to me that Abdul Aziz could well have been speaking
on behalf of the Sikhs who had been attacked in northern India. No
one had been arrested for rioting against them, either.

I reminded the group that the Nehru family had always been
known for its commitment to secularism. Shouldn't Rajiv Gandhi,
India's new prime minister and grandson of Jawharlal Nehru, be
given a chance to demonstrate his own commitment?

"Of course," said Mehboob Khan. "But the question is, will Rajiv
be able to break away from the communalist hold over the Congress
Party? We used to vote for the Congress because we felt that the
other political parties had become polluted with communalism. Now
look what has happened."

I asked the group if they considered themselves Indians.

They seemed stunned.

Mehboob Khan finally said: "This continuing suspicion of Muslims in India must stop. What have we done that is antinational?
How many Muslims have been involved in espionage? Is there really
a basis for suspicion? Did we not fully support the government when
there were wars? Did we not contribute to the national defense fund?
Did we not send our men to fight for our homeland? So why are we
still suspect? What more do we need to do to establish our bo-
nafides?"

The birthrate among Hyderabad's Muslims is high; Islam permits
a man to have up to four wives at the same time, and many Muslims

exercise this option. The average Muslim family in Hyderabad is said to have eight children. (The average Hindu family has four children.) Hindu chauvinists have long expressed public alarm over the Muslims' proclivity for procreation. Their argument is that the Muslim hordes could again overrun India—as they did starting in the tenth century, when Muslim invaders came pouring in over the Khyber Pass and defeated squabbling Hindu rulers.

The Hindu's racial memory is long and strong, and these days it is constantly pricked by irresponsible communalist organizations that have sprung up in many parts of the country. The leaders of these groups tell the Hindu that he must neither forget nor forgive the butchery and bloodshed that the Muslim conquerors brought wherever they went. In the western Indian state of Gujarat, for example, they tell horror stories of Mahmud of Ghazni, a Muslim tyrant who plundered the fabulous Hindu temple of Somnath, and also destroyed ten thousand other Hindu shrines in the province of Kanauj. Mahmud's armies swept through the area in 1025 A.D. So passive and pacific were the Hindus that they simply stood by while Mahmud's men ravaged the temples, slaughtered Hindu males, and raped and carried away Hindu women. The pillage of Hindu temples was especially favored by Muslim invaders because these temples were rich with the offerings of their devotees; and the rape of the Hindu women was an attractive proposition, too, because they were beautiful and submissive. The Muslim plundering of India continued vigorously through much of the next six hundred years: nearly six centuries after Mahmud of Ghazni's raid of Somnath and Kanauj, the Mogul emperor Aurangzeb would ruthlessly put to the sword Hindus who refused to be converted to Islam.

During my travels through India, I came across many fellow-Hindus who said that such historical wrongs had to be corrected.

"But what fault is it of today's Muslims—the majority of whom were born after independence?" I said one afternoon in Hyderabad to a local Hindu civic leader. "Why should majority Hindus now hold Muslims accountable for this terrible past? The Muslims of today want to live in peace."

"I agree it's not their fault," he said. "But sons have to pay for the sins of their fathers."

These are attitudes you cannot easily hope to overcome. Organizations such as the *RSS* flourish because of strong anti-Muslim ideology. Now the ruling Congress Party seems to have come around to embracing naked communalism. The votes, after all, are with the majority Hindus—this was quite clear in the December 1984 national elections.

As economic opportunities declined for ordinary Muslims, they were faced with three choices: to emigrate to Pakistan; to join the underworld in India; or to take up jobs in the oil-rich states of the Arabian Peninsula. Aziz Rahim did the first, Haji Mastaan did the second, and Syed Abdullah Barabood did the third. Each became affluent in the process.

Aziz Rahim was born and brought up in free India. But he found that his career in banking in Bombay was increasingly being stymied. He moved to Pakistan, married a Karachi debutante named Zubeda Mawjee, and soon obtained a job with a subsidiary of Citibank, the American multinational corporation. He did well with Citibank in Karachi. The bank then posted him to Bahrain, Beirut, and Nairobi. Aziz and Zubeda Rahim now live with their three children in Haworth, New Jersey. Rahim is a senior executive with Citibank in New York and visits Pakistan frequently. He and Zubeda often travel to India, too. It is a nice place to go as tourists, the Rahims say, and the shopping is still reasonable. But it is unlikely that Aziz Rahim would have done as well as he did professionably had he stayed on in Bombay. "There were opportunities in Pakistan—and I grabbed the chance," Rahim says.

Haji Mastaan prospered by staying on and becoming an underworld kingpin. His life story inspired a film producer to make a box-office hit. Mastaan lived as a boy in a packing crate on the Bombay docks. He joined a street gang, following the example of many Muslim youths from destitute families; he quickly rose to become its leader, then entered the lucrative world of gold smuggling. There was a real-life confrontation Mastaan had with a top government official who threatened to have him arrested. The rising young gangster said to the official: "For the record, I don't know what smuggling is. Between you and me, I've always been a smuggler. I am a smuggler. And I will always be a smuggler. Let's see what you can do about it, big shot! Do you think you can put me in jail? Do you think you can have me hanged? Let's see if you can find the proof. The only way you can stop me is if three or four of you guys get together and decide to pump a few bullets into my body. But you won't, will you? You guys don't have the guts."

Mastaan says eventually gave up his life of crime—but only after he'd made millions. He now devotes his time to "philanthropy" and "social work" in Bombay. He also harbors political ambitions.

Syed Abdullah Barabood of Hyderabad found that he was simply unable to support his three wives and eleven children on his four hundred rupees monthly salary (the equivalent of $40) as an elevator operator in a government office. He heard that job recruiters from Kuwait were coming to Hyderabad; while anybody could apply for these manual jobs, Islamic Kuwait especially welcomed Muslim workers; the oil-producing Persian Gulf state had ambitious development plans but a shortage of indigenous labor.

So Barabood wound up in Kuwait. He worked there for five years as an elevator mechanic. He earned about $3,000 a month—or thirty thousand Indian rupees. By the time he returned to Hyderabad, he had become a wealthy man in Indian terms. Now he sits at home all day, smokes his hookah, visits friends, plays with his children, and let his money accumulate interest in the bank.

I went to see Barabood in a neighborhood of Hyderabad known as Barkas. It consists of low-slung brick buildings, most with neat courtyards. Ten years ago Barkas was a Muslim slum, with open sewers and muddy roads. Its residents tended guava orchards and sold their produce to Hindu middlemen, who then marketed the fruit for a profit all across Andhra Pradesh. But then came opportunities to travel to the Gulf. The men of Barkas who went overseas started sending remittances home. It is estimated that in the Hyderabad area alone, more than $600 million was remitted by Muslims, in the last decade.

The guava orchards of Barkas are mostly gone now, replaced by playing fields and new houses. The roads have been paved. Several mosques have been built. I was brought here by a man named Mir Asad Ali, a local insurance agent. He wanted me to see how a poor Muslim neighborhood had prospered because its males went away to work abroad. On the way to Barkas, we drove through several other predominantly Muslim communities. Ali excitedly pointed out men who he said had returned from the Gulf.

"How can you tell them apart?" I asked.

"Easy, just look closely," Ali said. "You can tell from the way they're dressed."

Sure enough, I spotted droves of men wearing T-shirts that said "I Love New York," or "Kiss me, I'm Cute." They sported fancy Ray-Ban sunglasses, or solid-gold Rolex watches. Virtually all wore jeans, in contrast to other men who presumably hadn't had the opportunity to travel overseas and who therefore hadn't graduated beyond the traditional Hyderabadi sarongs and smocks. From time to time I saw men in Arab headgear and gowns. Were they Arabs visiting Hyderabad, or only local men who fancied the costumes of the lands they had visited? Ali told me that Hyderabad attracted a lot of Arabs who came here to buy brides. They would marry pretty local girls, give handsome presents to their parents, and whisk away the women and sometimes force them to work as maids in the bridegrooms' countries.

"But isn't there resentment over such practices?" I asked.

"No, not at all," Ali said. "Because economically these women are still better off working as maids abroad. A girl who's never even seen a string of beads now suddenly finds herself possessing a gold necklace."

Ali was taking me to the home of a man known in the Barkas neighborhood as Ustad. Not even Ali, who'd been acquainted with him for years, knew his real name. As I was to discover, "Ustad"—which translates from Urdu as "The Clever One"—was Barkas's chief of commerce. We parked in front of a grocery store whose glass cases contained stacks of Kraft Australian Processed Cheese, a particularly popular brand in the Middle East. Little boys played with toy cars that seemed foreign made; some of the boys wore smart safari suits. Every house seemed to have television antennas. We walked past a parking lot in which set rows of shiny Indian-made Ambassador cars. Ali explained that these were actually air-conditioned private taxis.

"Why aren't they out on the road?" I asked.

"They only go from here to Hyderabad's airport and back whenever the Bombay flights arrive and depart," Ali said. "You see, these taxis take passengers who leave for the Gulf, and they bring back those who've returned. No need for them to work at any other time. They charge two hundred rupees per person [the equivalent of $20] and each vehicle nets the owner two or three thousand rupees a day. That's a fortune."

Ali had wanted me to meet Ustad because Ustad, he explained, was in the business of obtaining anything for anyone—for a price. He was, Ali said, the Harrods and Macy's of Hyderabad: you could buy anything from a pin to a plane from Ustad. The fact that Ustad had prospered in Barkas indicated how prosperous its residents had become—they now had a continuing need for fancy appliances and textiles from abroad. Moreover, said Ali, Ustad's customers came from all over Hyderabad. For example, when a rich man on Jubilee Hills or Banjara Hills wanted to give his adolescent son a Japanese video set or a German camera, he could come to Ustad and obtain one on the spot. Ali, a short man who wore a crisp white shirt and a dark blue suit, marched briskly. He exuded energy; he was a self-made man who put himself through college in Hyderabad and went on to do extremely well in the insurance business.

We walked through a maze of narrow alleys and at last came to the pseudonymous Ustad's home. He wasn't there. But his friends and factotums were. We were received warmly in a small room, whose carpeted floor was strewn with fabrics.

"What can we offer you?" a man who identified himself as Saleem, said. "Video? Watch? Gold? Diamonds? Camera? Motorcycle?"

Ali explained hastily that I had come merely as an observer.

"Then at least let me offer you tea," Saleem said.

The tea was served in little glasses, just as it is in the Middle East. In India, tea is almost always offered in cups. And, as is done in the Middle East, the tea was heavily sweet and black; in India, tea is seldom served without milk. Middle Eastern habits die hard, Ali said.

As we sipped the tea, Syed Abdullah Barabood walked in. He joined us on the floor, neatly tucking his heels behind his haunches. I marveled at the flexibility of his bones: Barabood seemed to be at least fifty years old. He wore a white skull cap, a see-through linen shirt, and a checked sarong which local Muslims call the lungi.

"Why did you return home?" I asked him, after he told me about his experiences in Kuwait.

"What's the use of making all that money and not being able to see your family?" Barabood said. "I never saw them once in the long years that I was away. Now I can enjoy my wives and children, and they can enjoy the money I made for them."

Ali and I got up to leave, for we were already late for lunch at Ali's home.

"I am sorry I cannot invite you to my own home," Barabood said, with some embarrassment. "But you see, I am redoing everything. Everything is in a mess. We just got the replacement dishwashers yesterday, and later this morning the new air conditioners will be installed. The house is in a mess, you see. We haven't finished building the new floor yet."

As Ali and I stepped out of Ustad's home, Barabood said: "The next time you will be welcome guests in my home. I will personally cook a mutton biryani for you. I have just got a new microwave oven."

The casual visitor to India seldom gets to see how and where the majority of Indians live. Hyderabad and Bombay and Calcutta may seem crowded and overwhelming, but the country's cities and towns hold barely 30 percent of India's 800 million people. The rest of the population lives in 576,000 villages, fewer than half of which are electrified. Nearly 400 million Indians, or fully half the country's population, live below the poverty line—which is to say that the average annual income of these people is less than $125 per person. Some of these Indians earn less than twenty cents a day.

In Hyderabad, I was urged by Potla Sen, a former chairman of Indian Airlines and of the Food Corporation of India, not to neglect traveling through India's countryside. Sen informed me that India had a cultivated land area of nearly 150 million hectares, roughly the same as the United States. But while only four million American families depended on agriculture for their livelihood, in India the figure was seventy million families! There had been projected in the Western world an erroneous image of an India constantly hit by famine, Sen said. In reality, one of the most spectacular achievements of post-Independence India had been in agriculture, he said.

When the British left the subcontinent in 1947, annual food production in India was about 50 million metric tons. By December 1984, the figure had increased threefold. The only serious famine since independence occurred in the eastern state of Bihar in 1965 because of drought: that year, the national grain production fell to 76 million metric tons, a drop of 12 million tons from the previous year. President Lyndon B. Johnson complied with a request from Prime Minister Indira Gandhi to make up this shortfall with an emergency shipment of 12 million metric tons of wheat. Widespread famine was averted, although hundreds of Biharis perished before the grains could reach them. Now India maintained a buffer stock of 22 million metric tons, seven million metric tons more than the minimum level established by the government, Sen said. The danger to Indian grain production is less and less from drought because of new irrigation techniques; the danger is increasingly from rodents who often rule warehouses. It is estimated that more than 15 percent of India's annual grain production is destroyed by rodents.

And the danger now is that more and more of India's farmers are being driven toward the "poverty line" because of sharply increasing fertilizer costs and lagging grain prices. (A government-appointed Agricultural Prices Commission sets these prices on the basis of a complex and highly disputed formula.) The leading spokesman for Indian farmers, Sharad Joshi, claims that despite impressive strides in agriculture, the Indian farmer is not a prosperous individual. He says that more than 25 percent of the farmers in the Punjab— considered India's showcase of agricultural development—now live below the poverty line. A study done by the Agricultural Prices Commission in 1979 showed that farmers owning up to 7.5 acres of land had "negative household savings" each year; those owning between 7.5 acres and 15 acres, saved up to $250 annually; and those farmers owning between 25 acres and the national land ceiling of 80 acres per individual, saved at the most $2,000 a year.

Since 1979, fertilizer prices have risen by nearly 35 percent, so that the Indian farmer now pays the equivalent of almost 75 cents for a kilogram of nitrogenous fertilizer. Sharad Joshi says that while such costs have escalated, the wheat procurement price is now only $1.50 a kilogram—representing only a doubling since 1967. Farmers in India's most productive agricultural zone, the Punjab, have been especially hard hit. In the Punjab, which produces 60 percent of India's food grains, the consumption of fertilizers is particularly high —134 kilograms per acre, compared to the national average of 36 kilograms. Farmers are finding that they are no longer getting remunerative prices for their production. This has fueled a great deal of resentment. Joshi has asked farmers to switch to nongrain production where they might obtain better revenues: forests for lumber, horticulture, and oilseeds. As a last resort, Joshi has said, farmers could even leave some of their land fallow.

I found during my travels across India that farmers were increasingly being organized politically, a new development in post-Independence India. Their cry: We want a fairer shake. The farmers were formally banded together in early 1984 in the southern state of Tamil Nadu under the aegis of the Bharatiya Kisan Union (BKU). So popular did the organization become (its name translates as the Union of Indian Farmers) that soon branches were started in other states. But Sharad Joshi is truly the national leader of India's farmers.

Joshi, a slim, intense man, used to work for the International Postal Union. He had a brilliant academic career and joined India's elite civil service before being deputed to the I.P.U. He decided, however, that he'd rather be an activist than a paper pusher. He'd always been concerned about such things as better health care for rural families and better economic development in the countryside. So he started a lobbying group in 1980 called the Shetkari Sanghatana (which means Fraternity of Farmers). It was his nationwide agitation on behalf of farmers that forced the government to recently create a commission to investigate farmers grievances.

But remuneration for grain production and the rising cost of fertilizers are not the only main issues that affect India's countryside. Almost forty years after independence, the question of land reform continues to be controversial. As the British consolidated their colonial rule, India's traditionally self-sufficient village system began to disintegrate. In 1830, Sir Charles Metcalfe, one of the ablest British civil administrators of his time, wrote: "The village communities are little republics having nearly everything they want within themselves; and almost independent of foreign relations. They seem to last where nothing else lasts. This union of the village communities, each one forming a separate little state in itself, is in a high degree conducive to their happiness, and to the enjoyment of a great portion of freedom and independence."

Within a few years, the village system that Sir Charles described had changed dramatically. In *The Discovery of India*—probably the best literary work of history about India—Jawaharlal Nehru writes: "The destruction of village industries was a powerful blow to these communities. The balance between industry and agriculture was upset, the traditional division of labor was broken up, and numerous stray individuals could not be easily fitted into any group activity. A more direct blow came from the introduction of the landlord system, changing the whole conception of ownership of land.

"This conception had been of communal ownership, not so much of the land as of the produce of the land," Nehru continues. "Possibly not fully appreciating this, but more probably taking the step deliberately for reasons of their own, the British governors—who themselves represented the English landlord class—introduced something resembling the English system in India."

The British at first appointed agents, known as revenue farmers, who collected land tax from peasants and delivered it to the government. These agents developed into landlords. The village community now was deprived of all control over the land and its produce, Nehru says, and "this led to the breakdown of the joint life and corporate character of the community; the co-operative system of services and functions began to disappear gradually." Big landowners were created by the British after their own English pattern, according to Nehru, chiefly because it was far easier to deal with a few individuals than with a vast peasantry. "The objective was to collect as much money in the shape of revenue, and as speedily, as possible," he writes. "It was also considered necessary to create a class whose interests were identified with the British."

That class, the landlords, steadily gained in power and prestige. In Bengal they were called zamindars; elsewhere the word for them was malik. They exploited the peasantry. They accumulated vast fortunes. They were often cruel. But they were loyal to the British, and that was what mattered. During the British Raj, feudalism became a solid institution. The landlords did not whole-heartedly support the freedom movement—not the least because its leaders, such as Mahatma Gandhi and Nehru, were committed to instituting land reform once independence was achieved. The Congress Party had pledged to abolish absentee landlordism; the party's leaders assured peasants that they would secure for them permanency of tenureship and a fair share of the crop.

The late Krishan Bhatia noted in *The Ordeal of Nationhood* that in Nehru's home state of Uttar Pradesh, during the years that the Congress held limited local power before independence, it had enacted legislation for the abolition of the zamindari system. Bhatia, the former editor of the *Hindustan Times* and that Delhi newspaper's Washington correspondent for many years, wrote that the law protected the cultivator from the landlord's high-handedness by assuring him permanence of tenure as long as he paid a reasonable rent for the holding. The tiller was also given the option to own the land he worked on by paying moderate compensation to the absentee owner.

Independence came—but years went by before there was any significant land and tenancy reform or meaningful land-ceiling legislation that would limit the size of a landlord's holdings. In countries where there has been noteworthy land reform—such as Sri Lanka, Malaysia, and Thailand—the tiller was always given ownership so that he put in his best effort. It has been widely recognized that to maximize production you must make the tiller the owner of his land. But since the British took over India, the farmer has depended for his livelihood not just on the quality and quantity of his production but, more importantly, on the whims of the landed aristocracy. Moreover, antiquated social customs among India's peasants had resulted in fragmentation of land holdings where tillers had possession of property: fathers would bequeath land to their sons, who would divide up the property into small and uneconomic plots.

In the early years after independence, no sweeping land reforms were possible for a variety of reasons: land records were poorly maintained, deeds were fudged, and it was difficult to accurately establish ownership; there was considerable absentee landlordship; there were fraudulent practices such as "gifting" land to peasants who were in truth the landlords' serfs. Landlords developed cozy relationships with India's new rulers; they started contributing heavily to the ruling Congress Party. Krishan Bhatia writes: "Before 1947 the Congress Party was a mass movement and not the Establishment. Its sense of social justice was strong and its concern for the underprivileged in the rural areas genuine. The landlords then stood by the British Government." The dividing line disappeared after independence, when the landlords joined hands with the Congress chieftans.

For almost a decade after independence, there was not even a new land-ceiling law in many Indian states. Land reform was always a subject to be handled by the state governments, unlike foreign affairs or defense of telecommunications which were the prerogative of the central government. It was only in 1957 that relevant legislation came into being in these states—but it was so lenient toward landlords that tenants and tillers actually suffered under its terms. Landlords were now allowed to select between thirty acres in some states and two hundred acres in other states for personal cultivation; landlords could also parcel out property to family members. As a result, what was meant to be reform legislation resulted in a situation where landlords actually could legalize large holdings in their own names and in the names of relatives; the landlord was also permitted to throw out existing tenants from the portions of his property he had chosen for "self-cultivation."

"Instead of bringing greater security to the real cultivators of land, the reforms only added to the numbers of landless peasants and sharecroppers," Krishan Bhatia wrote. "Most state governments conveniently looked the other way while this process was occurring."

By 1971, nationwide concern mounted over the question of land reform. In many states, absentee landlords controlled large chunks of land; their tenant farmers languished. Regional newspapers—particularly those published in vernacular languages—highlighted abuses in areas such as eastern Uttar Pradesh and Bihar. Even Mrs. Gandhi, who seldom believed anything that appeared in the media, was forced to acknowledge that landlords were exploiting the peasantry in some parts of India.

Mrs. Gandhi had, by 1971, consolidated her personal authority within the Congress Party. She had broken away from the old party chieftans who had installed her as prime minister in January 1966. She was aware that there was little a national government could do to push through land reforms; but since her Congress Party also controlled many of India's states, the prime minister could apply pressure on her local representatives. She did so in an imaginative manner.

She issued a new rallying cry for Indians: *"Garibi Hatao!"* or "Remove Poverty!" The prime minister's public relations campaign glossed over the fact that the Congress Party's economic policies had exacerbated poverty since Independence; these policies had promoted the development of heavy industries at the expense of light and consumer-oriented industries, which create more jobs. With the exception of a much-publicized dam or hydroelectric project here and there, or some irrigation scheme, the Congress had also generally neglected rural economic development. Mrs. Gandhi's "Garibi Hatao!" call could be seen as an indictment of her own policies, and, indeed, some of the prime minister's political opponents as well as some figures in the intellectual community were skeptical. But it wasn't taken that way by ordinary Indians. They were thrilled at this new theme the prime minister was sounding.

Implicit in the *"Garibi Hatao!"* call was a promise of further land reform. With great fanfare, Mrs. Gandhi launched in 1974 India's Fifth Five-Year Plan. It envisioned the expenditure of $10 billion by 1979 on agriculture projects. The assumption seemed to be that if agriculture was formally highlighted in the government's economic program, then things like land reform would follow. (India's five-year plans set production targets; they are also a statement of the government's broad economic and social policies. The documents are mostly unreadable.) Some states acted on land reform; some states ignored the subject altogether. You can still visit regions like Bihar and come across landlords who control two-hundred-acre properties.

I decided to see for myself the impact of Indira Gandhi's agricultural and rural policies. I went to Medak, an economically backward area in Andhra Pradesh. Medak had been Mrs. Gandhi's last constituency. She was elected from there in 1980. For years she had contested parliamentary polls from the northern Indian state of Uttar Pradesh. But she had moved to Medak not only because it was considered a "safe seat" for her. She wanted to demonstrate that she was truly a national leader, that she could be elected from all parts of the country—that Indians anywhere would respond favorably to her.

I was driven to Medak by Pramila David. She was gracious enough to take time off from the Shilpa Clinic in Hyderabad, where she runs innovative family planning programs for the poor. People who come to the clinic can also sign up for free vocational training projects. Dr. David is a wellknown figure in Andhra Pradesh because she has helped thousands of destitute men and women in cities, towns and villages to find jobs, and thus gain self-respect. She has particularly assisted Harijans, or India's long-suffering "untouchable" community.

There are more than a hundred million of these Harijans in India today, an overwhelming number of them in southern states like Andhra Pradesh. The origins of untouchability lie in Hinduism's rigid and unrelenting caste system, according to historians like Romila Thapar. This institutionalized intolerance, she has said, was a result of the early Aryans' prejudice against the darker races they encountered during their conquest of northern India. The Chinese traveler Fa-Hsien, who came to India in the fifth century A.D., wrote that the persons who removed human excrement were considered untouchable by India's majority Hindus.

The Hindu caste system was essentially four-tiered: at the very top were the brahmans, the priestly class who studied and interpreted the religion and its scriptures; then came the kshatriyas, or the rulers and administrators; next on the totem pole were the vaishyas, or the merchant community; finally, there were the shudras, who performed manual labor. The "untouchables" were outside this four-tier system: they did all the scavenging and cleaning work. They were required to live and eat separately. If a brahman as much as spotted an untouchable on the street, he would at once return home to bathe his "pollution" away; even the mere shadow of an untouchable polluted his high-caste soul, the brahman believed. Untouchables could marry only other untouchables. They had few rights, only duties. Educational opportunities were denied to them, as were jobs in anything but sanitation, tanning, and shoemaking. They were not allowed to own property.

It was Mahatma Gandhi who started calling the untouchables "Harijans," or "Children of God."

"The moment untouchability goes, the caste system itself will be purified," the Mahatma said.

He invited hundreds of Harijans to accompany him during his travels around India. He ate with them. He took them along to political rallies, to temples, to the homes of brahmans. And in the southern princely state of Travancore, Gandhi ran into resistance from the royal family and its brahman allies in Travancore and virtually all of the Kerala region, of which Travancore was a part. Travancore's royalty and brahman hierarchy went to the extreme of requiring untouchables to carry bells to warn other pedestrians that they were coming. Whenever Hindus heard these bells, they scattered for cover.

Since late 1923, a campaign had been underway in Vaikom, a community in Travancore. The campaign was led by a Tamil from the neighboring Madras Presidency, a man named E. V. Ramaswamy Naicker. Naicker, or EVR as he was widely known, agitated for better living conditions for the untouchables of Vaikom. Specifically, he wanted untouchables to be allowed to traverse the road in front of Vaikom's great Hindu temple. EVR's friend, the maharaja of Travancore, became so upset over the agitation that he imprisoned Naicker. Mahatma Gandhi arrived in Vaikom to protest on behalf of the local untouchables. The maharaja's police put up barricades on the roads in front of the Hindu temple. Even Gandhi was not allowed access to the temple.

"My agitation here is nothing less than to rid Hinduism of its greatest blot," the Mahatma declared. "The curse of untouchability has disfigured Hinduism."

He negotiated for months with the maharaja, who finally relented. Travancore's authorities now agreed to open up the roads on three sides of the temple to all people, including untouchables; the fourth side was barred to untouchables. It took another decade of agitation on Gandhi's part to ensure that Harijans could not only walk on the roads outside temples but also worship inside if they wished to.

If Gandhi's efforts led to increased social acceptance of Harijans, it was the work of a man named Bhimrao Ramji Ambedkar that eventually resulted in positive economic and political gains for them. Ambedkar was a lawyer with a doctorate from Columbia University. He helped draft India's Constitution in 1949, which formally outlawed untouchability. He was also an untouchable. Ambedkar organized civic associations for the welfare of India's Harijans. He influenced newspaper publishers to write editorials urging the end of discrimination against untouchables. Ambedkar rejected Hinduism, embraced Buddhism, and persuaded hundreds of thousands of Harijans to convert. He even formed the Republican Party of India to ensure that Harijans join independent India's political mainstream.

Largely because of Ambedkar's work, the national government decreed that affirmative action be undertaken on behalf of Harijans. Special job slots were set aside for them in public sector industries. Air India, the government-owned airline, was ordered to step up its hiring of Harijan stewards and stewardesses, a directive that caused considerable grumbling among the upper-class people who traditionally joined the airline for its glamour: many of these non-Harijans felt that the new employees simply weren't bright or beautiful enough.

Resistance to the emancipation of Harijans continued in many quarters. When Acharya Vinobha Bhave, a respected social activist and disciple of Mahatma Gandhi, tried to lead a group of Harijans into a Hindu temple in Deogarh, in Bihar state, brahman priests physically attacked the frail Bhave. The incident shocked the nation. Prime Minister Nehru's administration immediately drafted a bill that made the practice of untouchability a criminal offense.

But discrimination against Harijans persists in India. Once in a while the newspapers carry gory accounts of Harijans being beheaded in remote areas by high-caste Hindus; or there are articles about the disfiguring of Harijan women. In Tamil Nadu and Andhra Pradesh, there have been incidents where entire rural neighborhoods of Harijans were set upon by Hindu hordes, who then burned down homes and killed residents.

It would be a very long time before the spirit of corrective legislation was mirrored in broad social attitudes toward Harijans, Pramila David said to me as we drove toward Medak. The countryside seemed dry; it hadn't rained for months. Indeed, drought had affected twelve of Andhra's twenty-three districts, and the state's food production was expected to fall substantially short of the 1984–85 target of 1.25 million metric tons. Peanut, rice, sorghum, and millet yields were not expected to equal the previous year's harvest. Many villages were running out of potable water. In the Telangana region of the state, villagers traditionally held an annual festival of flowers in honor of Batakamma, the local goddess of life. But, Dr. David told me, this year there hadn't even been enough water for the ritual bath given by priests to the goddess, who is supposed to usher in a year of abundant harvests. The lack of water was viewed by villagers as a bad omen.

We arrived in a village called Brahmanpalli. We went to the home of a man named Krishna Reddy, whose family had once owned hundreds of acres of land here but whose property now had shrunk to eighty acres because of Andhra's land-ceiling regulations. Reddy wasn't home, but his Australian-born wife, Joan, welcomed us to their ranch-style house. A group of local peasants had already assembled in anticipation of our visit (Pramila David had telephoned the Reddys the previous day). They sat on the stone floor of Joan Reddy's veranda, not exchanging a word with one another. The women sat separately from the men, at some distance.

I talked with Gajam Balaram, who belonged to the weaver community. He was a tall, thin man who wore a white dhoti, or sarong, a long white shirt, and thonged sandals. He had a cadaverous face, which appeared ghoulish because of white holy ash he had daubed on his forehead.

He was extremely worried, Balaram said. The crops on his two-acre plot were failing because of the drought. Villagers did not have enough cash to spend on themselves, so his family's textile retail shop simply had no business these days. He had to abandon weaving because of competition from Hyderabad's textile mills.

"Our life is no better than when I was a child," Balaram said in Telugu, which Pramila David translated for me. "In fact, my childhood was happier than the life I am able to give to my own children."

But hadn't this been Indira Gandhi's constituency, I said, surely she must have helped people here?

"Politicians!" Balaram said. "We can never believe any of their promises. They say so much during election time, then they vanish."

The acute need in the Brahmanpalli area, he said, was for better drinking-water supply, for sewage pipes, and for a hospital. The ten thousand residents of the area had been clamoring for these for many years, Balaram said, but to no avail.

"What good is it to us even if our representative was the prime minister of India?" said a man named Nandi Narasingrao. He had completed high school but could only find a job on a rice farm. He had recently gotten married, Narasingrao said, but now he was finding it difficult to feed his new bride. "What face do I have to show before my in-laws?" he said.

I asked a woman named Mutuah if Mrs. Gandhi was going to be missed in this area.

"Why should we miss her?" Mutuah, a Harijan, said. "Her death makes no difference to our daily lives. Our struggle to survive goes on regardless. Did Indira Gandhi truly care for us here?"

And it went on that way from village to village in Medak. In Islampur, Paddalpalli, Topran—in community after community of mud and brick homes, dusty roads and dry, brown fields, I heard the same sentiments. The need was not only for improved health-care facilities and better schools; it was also for bank loans to develop farms and local businesses. The need was for jobs. The need was for someone to come and listen to these villagers, but Mrs. Gandhi hadn't been here for many months and now, of course, she was gone.

The men and women of Medak were concerned with health care, better sanitation, more employment, schools. These concerns are replicated in virtually all rural areas of India's states. National politicians always pay lip service to the "needs of the peasant." But the life of the ordinary peasant hasn't improved much since independence: there now were more people than ever before who lived below the poverty line—who couldn't adequately feed, clothe, or house their families.

As Pramila David and I headed back toward Hyderabad, it occurred to me that there now were more people in India below the poverty line than the entire population of the country at indepen-

dence. In another fifteen years' time, there will be at least a billion
people in India; half of them certainly will be born into crushing
poverty, if current trends hold.

I suddenly remembered a sobering conversation I had in Delhi
some days back with Hugo Corvalan, the India representative of the
United Nations Fund for Population Activities. I had first met Corvalan, a Chilean physician, when he was stationed in Ecuador some
years ago for the United Nations. He had impressed me then as a man
who passionately cared for the poor and who was deeply worried that
the population growth rate in many of the world's poorest countries
was galloping beyond control.

I found Corvalan even more troubled when I went to see him at
the United Nations office in Delhi's fashionable Lodi Estate. He had
asked for the India assignment because of its challenges. India, after
all, had been the first Third World country to have formally made
family planning a matter of national policy. It had launched with
much publicity a nationwide sterilization drive. It had persuaded the
United States and other Western donors to pump more than three
billion dollars over the last two decades into population-control programs. And still, the population was growing each year at a rate of
more than 2.1 percent. The largest number of babies were born in
areas where there already were the most people—the rural countryside, where 70 percent of India's population lived. Moreover, improved health care had lowered the death rate in many parts of the
country; killer diseases like smallpox had been eradicated. Infant
mortality had been brought down. The life expectancy of the average
Indian had increased from 32 years at Independence in 1947 to more
than 54 by 1984.

Corvalan told me that at present the average married Indian
woman produced five children. If the Indian government's efforts to
reduce average family size to two children was successful by, say, the
year 2040, India still would have a population of 2.5 billion.

I wasn't sure I'd heard Corvalan correctly.

"Did you say 2.5 billion?" I said.

"Yes," Corvalan said.

And he now went on to give me more gloomy information: fewer than 35 percent of the country's 122 million married people used any form of contraception. In order to ensure that India's population does not surge beyond a billion by the year 2000, contraception prevalence must be extended to at least 60 percent of these married people.

Were the Indian authorities capable of extending family planning so dramatically?

The plain truth is, the Indian government has bungled population control from the very start. Nehru was a relatively late convert to the idea of family planning, even though his government instituted a formal population policy in the early 1950s. The resources that could and should have been channeled into population-control measures right from independence were never forthcoming. Nehru's first minister of health and family planning was a spinster of great rectitude who privately endorsed Mahatma Gandhi's oft-quoted view that celibacy was the best contraceptive. Massive grants that later were given by Western donors were mischanneled—which is to say, a lot of the money went into the pockets of politicians and top bureaucrats.

Mrs. Gandhi dithered over family planning. It was not until the "Emergency" of 1975–77 that the government acted decisively. The actions, of course, proved highly unpopular because the prime minister's younger son, Sanjay, pushed through draconian sterilization programs. He meant well, but he was a young man in a hurry; Sanjay Gandhi, Indira Gandhi's heir apparent, wanted to bring down India's birthrate overnight. Truckloads of preadolescent boys were sterilized by overzealous functionaries in order to meet quotas. Mrs. Gandhi's defeat in the 1977 election was at least partly attributable to public revulsion over the family-planning excesses of the "emergency" period.

After Mrs. Gandhi returned to power in 1980, little was heard from her on population. She was not about to risk talking about that subject again! As a result, family-planning programs continued at a low pitch—when what was really called for was a renewed and rigorous commitment to reducing the population growth rate. Despite the fact that the national government had a budget of more than $250 million for distribution to the states for family planning, much of the money went unspent. The United Nations kept pouring funds into India for population projects—and the money languished in Delhi.

Even during the December 1984 election campaign, Rajiv Gandhi did not utter a word about what many people think is India's biggest problem, overpopulation. Perhaps he did not wish to antagonize the majority Hindu population, particularly in the rampantly breeding northern Hindi-speaking states, whose electoral support he sought. Now Prime Minister Gandhi is talking about doubling the family-planning budget to nearly $500 million a year. I don't think how much more he spends really matters: already, Indian states have more money than they know what to do with. What is really required is better management of existing programs.

A few days after my visit to Medak, I found myself in Bangalore, the capital city of Karnataka State. Pramila David had suggested that I look up a man named Palli Hanumantha Reddy. He was the head of the Population Center, which had been set up in the early 1970s with the help of money from the World Bank. The center was intended to conduct research into family-reproduction trends in Karnataka, a prosperous state of 38 million people. Now Dr. Reddy's center functions as an arm of the state government.

The center consisted of a long, low building situated in front of a playing field. The location was in Malleswaram, one of the most congested neighborhoods of Bangalore. In one corner of the field boys were battling it out at cricket; in another corner, young men were romancing young women; in still another corner, elderly citizens were taking their evening constitutional. Dr. Reddy was a middle-aged man with a shock of graying hair, spectacles, and an affable manner. He made it clear at the very outset that he didn't think that family planning in his state and all across the country suffered from overabundance of good leadership.

"In fact, I would even say that there is much negligence in this field," Dr. Reddy said.

The Karnataka government set aside more than $90 million a year on family planning, he said; yet, much of the money wasn't spent. State governments generally just did not have the imagination to spend money properly on family-planning programs, Dr. Reddy said.

What was needed, he said, was a system of financial incentives so that small clinics all over the country could induce more people to sign up for family-planning measures of their choice. Since state governments already had funds lying around, why not gift certificates or savings bonds for participants in family-planning programs? And why not equip family-planning centers with vocational training courses for the poor, as Pramila David had done in Hyderabad? Most state governments unwisely concentrated on promoting sterilization; they ought to encourage a range of other contraceptive measures that were not so final and terminal as sterilizations. More attention needed to be paid to child-care programs: it had been proven in rural areas particularly that mothers listened to midwives and nurses. So why not train more nurses to spread the message of family planning? Why not train agricultural extension workers to inject a family-planning component into their daily dealings with peasants?

Palli Hanumantha Reddy made a lot of sense. So why wasn't the Karnataka government listening to him? Or Rajiv Gandhi's administration?

Reddy shrugged, then raised his hands to the heavens.

I flew from Karnataka to Kerala, India's southernmost state. It is a gem of a place, emerald green, scored with lagoons and canals and inlets, festooned with miles of coconut groves. The Indian Airlines airbus from Bangalore cruised over Kerala's inland mountains, which were carpeted with rubber, tea, and coffee plantations. A Keralite stewardess informed me that alongside these plantations were acres of pepper and cardamom and cashew nut fields. As the plane descended toward Cochin, an ancient coastal city where I planned to meet friends, I had to pull my eyes away from the window because of the violent glare from the vegetation down below. When I looked out again, we were just over the city itself. There seemed to be miles and miles of dwellings closely packed under swaying palm trees. The stewardess, who said she had recently completed college in Trivandrum, told me that Kerala had the highest population density in India —some 1,200 persons to the square mile, or four times the national figure. Despite a falling birthrate, she said, the state's population had pushed past thirty million.

In the Third World, Kerala long ago became a metaphor for literacy and excellent health care. By 1955, when most states of the Third World were still backward, miserable places—and still under their colonial yoke—Kerala already had achieved the highest literacy rate of any region in the developing world, an astonishing 95 percent.

The Christian missionaries who arrived in the eighteenth and nineteenth centuries had established English-language schools. Kerala's two princely states, Travancore and Cochin, were traditionally governed by rulers who promoted literacy, especially among women. The Hindu Nayars, an ethnic community, also vigorously pushed for education. Because Kerala had no industries until well into the 1960s, government service was the most sought-after career for the young. So they studied hard for the competitive entrance examinations—and the competition among Kerala's people (who were 50 percent Hindus, 25 percent Muslims, and 25 percent Christians) in turn helped push ever upward the quality of education. The state decreed that all education through high school would be free; moreover, even the salaries of teachers in many private schools were paid by the state from tax revenues. In addition, health services were free. The first public clinics for administering the smallpox vaccine were established in Travancore and Cochin.

Kerala was unusual in other ways, too. In the rest of India, women were largely confined to home and hearth; but in this state they were encouraged to study and to get jobs. The high status of women mostly stemmed from the fact that much of Kerala's majority Hindu society was matriarchal.

But Kerala also became a metaphor for something besides high literacy and good health care.

It was the first state in the world where the Communist Party obtained power through legitimately held elections. That occurred in 1957. As literacy spread, Keralites started to harbor higher and higher economic expectations. But the system could not deliver. Because of the nature of the terrain, virtually all economic activity was confined to land cultivation or fishing. Yet each year the schools and colleges were turning out thousands of graduates. Unemployment rose beyond 15 percent, and soon there were violent demonstrations against the ruling Congress Party of Jawaharlal Nehru. A local Communist leader named E. M. S. Namboodiripad accused the Congress of "class exploitation." At rally after rally, he equated the Congress rule with British imperialism. Namboodiripad's rhetoric, combined with the growing unemployment and the rising expectations of Keralites, helped put the Communists into power. Namboodiripad's government was the first constitutionally elected Communist administration in history.

Prime Minister Nehru actually seemed to be proud of the development. He told Krishan Bhatia of the *Hindustan Times* that perhaps now Communists all over the world would realize that they could attain power through the ballot box and become more tolerant of democratic political processes. Dom Moraes, in his biography of Indira Gandhi, *Mrs. Gandhi,* recalls that the Fabian Socialist in Nehru even seemed delighted that a leftist government had come into being through democratic means; Nehru, according to Moraes, hoped that Kerala could be the precursor of other democratically elected Communist governments all over the world.

Mrs. Gandhi had become president of the Congress Party by now. She wanted to revitalize the aging organization. She did not subscribe to her father's live-and-let-live attitude toward opposition parties, much less applaud the takeover, however democratic, of an Indian state by the Communist Party. She advised the Kerala unit of the Congress Party to prepare for a nasty battle with Namboodiripad's government. The Congress threw in its lot with the Nayars and the Christians of the state, who felt discriminated against by the Communist government; Namboodiripad's party had instituted radical land reforms, pushed out many influential and established Nayars and Christians from the bureaucracy, and tried to bring about structural changes in the educational system over which the Nayars and Christians had long held sway. The Communist government even tried to take over the parochial schools operated by the Christians and Nayars.

Rioting now occurred. There were Congress-sponsored demonstrations all over Kerala. Police fired tear gas at mobs. Then orders were given to shoot uncontrollably violent demonstrators. Several civilians died in melees. It was clear to many observers at the time that Mrs. Gandhi was calibrating the demonstrations from Delhi so as to ensure that the law-and-order situation deteriorated rapidly. She could then persuade her father, the prime minister, to dismiss the Kerala state government on the ground that it was unable to check the spreading lawlessness.

That is exactly what Mrs. Gandhi did, and Prime Minister Nehru accepted her recommendation. On July 31, 1959, the Namboodiripad government was deposed under a presidential order. But the lawlessness continued, this time fueled by the disaffected Communists. The Nehru–Gandhi axis ordered elections six months later. But in order to win the poll, Mrs. Gandhi had to make alliances with the Socialists and with the Muslim League. This was the same Muslim League that less than two decades ago had agitated so fiercely for the partition of Greater India into India and Pakistan. Mrs. Gandhi's political marriage of convenience with the Muslim League distressed many of her supporters within and without the Congress Party. The Congress formed a coalition government with the League and the Socialists.

The Communist Party subsequently split into a wing favoring the Maoist version of Marxism and another wing that leaned toward Moscow. (The split had more to do with the estrangement between Moscow and Beijing, rather than developments in Kerala; but it further weakened the previously monolithic Communist movement in Kerala.) Over the next twenty years, both Communist wings held power as members of various coalition governments—but the supremacy that Namboodiripad enjoyed between 1957 and 1959 was never quite replicated. It would not be incorrect to say that Indira Gandhi ushered in an era of coalition governments in Kerala; since 1960, in fact, the Congress and the Marxists have had to woo smaller regional and communal parties in order to form coalition governments. Tenuousness, not stability, has usually been the main characteristic of these administrations.

I got to Kerala a couple of days after the December 1984 national parliamentary election. The leading newspapers, such as the *Malayalam Manorama,* were asking in their editorials whether the Communists were a spent force. Of the 20 parliamentary seats in Kerala, Rajiv Gandhi's Congress Party won an unprecedented 13. Namboodiripad's Communist Party, known as the cpi(m) [the (M) stands for Marxist] won only one seat; the other wing of the Communist Party, known as the cpi, was completely shut out. "We never expected an Indira Wave in Kerala," said one of Namboodiripad's former key lieutenants and a former chief minister of the state, P. K. Vasudevan Nair.

Even in death, Mrs. Gandhi had defeated and demoralized Namboodiripad.

Kerala may have looked green and inviting from the air, but Cochin was hot, sticky, and dusty. I waited almost an hour for my baggage to appear; the delay, I was told, was on account of several large crates that had arrived by another plane from the Middle East.

"These days there is nothing but crates from the Gulf that come here," an Indian Airlines official said, wearily. "Big crates, too. We don't have the machinery to haul them. How much pushing and pulling can my men do with their bare hands?"

The crates, containing such things as television sets, dishwashers, and stereo sets, had been arriving from Middle East countries where, in the last ten years, more than 500,000 men and women from Kerala found lucrative work. Not only Muslims—known here as moplahs—traveled abroad; so did tens of thousands of Kerala Christians and Hindus. Their El Dorado was the Arabian Peninsula, whose oil-rich states were in need of manpower. Carpenters went from Kerala, and plumbers, technicians, schoolteachers, professors, physicians, nurses, drivers, even maids. The traffic from Kerala was so heavy that Air India started special thrice-weekly flights from Trivandrum to the Gulf. The emigration, however temporary, eased the unemployment problem in Kerala; and it showered upon the state a financial windfall —the Keralites who went abroad remitted money home, so that since the mid-1970s the state has received more than four billion dollars. The money has resulted in new homes, better neighborhoods, and a spree of spending on such things as cars and scooters.

I had trouble finding a taxi outside the Cochin Airport. I was told that many taxi drivers had moved to the Middle East. The drive to the Grand Hotel, where I was booked, took an hour because the road leaped over a number of bridges that could accommodate only one traffic lane. Had traffic moved at this pace in most other Indian states, there would have been mayhem, and probably a murder or two. But Keralites seemed quiet, peaceful people—at least on their roads. My taxi driver, a reedy man named Bala, did not even curse or mutter under his breath.

I couldn't stand his silence and stoicism any longer.

"Is traffic always like this?" I asked.

"Always, sir," Bala said.

"Is anything being done about it?"

"No."

"Isn't it frustrating to be on such roads?"

"Yes, sir."

We drove past a large naval yard. Cochin is the headquarters of the Indian Navy's southern fleet. There seemed to be more churches inside the yard than sailors. Christianity was said to have arrived in Kerala even before it was identified with Rome. John Keay, in *Into India*, writes that a mysterious Thomas founded what is called the Syrian Church of South India. The Cambridge History of India quotes from the Apocryphal Acts of the Apostles 2 an anecdote relating to Thomas, the doubting one of Jesus' twelve Apostles. "Whithersoever thou wilt Lord, send me," Thomas says. "But to

India I will not go." He is eventually said to have been sold to an Indian who wanted to take home a carpenter, John Keay writes. Was the Thomas who came to Kerala the Thomas of the Apostles? Theologians in India and elsewhere still debate that one.

The early Christians of Kerala recognized the authority of the Nestorian Patriarchs of Babylon rather than the Bishop of Rome. When Vasco da Gama and his Portuguese fleet arrived in Kerala in 1502, they were angered by the Kerala Christians' rejection of the Bishop of Rome. So they began a program of conversion. The Keralites who resisted the Portuguese formed what is now known as the Chaldean Church of India. But those who were "persuaded" by the Portuguese to switch their affiliation to Rome are the present-day members of the Syrian rite of the Roman Catholic Church of India. There was further fragmentation of the Christian community over the years. In addition to the Catholic and Syrian churches, there are many other Christian denominations: Jehovah's Witnesses, Lutheran, Baptist, Methodist, Anglican and Seventh-Day Adventist, to name a few.

I had come to Kerala because my friends Kutty and Bhavani Narayan had suggested a meeting with members of India's most rapidly dwindling community, the Jews of Cochin. The Jews are said to have come to India in 72 A.D. They established themselves mainly as traders and teachers in Cochin and Bombay. Before 1948, which is to say before the state of Israel was created, there were nearly 50,000 Jews in India, most of them in Bombay; in Cochin there were some 3,000 families. The Cochin Jewish community was divided into "White Jews"—who were the more affluent ones—and the "Black Jews," who weren't so well off. After 1948, the Jews of Bombay and Cochin started migrating to Israel. Now there are barely 7,000 left in Bombay, and just about 100 in Cochin.

Shabdar and Gladys Koder have refused to leave their ancestral home here. For one thing, they own a chain of food and supplies stores in Kerala; for another, they are well into their seventies and do not fancy the prospect of making a fresh start in an alien land. There is still another reason why they have not migrated to Israel: the

Koders see themselves as Indians. Their roots are here. (Shabdar Koder's great-great-grandfather came here 300 years ago from Baghdad via Burma to set up a trading business, which is still thriving.) They think that exciting times lie ahead for India and they want to be around to see Rajiv Gandhi succeed.

I went to see the Koders in their one-hundred-year-old house in an area known as Fort Cochin. The house had three stories and it overlooked a bay. Coconut trees rose behind the Koders' home, and in front there was a large park. Most of Cochin's one hundred remaining Jews live in this neighborhood. It was the bewitching hour of sunset when I showed up. The thin light made the pink walls of the house glow softly. There was an enormous, ornate wooden door that a saree-clad maid opened. I was led up a wooden stairway to the second floor where Shabdar Samuel Koder was waiting for me in a huge sitting room.

He was a tall man, balding, with a strong handshake and a friendly face. His wife, Gladys, immediately brought out a tray of savories and sweetmeats. The tray seemed bigger than she was. The food, she said, was all homemade. Then she insisted on showing me the Koders' collection of antique Chinese porcelain. They possessed dozens of early Ming dynasty vases, Ching dynasty plates, and Tang horses. It was a museum that they had there. I told them that I was impressed indeed.

"Ah, so was Rajiv," Koder said.

"He was here?"

"Yes. And he brought along his wife, Sonia."

The Gandhis had come to Cochin several years ago as tourists. Rajiv Gandhi was still a pilot for Indian Airlines then. They visited the synagogues in the area in the company of the Koders. Sonia Gandhi, a collector of antiques, stopped off in a curio shop not far from the Koder home. She fancied a Chinese porcelain plate, but Shabdar Koder thought the storekeeper was asking too much for it. He tried to bring the price down, but the seller would not budge.

"Why don't you come and see our collection?" Gladys Koder said to Sonia Gandhi.

The Gandhis stayed for tea. Sonia Gandhi liked a particular porcelain item, and the Koders said they gave it to her. Was it from the Ming period, or the Tang period, or even the later Ching period, I asked, for porcelain items from any of these eras—but particularly the first two—would ordinarily be extremely expensive. The Koders smiled and declined to answer my question.

"Charming couple they were," Shabdar Koder said. "I remember clearly Rajiv telling me he wasn't interested in politics at all. Of course, in those days his younger brother Sanjay was still alive and everybody thought that he would succeed Mrs. Gandhi. Who could have predicted this bizarre turn of events?"

"We think that Rajiv has a really good future ahead of him—but he must act fast to get rid of corruption in government," Mrs. Koder said. "What a mandate! What a golden opportunity!"

Koder may be a Gandhi well-wisher, but he is also distressed by the Indian government's long-standing policy toward Israel. Indian representatives at the United Nations have vigorously supported various Arab-sponsored resolutions against Israel—but have either resisted or ignored Israeli condemnations of Arab terrorist acts. Indian officials say privately that India's policy toward Israel is in its own best "national interest": these officials point to the fact that tens of thousands of Indian migrant workers are employed in the oil-rich countries of the Middle East and that the annual remittances of these workers help enlarge India's foreign reserves. They also note the fact that Indian construction companies, have billions of dollars in contracts with such countries as Saudi Arabia, Iraq, and Libya.

Not long after Rajiv Gandhi's electoral victory in December 1984, the chairman of the Conference of Presidents of Major American Jewish Organizations wrote to the prime minister to congratulate him. The official, Kenneth J. Bialkin, also relayed to Gandhi the concerns of the American Jewish community. He noted that on numerous occasions the Indian government had denied visas to Israeli athletes, scientists, jurists, and even diplomats.

This discrimination together with India's unceasing condemnations of Israel at the United Nations and within the nonaligned movement and its one-sided identification with the Arab and the Palestine Liberation Organization had undermined "India's ability to assume an honest and constructive role in Middle East peacemaking," Bialkin wrote. "Moreover India's hostility toward a vibrant sister democracy and a staunch American ally has affected the attitudes of many in this country who would like to identify more with Indian causes and concerns," Bialkin said.

As of March 1985, Prime Minister Gandhi had not acknowledged Bialkin's letter. And I doubt whether the Indian government's official policy toward Israel is going to change.

I asked the Koders what future they saw for Cochin's Jews.

"What future?" Mrs. Koder said, slowly and so softly that I had to edge closer to her on the damask sofa we shared. "The Jews here have no future. We are a dying community. We can hardly even call ourselves a community anymore. You know, I really miss our numbers. There used to be so much laughter here, and joy, and good living. Then one by one the families started leaving. Now we feel so alone. Those of us who have remained here are old and lonely."

Soon their married daughter might leave for Israel, the Koders suggested. Then what?

They told me that one reason emigration to Israel from Cochin accelerated was that families could not find husbands for their daughters here. There was a fourteen-year period when, strangely enough, only girls were born into Cochin's Jewish community. Emigration did not occur because of any anti-Semitism in Cochin. In fact, the Koders said, India was probably one of the few places in the world where Jews lived in complete harmony with non-Jews.

I asked about the synagogues in Cochin. Who supported them? Shabdar Koder said that the synagogues were maintained through income generated from rental properties that the institutions owned around Kerala. But there had been no rabbis at these synagogues for many, many years, he said. The community could not afford them. Any theological or social disputes that arose in the community were referred to rabbinical authorities in Jerusalem or Britain.

"Our synagogue services have been hit very badly," Shabdar Koder said. Jewish custom called for a minyan, or quorum, at religious services, of at least ten men above the age of seventeen. It was often difficult to raise such a quorum, Koder said.

"We are a people of the past here," he said. "It is ironic, isn't it, that we Jews prospered in India, we were always a part of the society here, we were never ill-treated—and now we are disappearing from the one country where we were always secure."

5

The Magic of Culture

I T happened like this. I returned to Bombay one morning from
Kerala, and found a message from my friends Vir and Malavika
Sanghvi that I should join them for lunch. The meal was to be at the
home of Vinod and Saryu Doshi, one of the city's well-known couples. I was puzzled at the invitation. I had never met the Doshis
before; they and I moved in different circles. Vinod Doshi was a very
rich man who headed Premier Automobiles, one of India's biggest
automobile manufacturers. Saryu, who held a doctorate in art history
from an American university, was editor of a respected art journal
called *Marg* and also an art collector in her own right. Invitations to
their home were prized by *le tout* Bombay. I had heard that the
Doshis entertained frequently but selectively.

"It's supposed to be quite an event," Vir Sanghvi said. "In fact,
the Doshis are keen to meet you—I've told them about you so often.
And I think you'll enjoy meeting their other guests."

I wasn't particularly anxious to meet *le tout* Bombay, but I decided
that I would accompany the Sanghvis. I enjoyed their company. Vir
Sanghvi, who ran *Imprint,* was a personable young man bubbling
with ideas and initiatives. Malavika was equally charming and sophisticated. We'd been friends for many years, and I spent a lot of my

time with them whenever I was in Bombay or when they visited New York City. Both were younger than I; they showed concern for my well-being as if I were a sibling. Few of us acquire solid new friends after our school days but the Sanghvis had come into my life long after college.

The Doshis lived in a tony neighborhood in the Pedder Road section of Bombay. Vinod Doshi, a short, stocky man, opened the door to his apartment. He crushed the Sanghvis in a hug that reddened his face from the effort, shook my hand warmly, and waved us inside. Doshi's living room was large and it opened out into a terrace beyond which was the azure Arabian Sea. White-liveried waiters glided around serving drinks and appetizers. The art on the walls was eye-catching: large Husain paintings, exquisite Mogul miniatures, glass portraits from Gujerat, richly-colored cloth hangings. It took an effort to tear my eyes away from these walls. Malavika Sanghvi nudged me in the ribs and nodded toward the other guests.

In one corner stood Rudolf Nureyev. He was chatting with Ravi Shankar, the sitarist. Listening in was Shashi Kapoor, the movie star. In another corner was Govind Nihalani, a top film director. He was in deep conversation with the actress Simi Garewal. Vinod Doshi's wife, Saryu, was talking with Bakul Patel, the widely known social worker and management consultant. Santosh Verma, a photographer specializing in celebrities, stood in the middle of the room on an antique Persian carpet, surveying the scene.

Nureyev had come to Bombay not only to break bread with Vinod and Saryu Doshi. He had brought along the Paris Ballet Company, of which he was now the director, for a series of Indian government–sponsored performances around the country. He was accompanied to this lunch not by his troupers but by an eager Indian government official who encouraged Verma to take pictures of him with his ward. Nureyev and the official were invited guests, of course, but the local French Consulate functionaries who turned up along with the dancer had not been expected. Saryu Doshi, an elegant woman with a stunning yellow-green saree, was being polite to the party crashers, but clearly she was annoyed. Most Indian hostesses resign themselves to the possibility that any or all of their guests will bring along a guest or two of their own without first asking; but the French consul general, himself uninvited, had shown up with a dozen.

I asked Nureyev whether he had been to India before.

"Ah yes, of course, and I loved every minute of it," he said. He said this pleasantly, although he kept looking at the sea. "But it was only a brief stopover, maybe half a day or so, on my way to Australia."

"Where did you stop over?" I said.

"Karachi," Nureyev said.

I told him that Karachi was no longer in India. For the last thirty-seven years it had been a part of the neighboring state of Pakistan.

"I loved it anyway," Nureyev said, gamely.

Ravi Shankar had caught a bit of this exchange. He looked at me and smiled.

"Poor fellow," he said in Hindi, looking in the general direction of the Russian exile.

The publicity photographs of Ravi Shankar seldom show him standing up, and perhaps with good reason. He is a very short man. He has a large head, a wide forehead, and eyes that are lively with feelings. His hands are big, with long, slim fingers. I had expected him to be a distant, even forbidding figure. But he was extraordinarily friendly.

"Let's have a chat about the Indian cultural scene," Shankar said, after I told him that I was writing a book on India. I told him that I'd read his own book years ago. "Why don't you stop by the apartment tomorrow morning?"

Shankar, it turned out, was visiting Bombay for a sitar recital. He ordinarily lived in Delhi. The friend's home where he was staying was clearly the abode of a classical music aficionado: there were pictures of Ravi Shankar and other greats all over the place, and a variety of musical instruments such as sitars, veenas, and tablas, the Indian drums. When I arrived, Ravi Shankar has been performing a pooja, a devotional ritual in front of a small altar. I observed him praying and was moved. The very act of genuflecting in front of his Hindu deities made him seem such a humble man. Here was a man who, more than any other, had put India's music on the map of the world. Here was a man who was a living legend, who could attract large audiences wherever he went, whose records and cassettes were available in stores all over the world, a man who had been honored and applauded by scores of governments. I caught a snippet of Ravi Shankar's prayer: "Lord, give me strength to be simple and modest."

The words were in Sanskrit, and they were part of a slokah, a verse that was probably as old as Ravi Shankar's music itself. What is now called classical Indian music, in fact, flowed from the scriptures and prayers of the ancient Aryans who spilled into India thousands of years ago and settled first in the Indus Valley region. Since that time, Indians have used song, music, and dance as an integral part of their religious worship. It is customary for every Indian artist to start his performance with a religious invocation of some sort: dancers, for example, bow before a statue of Lord Nataraja, a reincarnation of Shiva; singers pray to Saraswati, the goddess of music and poetry and knowledge. The scriptures of the Aryans dealt with worship of the Almighty and also with human behavior norms for human conduct. And classical music, through its ragas, or notes, was also about human emotions and about the seasons in a man's life.

"When I sit down with my sitar, I go back centuries," Ravi Shankar said. "Indian music is eternal. It is as if it springs from a fountain of eternal youth. It constantly rejuvenates itself. I think the reason why people all over the world have responded to Indian music is that it reaches into everyone's hearts and souls. Indian music is spiritual. It is also sensual. I think the reason why Western audiences have responded to my music is that at my concerts the spiritual and the sensual find a meeting place."

Ravi Shankar worries that at his concerts the young people of the West find it fashionable to smoke pot and use drugs to "get high." He does not encourage such things, he told me, and he finds drugs a violation of the spirit of his concerts. I recalled to him that during my own college days in the late 1960s in the United States, it was very common to attend his recitals while stoned.

Ravi Shankar's exposure to the West did not start only when he exported his sitar music. He spent many years in Paris as a child because his older brother, Uday Shankar, lived and taught Indian dance there. It was Uday Shankar who raised him as his own child and who instilled in Ravi Shankar the great discipline it takes to become a great sitar player. Many Indian musicians lack such discipline, Shankar told me. They have seen how receptive the West is to Indian classical music and so no sooner than they learn to hold an instrument correctly do they take off for Western shores, lured by dollar signs.

"Among many musicians today, there is both the absence of discipline and the lack of modesty," Shankar said. "That amazes me."

I asked him how he would like to be remembered.

"I would like to be remembered as someone who served music during every moment of his life," Ravi Shankar said. "I would like to be remembered by future generations as someone who enriched music in the international sense, as someone who blended the classical with the modern and yet who did not abandon traditions. In my music, I have tried to keep the balance between traditions and innovative creativity. I am a purist but I am also an experimenter."

Now Ravi Shankar has started a series of schools around the country to strengthen classical norms of music. It is not enough to know techniques, he says, it is just as important to be imbued with values.

"People talk about this post-Indira age, about vast technological changes, about the computer era," Ravi Shankar said. "All that is fine, of course. But the real strength of India has been its traditions. I hope the young people around Rajiv Gandhi don't abandon this heritage. I think Indira Gandhi was such a marvelous blend of a scientific mind and a heart that cared for India's cultural heritage and traditions. Whatever her politics, popular culture flourished under her. My prayer is that her son Rajiv similarly blends the ancient and the modern."

Later, I thought about how the vast Indian radio and television network has been supplementing the temple courtyard as the venue for musical performances. More than half of the government-owned network's broadcast time is devoted to musical programs. As I walked away from Ravi Shankar's apartment, I could hear someone's radio in the background: sitar was in the air.

I looked up a quotation from Arnold Blake's acclaimed *New Oxford History of Music.* Blake said: "It is impossible to divorce Indian music from the whole structure of Indian culture and philosophy. To the Indian student, music is not an isolated phenomenon but one directly and inextricably linked with philosophy and religion, and of cosmic importance. The right kind of music . . . serves to break the cycle of birth, death, and rebirth."

Ravi Shankar had spoken about blending the old and the new, a theme that I found recurrent in the India through which I traveled after the assassination of Indira Gandhi. It certainly seemed to be the dominant theme in Bombay's cultural circles, who have long set the pace and established the tone of the country's modern popular culture. The death of Indira Gandhi was felt keenly by Bombay's cultural czars, who now wondered if Rajiv Gandhi's commitment to supporting the arts would be as constant and consistent as his mother's. In the event, Prime Minister Gandhi made a reassuring statement that his government's support of the arts would be undiminished; Gandhi even personally took charge of the ministry that channeled funds to cultural organizations; he also announced that one of his first trips abroad would be in June 1985 to inaugurate the "Festival of India" in the United States.

Ravi Shankar, of course, was India's best-known cultural ambassador. It was his performances that activated the interest of millions of foreigners in Indian culture. Still, Shankar's was essentially a one-man show; it was only in recent years that the maestro had set up schools to further his art and to train students in the sitar. Indian classical music and dance are very much rooted in this tradition of knowledge —the acquisition of knowledge from a guru. The guru's given wisdom is then spread by his disciples through their own work. This centuries-old process and practice has been sustained remarkably by a man named Guru Kalyanasundaram Pillai.

Pillai is India's foremost teacher of Bharata Natyam, the solo female dance form that originated in the southern part of the country. This dance form dates back at least a couple of thousand years. Bharata Natyam was traditionally a temple art, performed by women called devdasis who, as votaries of the gods, dedicated their lives to religious service in South India. These women performed in the great temples of the south, such as Chidambaram and Tirupathi, and also at the royal courts of Tanjore. It was the rulers of Tanjore, in fact, who emerged as the leading patrons of this particular dance form over the centuries and who supported the nattuvanars, a community of dance masters and gurus. These nattuvanars then went forth to different parts of the country to establish Bharata Natyam academies. More than forty years ago, Pillai's father, an acclaimed dance master named Guru Kuppiah Pillai, settled in Bombay and formed the Raja Rajeshwari Bharata Natya Kala Mandir. Kuppiah Pillai was assisted by his son-in-law, Guru Govindraj Pillai, and by his son, Guru Mahalingam Pillai.

In those days Bombay was already a commercial metropolis but it had not acquired the reputation of being the country's cultural capital as well. Bombay, in truth, was one of India's newest cities in the sense that it was growing rapidly in population and land area: neighborhoods were going up overnight on land reclaimed from the Arabian Sea, thousands of people from the rural hinterland were flooding into the city in search of jobs, and clever entrepreneurs—who foresaw the need this growing population would have for entertainment—surged ahead in the development of the movie industry. The commitment was to the new: new neighborhoods, new buildings, new enterprises, new films. But Kuppiah Pillai brought the old to the new in an effort to reinforce the traditional underpinnings of society.

The dance academy he founded in Bombay at once attracted the daughters of Bombay's leading families. Kuppiah Pillai stressed that whatever the dancer's mother tongue, Bharata Natyam had only one language—the language of facial expressions, body movement, and hand gestures. His art was anchored in the certified teachings of Bharata, the great guru of the second century A.D., who wrote the Natya Shastra, in which he defined with extraordinary clarity the precise choreographic terms of Bharata Natyam: this dance form, according to Bharata, was a combination of rhythmic acting and pure dance, a dance form in which every movement would be minutely mapped and nothing left to impulse or chance.

Kuppiah Pillai's son, Kalyanasundaram Pillai, decided to continue his family's tradition of teaching the Bharata Natyam. And under him, the dance form has flourished. He has adapted the form's classicism to modern times by using not only the traditional language of Tamil for lyrics but also a number of vernacular languages. Not long ago, Pillai accompanied a troupe to neighboring Nepal, where he used several Nepalese songs as accompaniment.

In most Indian classical dancing, but especially in Bharata Natyam, the dance master, or nattuvanar, is not only the choreographer but also the symphony conductor: he plays the cymbals, he recites the rhythmic syllables known as the jattis that are played on a percussion instrument known as the mridangam, and sets the pace of the performer's movements. The orchestra follows his lead.

Pillai is a small, compact man with a skin that glows like phosporous. I met him at his academy, which occupies a couple of classrooms in Bombay's New Era High School. It was late evening, and Pillai was still instructing a group of adolescent girls who were to travel with him the next day to Jubbalpore for a performance. The girls were clearly tired, they were sweating; the pounding of their bare feet on the stone floor of the classroom must have been painful. But Pillai, ever the taskmaster, did not let up. Like a machine recording, he kept up the rhythmic adavus, the patterned movement of the guru's hands which is accompanied by the chanting of the rhythmic syllables, *ta tai tam-dhit tai tam.* These adavus add up to a hundred-and-twenty basic dance motifs—and it seemed to me that, even at this late hour, Pillai was testing his troupe with every one of them.

"In Bharata Natyam, every last detail has to be perfect—otherwise you lose the harmony of movement," Pillai said to me. "No one said this is easy work, either for the guru or for the disciple. But in the quest for perfection lies the pleasure of this dance form."

Pillai's students have given pleasure to audiences all over the world.

They have themselves started Bharata Natyam dance schools in the United States, Canada, and in Western Europe. Pillai often accompanies his India-based disciples to foreign venues for performances. There are those who even call him India's "jet-age dance guru." Sunil Kothari, a prominent dance critic, lauds Pillai for uniquely blending acient and modern themes in his choreography.

"The contribution of this dance school, and perhaps of myself, is the training and despatching of students to different parts of the country and the world," Pillai said. "We have shown that the classical traditions of India can be adapted to modern times without sacrificing their purity. We have shown that the old scriptures and the old mythological tales of India are still valid and applicable in this modern age of ours. Like our classical music, the power of this dance form lies in its capacity to hold audiences no matter what culture they hail from."

Now it was close to the midnight hour, and I took my leave. I had hardly stepped out of Pillai's classroom when I heard the resumption of his hand-clapping and rhythmic chanting. The responding tinkling of the ankle-bells worn by Pillai's dancers followed me for miles afterward.

One of Kalyanasundaram Pillai's most distinguished students is a woman named Protima Chowdhury. She now not only gives Bharata Natyam performances but also tutors young girls herself, in addition to assisting Pillai—whom she affectionately calls Masterji—whenever his troupe has concerts out of town. Chowdhury introduced me to her brother-in-law, a wealthy Calcutta businessman named Hari Pada Roy. He in turn insisted that I meet his spiritual mentor, whom he called Dadaji.

It is not uncommon for Indians to introduce other Indians or even foreign visitors to their personal gurus. The "guru" is an institution in India; even Indira Gandhi had her own, a man named Dhirendra Brahmachari, who came to wield great political influence in his time and expertly blended the spiritual with the temporal. Some gurus have prospered so much that India is no longer big enough for them:

they have established ashrams and hermitages abroad, as in the case of Bhagwan Shri Rajneesh, who bought vast property in Oregon and created virtually a new township to accommodate his doting devotees.

I was not especially enthusiastic about accepting Roy's offer. I had been exposed to a great deal of guruism during my growing up days in Bombay. The experiences weren't all pleasant. In my early teens, my parents had followed the advice of relatives who interpreted my temper tantrums and adolescent rebelliousness as the manifestation of someone's black magic on me; the relatives urged my parents to take me to exorcists. And so I was led through several months of dark rituals: lemons were squeezed over my head, vermilion was sprinkled on my hair; one exorcist, chanting Sanskrit mantras, pricked my finger and smeared the blood on his forehead. It was all very frightening, and for years afterward I could not shake off those dreadful images of sleazy men mumbling incomprehensible hymns and making magic on my body. My adolescent rebelliousness, of course, continued, and my relatives opined that that was because my parents hadn't subscribed to more expensive exorcism. The scholarship from Brandeis University was therefore a kind of deliverance for me, for once I left India for America I also left the sinister world of gurus far behind. In a country of immense financial disparities where the poor desperately want to improve their lot and where the rich are eager to consolidate their often ill-gotten wealth, the gurus offer instant spiritual salvation—for a price. The very poor and the very rich need to have faith, and the gurus of India are often the beneficiaries of such belief.

Hari Pada Roy, who has made millions from an automobile spare-parts import business, told me that Dadaji was not the conventional kind of guru. In fact, Roy said, he wasn't a guru at all but someone who helped people understand their inate spirituality. Roy added that no gifts or donations were required, and any such contributions would offend Dadaji.

Dadaji's real name is Amiya Roy Chowdhury, but he is no relation of Protima. He is eighty-four years old but doesn't look a day over fifty. He has deep, dark eyes and a gentle smile. He lives in a modest house in one of the busiest sections of Calcutta, with the clangorous traffic providing a constant soundtrack to his meditations. He is married, has two children, and earns a decent income from a family-owned toy shop. The day I went to see him, Dadaji—"Dada" is a term that means Elder Brother; "ji" is an honorific of respect—was reclining in his living room, wearing a loose sarong and a vest. He seemed to smile a lot and frequently joked with several visitors, all of whom, like me, were sitting on the carpet. Dadaji turned to me.

"You are a writer," he said.

I was startled. Hari Pada Roy had told me that Dadaji didn't like to be informed in advance who his visitors were going to be.

"How do you know that?" I said.

"It is written all over you that you are a writer," Dadaji said, with a huge smile.

He rose from his divan and beckoned me to follow him. I was led into an inner room, which was furnished with just a cot. On one wall was a framed painting of Dadaji's own spiritual mentor, Sri Satyanarayana. It is said that there really was no such person as Sri Satyanarayana (the name means He Who Knows the Truth) and that Dadaji rendered the image from his subconscious.

Dadaji asked me to sit in front of this portrait, which was of an old man in white robes. Sri Satyanarayana's expression was subdued and unsmiling. Dadaji then picked up a small writing pad and asked me to pluck out one sheet. The sheet was the size of a business card. He asked me to hold this sheet, which was perfectly blank on both sides, to my forehead and then bow before the portrait, while pressing the sheet to the floor with my forehead.

I could feel Dadaji's fingers on my spine, kneading the vertebrae.

Dadaji directed me to rise. I removed the paper from my forehead, and looked at it.

Written on one corner was a two-word "mahanam," or personal

message. I couldn't believe my eyes. Dadaji asked me to memorize the two words, saying that this message was my own inner mantra. No two people would have the same mantra, he said. The message was written in red ink in capital letters. Dadaji asked me to fold the paper. I did so, then was asked to straighten out the sheet. Now the mantra in red ink had vanished. The sheet was perfectly blank again.

As Dadaji led me out of the inner room, I became aware of a powerful fragrance emanating from my body. I could smell a mix of sandalwood and jasmine. The fragrance stayed with me for days afterward, through innumerable showers and swims.

"The mahanam, the mantra, comes from within you," Dadaji said later. "I am not your guru. The Lord residing within you is the only Guru."

I told Dadaji about some of my early experiences in Bombay, and he didn't seem surprised.

"What outlandish and preposterous practices are furthered in the name of the Lord!" he said. "All those who claim to be gurus and reside in ashrams and temples are misguided souls who in turn misguide their unsuspecting followers and seekers who thus become victims of traditional superstition. Our scriptures have been misinterpreted to suit the convenience of a few religious heads who have vested interests in organized religion. You need not don ocher robes, sport long beards and matted hair, or renounce worldly duties and live in seclusion from society for the sake of Truth."

I asked Dadaji what I should do with my mantra.

"Recite it slowly whenever you need peace and strength," he said.

The India of gurus and swamis is one India, and one with which the outside world is familiar because of the publicity generated by peripatetic godmen like the Maharishi Mahesh Yogi, the guru of the Beatles. Many non-Indians are unaware of the multidimensional nature of Indian culture. Indigenous Indian drama and literature are thriving as never before, and the Indian film has emerged as a powerful medium of social inquiry.

Although successive governments have vigorously promoted cultural activities, the arts in India are traditionally regional in nature —which explains their vitality: state governments in the country spend large sums to encourage the establishment of drama, dance, and literary academies; government awards are given to playwrights and writers and poets. Patronage of the arts, in fact, is an ancient tradition in India. The rajahs and maharajahs of the country supported court poets and writers and musicians. Why? Because such patronage assured them a good reputation. The scribes and musicians praised their patrons; they raised the rajahs to the level of legend; they mythologized their deeds; they gave them an eternal life. In Sanskrit, the process of such praise was called "stuthi pathak" ("praising the sponsor")—a cheeky term, actually, and one that subtly alluded to the fact that even those who praised sometimes injected veiled criticism of their patrons's ways.

As the power and the influence of India's royalty waned during the ascendancy of the British Raj, regional literary activities correspondingly declined—but did not die. In thousands of villages all across India, peasants fashioned entertainment for other peasants by putting on plays based on religious and mythological themes. This village tradition came to be known as "lalith." The players would daub their faces with colored paste and assume the roles of mythological figures. The theme of such entertainment almost always was the triumph of good over evil. These village plays were not merely straight narrative; music, too, was incorporated into the entertainment. Complementing the village plays were the troubadours, who traveled from community to community, and sang songs with mythological themes. This oral tradition still lives on in India's villages.

Toward the end of the nineteenth century, the social reformist and nationalist movements that had sprouted in areas such as Bengal and Maharashtra helped to give a fresh stimulus to literature and drama in the Indian languages. Writers helped to generate a new wave of awareness concerning injustice and such pressing social problems as child marriage, bride abuse, and neglect of women's social and educational status. Even as people like Bal Gangadhar Tilak and Mohandas

Gandhi—soon to be known as the "Mahatma," or great soul—were developing a national political movement that would years later culminate in independence, a number of literary giants were sculpting formidable reputations and gathering large numbers of followers: Bharatendu Harishchandra, who wrote in Hindi; Bankim Chandra Chatterji and Sir Rabindranath Tagore, the Bengali writers; Veeresalingam, the Telugu scribe; Subramanya Bharati, the Tamil writer; and Chiplunkar, Kirloskar, Deval, Khadilkar, Sripad Krishna Kolhatkar, and Ram Ganesh Gadkari, the Marathi writers.

The chief contribution of these writers lay not only in the delight they gave to their audiences through plays and novels and poems and essays. It was these writers, perhaps more than the political activists, who brought about an extraordinary social awakening in Indian society. The Maharashtra playwright Deval wrote a play called *Sharda* that dealt with the taboo topic of child marriage. It was not uncommon during the nineteenth and early twentieth centuries for elderly brahmans to marry prepubescent girls. The bridegrooms would often die, leaving their child brides destitute and uncared for: remarriage was frowned upon, and these "widows" wound up as beggars—they were required to shave their heads and wear only white sarees. *Sharda* was so powerful a play that it resulted in a series of government measures forbidding child marriages. Another writer, Ram Ganesh Gadkari, depicted the evils of drink in *Ekach Pyala* ("Only one drink"), which contained so strong a social message that civic societies were formed to crusade against liquor consumption. Marathi-language literature, along with Bengali literature, flourished because Maharashtrians and Bengalis had a shared tradition of high literacy, concern with social issues, and of political awareness.

I particularly cite Marathi literature because it remains in my view the most vibrant and creative regional cultural exposition in India. It was the dramatist Khadilkar who introduced political satire aimed at the British colonial rule. He cleverly disguised his barbs in a play called *Kichak Vaad*, which employed mythological themes but which was a veiled attack against the tyranny of foreign rule. The play, in fact, was subsequently banned by the British, who had caught on to its real message. The first truly good humor was also seen on the Marathi stage, in Gadkari's *Vedyancha Bazaar,* which poked gentle fun at contemporary social mores. Complementing Marathi drama and literature were journalistic writers such as Agarkar and Phule, who also helped to increase social attention on injustices through theri thundering editorials.

"Today's writers owe a great debt to these early pioneers," says Charusheela Gupte, my mother and author of nearly one hundred Marathi novels, plays, and children's books. "These pioneers laid a very strong foundation for subsequent social inquiry through drama and literature. Literature reflects life, and writers like Khadilkar and Gadkari and Hari Narayan Apte painted word-portraits of the society that existed during their time. Their technique was to compare the circumstances of their time with India's golden past, and to draw from such comparisons lessons for the future."

This technique has been borrowed by such contemporary writers as Gopal Sharman of the Akshara Theater in Delhi. Sharman is best known for his version of the *Ramayana,* India's great epic. Sharman is essentially a classicist steeped in Sanskrit scriptures, and he was intrigued by the story and plot of the *Ramayana.* The epic's origins are shrouded in mystery, although many Sanskrit scholars say that it was composed by the poet-sage Valmiki before 500 B.C. The story is simple: King Rama of Ayodhya (a part of what is now called Uttar Pradesh state) and his lovely wife, Sita, daughter of King Janaka of Videha, have been exiled by Rama's weak father, King Dashratha, at the behest of Dashratha's wife, Kekeyi. Sita is then kidnapped by King Ravana of Lanka. Ravana is popularly depicted as a multiheaded demon, not unlike Shakespeare's "hydra-headed monster." Rama sets out in pursuit of Ravana and enlists the assistance of Hanuman, a monkey god. Eventually, Ravana is found and killed, and Sita is reunited with her husband. But Rama now suspects Sita of infidelity and banishes her. The final reunion occurs in heaven. The plot of the *Ramayana* has been interpreted by many scholars as an allegory of Aryan and pre-Aryan conflict, which ended in the Aryan conquest of much of India's south.

The *Ramayana* was a mirror of its time. Stanley Wolpert, the California historian who researched the epic, says that the *Ramayana* gives many insights into the character of later Aryan court life. It tells of the machinations and endless intrigue of the aging King Dashratha's three wives, who struggle and conspire to place their own sons in the position of heir apparent. Wolpert points out how powerful a force religious law, or dharma, had become in dictating "proper" behavior for both the common man and for monarchs. The *Ramayana* shows the contrast between the decadence of the royal court and the austerity of forest hermitages. "The spiritual as well as economic interdependence between the settled city and the untamed forest regions of the still predominantly wild Gangetic plain helps us understand better the process through which the gradual socioeconomic transition of North India was affected in this epic era," declares Wolpert.

The *Ramayana* is India's most popular epic, a romance that has been told and retold over the centuries in drama, poetry, novels, and films. But Gopal Sharman felt that it needed a new interpretation for modern times. So fourteen years ago, he wrote his version of the *Ramayana*, in English—as an one-actor play. Sharman's wife, the noted actress Jalabala Vaidya, was cast in all twenty-two roles. The play has since been performed fifteen hundred times in India and abroad, and has become the most successful single production in the history of the Indian theater. One reason for Sharman's success is the fact that his *Ramayana* cuts out the epic's original medieval and fairy-tale qualities. Rama and Sita are presented not as awe-inspiring mythological figures but as flesh-and-blood human beings who are undergoing severe trauma in their personal lives. There are allusions in Sharman's play to contemporary stresses on domestic life, so that the *Ramayana* is far more relevant to today's audiences than the earlier versions, which tended to merely glorify the central characters.

"The questions I had in mind when I wrote my *Ramayana* were: what does all our inherited spiritual mumbo jumbo mean? Does India's mythology have any relevance for modern times? Should we be simply inveigling audiences into suspending their disbelief? Or should we invite their participation by presenting historical themes in a contemporary light so that the past and the present are fused?" Sharman said, as we sat one afternoon in his Delhi garden under pipal and neem trees. It was hard to believe that we were actually right in the middle of Delhi's busiest neighborhood: Gopal Sharman and Jalabala Vaidya own a quaint bungalow that the architect Lutyens built for his engineers while they were at work on constructing New Delhi. Once there were many such bungalows in this area, but now only the Sharmans' one remains—the rest have been torn down to make way for expensive apartment blocks. The success of his *Ramayana* has enabled Sharman to design a small theater on the premises, where his Akshara Theater Repertory puts on his works (he has written a dozen plays and is now working on one based on the life of Indira Gandhi). Sharman is a skilled carpenter and self-taught electrician, among other things, and every seat in the auditorium, every gadget, and every spotlight were personally fashioned and installed by him. The stunning posters and brochures of his plays are similarly designed by Sharman, with help, of course, from Jalabala Vaidya and her daughter, Anasuya, who runs the repertory's commercial side. Patrons at the performances can not only enjoy themselves during intermissions in the Sharmans' garden, they also are given soup that Jalabala Vaidya makes from vegetables grown in her own garden.

Sharman is angered by the fact that many theater groups in India have been deeply politicized. He is especially troubled by the export of these groups's products, which seem to say that all is unwell in the country. "We decided a long time ago that even though we get frequent opportunities to travel abroad, we wouldn't go around telling the world this was a wretched country—it is very fashionable among some in the theater crowd to denigrate India in their work," Sharman said. "We simply aren't part of the anti-Establishment Establishment." Through his plays, Sharman has openly portrayed India's social ills—such as the increasing strains on family cohesion, the question of drug abuse among the affluent young, sexual promiscuity in the cities. Sharman is attempting to generate social dialogue in the country through his plays; but the bottom line is always renewal of hope and faith in traditional Indian culture. Jalabala Vaidya said: "We want our theater to be a home for the mind of India."

Sharman had spoken about certain theater groups that went abroad and denigrated India. But there are these days many more troupes setting forth from Indian shores to project a less political and less ideological image of the country abroad. The man in charge of such sanitized cultural exports is Pascal Alan Nazareth, India's cultural commissar. Even among the highly critical and inbred community of top government bureaucrats in Delhi there is general agreement that Nazareth, a member of the Indian Foreign Service, has worked wonders as executive secretary of the Indian Council for Cultural Relations. The council is a government-funded autonomous body which coordinates all projects concerning the projection of Indian culture abroad; it also handles the visits of foreign artists to India. While I was in Delhi, the Bolshoi Ballet was giving performances under the auspices of ICCR, and some days later, Nureyev and his Paris Ballet Company turned up in the capital city, as the council's guests.

I had known Nazareth when he was India's high commissioner, or ambassador, in Ghana; I was the Africa correspondent for the *New York Times* in those days and would occasionally visit Ghana on business. Nazareth had impressed me as a dedicated envoy who worked terribly hard to further India's diplomatic and commercial interests, and I felt that he would go far in the foreign service. His appointment as India's chief cultural official, therefore, was no surprise to me. But perhaps even Nazareth, familiar though he was with the ponderous ways of government bureaucracy, was not prepared for the mess the council was in. When he took up his post in Delhi, there was a huge backlog of bills payable; there was little coordination between the council and its external representatives; favoritism was rampant, and mediocre artists often got sent abroad because they had good political connections. And third-rate, unheard-of performers from abroad frequently got invited to India, often because some cabinet minister enjoyed dalliances with someone connected with these groups.

What Pascal Alan Nazareth did, with verve and ruthlessness, was to streamline the council's operations. He introduced professionalism to the agency, whose annual budget of $3 million is entirely paid for by the government. By better management and closer attention to expenditures, Nazareth was able to triple the council's activities without increasing the budget. Nazareth was very selective about what foreign culture would be imported under official aegis: no more punk rock groups—in the last two years, Nazareth was able to attract to India the New York Philharmonic, the Metropolitan Opera, La Scala Opera from Milan, Nureyev, the Bolshoi Ballet, the Royal Ballet, and other top troupes. Moreover, Nazareth persuaded Doordarshan, the Indian television network, to broadcast live these performances so that the foreigners were assured of vast audiences all across India. For instance, it is estimated that more than 100 million people watched Zubin Mehta's televised concert. Nazareth has also persuaded several Western television networks to broadcast documentaries on Indian dance, drama, and music; he has sponsored seminars on Indian culture in Greece, Britain, Italy, the United States, and the Soviet Union; he has organized exhibits on India in Australia, Japan, and in several Latin American countries. "It was the coordinated effort that was really needed," Nazareth, a slim, balding man, told me. "I think we can confidently say now that India, in terms of credibility for cultural handling, has more than come of age." One of Nazareth's innovations was to bring private sector participation into the official cultural scene: he now farms out to private concerns such things as brochure production, tour group planning, and ticketing. Nazareth also persuaded the government-owned television network to broadcast Kenneth Clark's acclaimed series, *Civilization*. Nazareth has shown that imagination and innovation have a very large role to play in contemporary India, and I admire him for it.

Both Pascal Alan Nazareth and Gopal Sharman had a common patron saint: Indira Gandhi. It was Mrs. Gandhi who approved Nazareth's ambitious proposals concerning the council. Nazareth shrewdly cultivated such key Gandhi allies as Pupul Jayakar—long regarded as India's cultural czarina—who was instrumental in persuading the prime minister to channel funds into promoting cultural activities.

(Mrs. Gandhi made it a point to attend concerts and shows sponsored by the council, and often invited visiting foreign artists to her home for dinner. Nazareth told me about the time the prime minister asked Richard Kness of New York's Metropolitan Opera Company to her home because she had missed seeing him on stage. Ness was so touched that he got on his knees and sang a tune from *South Pacific*, "If I loved you." Nazareth recalls that Mrs. Gandhi blushed through the song. On another occasion, the Zimbabwe National Dance Company performed on her lawn at One Safdarjung Road, and the prime minister joined the dancers for a few steps, much to the visitors' delight.

(A number of people who knew Mrs. Gandhi well told me about her fascination with intellectuals and artists. Shehbaz Safrani, a scholar and painter who now lives in New York City, pointed to the prime minister's long friendship with Dorothy Norman, the New York photographer and writer, and with Buckminster Fuller, the architect. Mrs. Gandhi also corresponded regularly with Irish writer Darina Silone, the wife of the distinguished Italian novelist Ignazio Silone. Whenever Mrs. Gandhi came to New York, she would ask her friend and confidant Ralph Buultjens to arrange small dinners so that she could meet American writers and thinkers. "Indira Gandhi had a small but efficient culture network all over the world," Safrani says. "That is how she kept herself abreast of global literary and aesthetic trends.")

There are those who suspect—and I am among them—that Indira Gandhi will be best remembered for her attention to and encouragement of cultural activities. She was modern India's leading patron of culture. Back in the late 1970s, when Sir John Thomson, then the British envoy in New Delhi, proposed that an exhibition of Indian antiquities be held in London, Mrs. Gandhi shot back with the suggestion to instead host a "Festival of India," in which the entire, awesome range of Indian art, past and present, would be displayed before British audiences. Such a "festival" was held in Britain in 1982 —and it was hugely successful; in addition to reactivating Britons interest in the cultural heritage of their former colony, the festival helped to stimulate fresh commerce between Britain and India. The significant thing about the "Festival of India" was this: it gave a foreign audience a holistic sense of the continuity of Indian culture; and the "festival" was run not in the traditional, lackadaisical Indian bureaucratic manner, but in a modern, managerial way.

The success of the British "Festival of India" was not only because of Mrs. Gandhi's personal interest in celebrating Indian culture. It was also because of her choice of two key figures to help run the festival—Pupul Jayakar, and a young Indian Foreign Service officer named Niranjan Desai. Mrs. Jayakar conceived many of the main exhibits and arranged for priceless objets d'art to be shipped from India to British museums; because of her longstanding friendship with Indira Gandhi, Mrs. Jayakar was in a position to reflect in the organization of the festival the wishes of the prime minister herself. Desai, a low-key, gracious man with political savvy and managerial sense, was the day-to-day coordinator of the festival: it was Desai who rode herd, and who smoothed out the inevitable frictions arising out of managing such a large-scale enterprise. Naturally, Desai made a few enemies in the moribund Indian bureaucracy; but he ensured that the festival won for India millions of new friends in Britain.

The Pupul Jayakar–Niranjan Desai team was asked by Mrs. Gandhi to stage an encore in the United States. The team was assisted by some astute "culture-managers"—the Delhi designer Rajeev Sethi; S. K. Misra, a top bureaucrat in the Indian government; and Ted M. G. Tanen, a former American Foreign Service official, who now ran the Indo-American Subcommission for Education and Culture in New York. Their efforts resulted in an American "Festival of India," the biggest cultural happening of its kind in the United States, which Mrs. Gandhi's son and successor, Rajiv Gandhi, inaugurated in Washington on June 13, 1985, along with Vice President George Bush. President Ronald Reagan characterized the festival as a living memorial to Indira Gandhi—who had hoped to inaugurate it. Hosting art and other exhibits were institutions and museums in 90 cities in 36 states; on display were not only Indian antiques, but also rural and tribal art. Scores of Indian writers, poets, dancers, musicians, painters, and sculptors would be visiting the United States. The festival will run through 1986, and Desai says he expects that it will lead to an increase in commerce between India and her biggest trading partner, the United States (the two-way trade between the two countries now is estimated at $4 billion annually), and to an increase in tourism.

There has been criticism in India, of course, concerning the $5 million or so that the Indian government has invested in the $15 million festival—and there have been suggestions that Mrs. Jayakar has engaged in cultural empire building! But my own feeling is that such criticism is politically motivated and comes from people who are personally hostile to Mrs. Jayakar and resentful of her warm relations with the Gandhi family. I don't think that Pupul Jayakar, at seventy-one years of age, entertains grand dreams of empire-building. In my conversations with her, she struck me as a very knowledgeable person who is passionately committed to the proper projection abroad of India's extraordinary cultural heritage. And the evidence suggests that her approach to such projection—through "festivals of India" —is creating a new atmosphere of appreciation of India; in France, for example, a India festival opened in early June 1985 and was an instant smash hit. The Soviet Union and West Germany are in the process of fashioning similar festivals. And the Indian festival appears to have encouraged the Chinese government to want to stage a "Festival of China" in the United States in 1989.

I met Niranjan Desai a few days after the June inaugural of the festival at the Kennedy Center in Washington. He was uncharacteristically exuberant. For it had been a dazzling event—Ravi Shankar gave a sitar recital; Ali Akbar Khan performed on the sarod; and Alla Rakha and his son, Zakir Hussain, played the tablas. Desai told me that he hoped that the festival will take the mystery out of India and make her culture more intelligible to ordinary Americans. Mrs. Jayakar and Desai had expected that one of their biggest problems would be to attract media attention for the festival. But the plucky are sometimes lucky: a groundswell of interest in India was building up in the United States because of the wide popularity of the television series *The Jewel in the Crown,* based on the British writer Paul Scott's *Raj Quartet,* and of two award-winning films—David Lean's adaptation of E. M. Forster's novel *A Passage to India,* and Sir Richard Attenborough's *Gandhi,* a dramatic chronicle of the life of Mahatma Gandhi. Niranjan Desai says that by the time Prime Minister Rajiv Gandhi arrived in the United States in June 1985 to inaugurate the festival, "America was ready for India."

The "Festival of India" is the latest and the biggest display of Indian culture abroad, and it would seem that a country like India, with its ancient traditions and heritage, must have been putting on such grand cultural shows abroad for a long time. Not so. To be sure, various foreign museums from time to time hosted displays of Indian art. But it was only in 1978 that the Indian international airline, Air India, exported an exhibition of costumes and dresses called "Sringar"—which translates as "decoration." That show was seen by audiences in a dozen American cities, and has since toured all over the world.

One of the unheralded but dynamic forces behind the projection and promotion of Indian culture abroad in the last seven years has been a handsome, dimunitive Bombay-born woman named Pallavi Shah. She works for Air India in New York, and along with her colleague, Mahendrasinhji Chudasama, has conceived and actualized dozens of Indian cultural shows in the United States and elsewhere. Mrs. Shah's philosophy is simple: "You can continue being misunderstood—or you can do something about it." She has long felt that most Westerners simply do not know what Indian culture is all about. It is not only about gurus and mantras, Mrs. Shah says. "India is one of the cradles of civilization—and in contemporary India, a 5,000-year-old culture is alive, well, and flourishing," she said to me when we met in Bombay. "Maybe what puzzles many foreigners is that our 'culture' is not fossilized and preserved in museums—that it is a living culture!"

The innovation that Pallavi Shah has brought to India's "culture business" is in the use of modern marketing techniques. She seeks out museum officials all over the United States and persuades them to incorporate displays of Indian art or handicrafts or dances in their programs; she visits schools and gives demonstrations of such things as "rangoli," the Indian ritual of tracing decorative patterns on the floor with colored powder during auspicious occasions. Mrs. Shah also enlists the help of Americans in raising funds for Indian programs. "There is no better way to bridge alien cultures than through staging cultural displays and performances," she says.

As part of the "Festival of India," dozens of Indian films will be screened in American cities and towns. The film is the most popular form of public entertainment in India; television is still in its infancy, and dance and the theater are beyond the financial reach of most people. India turns out nearly a thousand feature films in a dozen languages each year, which makes it the world's biggest producer of films. In addition to the feature films, hundreds of documentaries are also made each year.

It is very big business indeed, with top stars like Amitabh Bachchan demanding and receiving from producers the equivalent of almost a million dollars per film; producers can afford to pay such prices because the inclusion or exclusion of top stars can make or break films at the box office. It is the practice among some stars to ask producers to cough up most of their fees in cash, some of it in hard currency such as the American dollar. Most Indian films, but especially the Hindustani ones manufactured in the Bombay film factories, are fashioned to a formula: two or three stars; lots of pathos; several violent fight scenes; suggestions of rape; a car chase; one or two deaths, preferably of a doting father or a devoted mother, at the hands of the villain; and at least a half-dozen shrill songs (virtually every Hindustani film is a musical). The Indian censors do not permit kissing scenes in Indian films on the grounds that such amorous public displays run counter to Indian traditions and sensibilities— although kissing and some nudity are permissible in foreign films shown in India.

The critic Amita Malik has remarked that when the Lumière brothers of France held their first bioscope show at the Elphinstone Theatre in Bombay in 1896, they could scarcely have anticipated that they were helping plant the seeds of the Indian cinema industry. The Frenchmen showed two films, *Arrival and Departure of a Train* and *Bathers in the Sea,* which were elementary works showing people and objects in movement. Malik says that the arrival of the cinema in India could not have been better timed: it was the turn of the century, and urban audiences clamored for mass entertainment. For these mass audiences, Malik says, the cinema with its direct visual impact, its easy accessibility, and its relatively straightforward themes seemed "the natural answer."

The commercial possibility of the film medium was not lost on a young Indian who had been studying engineering in Europe in those early days of the century. The student, Dadasaheb Phalke—later to be called the father of the Indian cinema—was so moved by a film he saw in London on the life of Christ that he forthwith returned home, sold his wife's jewels, and produced *Raja Harishchandra,* India's first feature film. The film dealt with the life of a mythological king who renounces worldly life and seeks solace in the wilderness. Phalke's script embodied the age-old "good-over-evil" theme, to which illiterate audiences responded mightily. As Amita Malik has written, Phalke lived long enough to see that the safest box office guarantees in India came from the mythological film.

The "Golden Age" of the Indian film is widely agreed to have been in the 1930s, when several large studios flourished not only in Bombay but also in places like Calcutta. Besides mythological themes, directors tackled such social topics as untouchability, child labor, and abuse of women. But in the wake of World War II, the studio system collapsed in India (the financial pinch of the war, and generally rigorous wartime conditions had started the decline of these great studios). Men who had made fortunes in the wartime black market now fancied themselves as bigtime producers à la Hollywood; they pumped millions of rupees into the film business, setting up the star system and devising the box office formula. With the lavish attention of these new film tycoons, the world of Bombay's movie industry started to grow very rich indeed. The movies these tycoons made were generally drivel—but that was exactly what India's overwhelmingly poor and illiterate audiences seemed to want.

"Most Indian films are pure fantasy," says Bhaichand Patel, who writes frequently on the Indian film scene. "They are fairy tales. They depict splendor and wealth that are beyond the grasp of most Indians. If you are an ordinary Indian who lives in a chawl, an urban tenement, or in some dilapidated village, then going to a film is an escape —an escape from the drudgery and terror of daily life. Indian films are really pure escapism—which, in an overwhelmingly poor country like India, explains why they are so popular with the masses."

These films continue to be popular with overseas Indians as well, who cannot seem to break the viewing habits acquired in their native land. There is a great demand for the latest Hindustani films from Indians who emigrated to the oil-rich states of the Middle East, and to the West. Even the Arabs are hooked on the Indian cinema— Hindustani film music, with its gay rhythms and lyrics, mirrors Arabic popular music. For instance, films made decades ago by the legendary producer-actor-director Raj Kapoor—such as *Awaara, 420,* and *Sangam*—are still packing 'em into theaters of the Middle East. How often have I traveled in taxis in Amman and Damascus and Cairo and Beirut and Bahrain and Casablanca and Tunis and Aden and heard cab drivers merrily whistling tunes from these films.

If Raj Kapoor is still the idol of millions of filmgoers in the Middle East and India who seek song-soaked and romance-ridden entertainment, Satyajit Ray remains the hero of the more serious movie fans. Among cognoscenti in the West, Ray, not Raj Kapoor, is the true artist. Influenced in his early years by the films of the French director Jean Renoir, Ray's own works have been masterpieces of humanism and cinematic technique: his films have been described by critics all over the world as possessing lyricism and a poetic quality, works of carefully constructed art that are played out at a leisurely pace. Not for Ray the cheap thrills and car chases of the commercial Hindi cinema; he shows in films like *Pathar Panchali* (The Ballad of the Road) and the Apu Trilogy the special impact that everyday problems of poverty and domestic strife have on ordinary people; in *Distant Thunder,* Ray dealt with the dread topic of famine—and how it could have been avoided had men been more humane to men. In *The Chess Players,* Ray captures the languor of a Muslim community in British India where the colonial rulers, their poor subjects, and the decadent local royalty lead lives that are compartmentalized, and strange and often bewildering to one another. Through his works, Satyajit Ray brought Indian films to the attention of a world audience. Moreover, by energetically promoting the Calcutta Film Society—which aims to make audiences more cultivated in their tastes —Ray has in effect raised the expectations of his audiences; there now are film societies all over India, and for their rapidly growing numbers of members film is now as much a medium of entertainment as it is a topic for vigorous intellectual discussion and analysis.

Ray has influenced a whole generation of filmmakers who view their medium as a powerful instrument of social inquiry—although by no means is Ray a fiery crusader for social causes. The work of these filmmakers has given rise to what is known in India as the "parallel cinema." Call it if you will cinema verité, or docudrama; but the productions of these men and women are sophisticated and focus powerfully on such ongoing social problems as bride burning, dowries, exploitation of women, alcoholism, child prostitution, gambling, and oppression by landlords. Perhaps more than any political rhetoric has, these films drew national attention to the problems of social inequity and injustice, sometimes resulting in corrective legislation. Some of the earliest exponents of the "parallel cinema" were Bengal's Mrinal Sen, Sayeed Mirza, Girish Karnad, and Mani Kaul (who once infuriated colleagues by declaring that he made films for his own satisfaction and that he did not care if people saw them or not!). Now there is yet another generation of "parallel cinema" directors: Gautam Ghosh, Govind Nihalani, Ketan Mehta, and Gopalkrishnan. Their films tend to be more politicized than those of their predecessors; and the new purveyors of the "parallel cinema" see themselves shaping audiences' social awareness and sensibilities, and also, of course, providing people with entertainment. (I should like to point here that although the cinema is India's most popular source of entertainment in cities and villages alike, it has brought about the death of an ancient source of entertainment in rural areas—puppetry. Ironically, the world's biggest collection of Indian puppets is no longer in India but at the American Museum of Natural History in New York City.)

The man who can be said to be a true inheritor of Satyajit Ray's mantle is Shyam Benegal of Bombay.

I went to see Benegal in his office on Tardeo Road in Bombay, a bustling commercial thoroughfare within sight of the Arabian Sea. The building was modern, but his suite was not—I thought for a moment that I was in some bus depot, so packed with supplicants, petitioners, and technicians were the three rooms used by the director. In one room, a film crew was shooting footage for titles; in still another room, an editor was splicing film. The spicy odor of curry suffused the suite. The walls were festooned with posters from Benegal's dozen films.

Benegal is a man of medium height with a cheerful manner and a bearded, high-crowned face that makes him look well beyond his age of fifty. He had just returned from a filming trip to Goa, and he was plainly tired. The last ten years have involved constant film production for him—not only his dozen feature films but also scores of documentaries and advertising shorts, which generate the wherewithal for Benegal's "parallel cinema" work. Benegal has also been producing instructional films for farming communities in different parts of India; the films employ a story line and their characters deal with such topics as peanut cultivation, animal husbandry, and pest control. Although most of these short films are made in Hindi, they are dubbed into nine languages. Benegal sees these films as not only offering instruction to peasants and farmers but as starting points for serious discussions on improving the quality of life in rural areas.

Benegal shot to fame when he made a feature film titled *Ankur,* which was about exploitation of women in rural India; it won several Indian awards and critical acclaim abroad as well. He subsequently made *Manthan,* depicting the lives of dairy farmers in the western state of Gujerat. No major stars were used in the film, only stage actors and real-life farmers. The film bagged several major Indian and Western awards for Benegal; perhaps more importantly, it consolidated Benegal's status as an innovative filmmaker. The critical and financial successes of *Ankur* and *Manthan* enabled him in subsequent films to continue exploring such controversial subjects as the failure of land reform and the cruelties of the caste system. Benegal went into India's villages to grasp and depict everyday realities of the rural poor. For him it was important to understand and tell the story of the great divide that exists between urban and rural life in contemporary India. Benegal was interested in the social arrangements between people in deprived communities; he investigated the codes of caste; he studied beliefs and attitudes. All along his central question was: am I getting the intangible essence of a situation?

"I like to think of myself as a chronicler of my times," Bengal told me, over successive cups of tea. "I am very interested in the forces, often unseen, that have shaped societies and individuals. In making my films, I set out to discover what are the reference points for individuals or social groups that make them what they are or that make them turn."

Benegal is fascinated by what he calls the "balance of life" in today's India—how people manage to retain perspective and hope even in the midst of soul-crushing poverty. He is excited by the political changes taking place, and he shares many of Rajiv Gandhi's goals of economic development. But he doesn't see himself as a political filmmaker. His role is that of someone who undertakes social inquiry.

"To help ourselves understand what this extraordinary mosaic called India is all about—that is how I see my role as a filmmaker," Benegal said. "We live in exciting and excitable times, and the responsibility of a filmmaker such as myself is now even greater to be rational, to be reflective, to never stop asking questions about where we are headed."

In asking his questions, Benegal worries that his films might get too simplistic. His obligation to his art, he says, is to strike a "balance" himself: the plots must not be complex, but the characters must be, for people are filled with complexities. His are not the kinds of films that owners of video cassette players in the expatriate Indian communities of the Middle East, London, and New York City necessarily rush out to acquire, of course. There are those critics who have expressed reservations over Benegal's cerebral approach to filmmaking—but his response is that films, especially those involving social inquiry, must make audiences both feel and think.

Such an approach also has attracted one of Benegal's great friends, Shashi Kapoor, to the "parallel cinema." Kapoor is a product of India's dazzling commercial film world, a man who has probably starred in more Indian films than anyone else. Kapoor, the younger brother of veteran filmmaker Raj Kapoor, was trained at the Royal Academy of Dramatic Art in London and for many years was part of a Shakespeareana touring company led by the famed Kendall family of Britain (Kapoor in fact married the boss's daughter, Jennifer Kendall; she died of cancer in 1984). When he found his personal finances languishing, Kapoor followed the lead of his father, Prithviraj, and his two older brothers, Raj and Shammi, and entered the world of the commercial cinema. His fresh, boyish face, his shy smile, and his youthful build helped catapult Shashi Kapoor to the top of the heap within a short time. Shashi Kapoor has also acted in and financially supported several art-house films made by James Ivory and Ismail Merchant of New York, including the critically acclaimed *Heat and Dust.*

Kapoor, of course, continues to retain one foot in the commercial cinema camp: that is where he makes his millions, which enable him to support such "parallel cinema" ventures as *Utsav,* a historical film

with contemporary themes. But Kapoor is finding that so commer-
cial-minded are India's major film distributors that no one is willing
to buy the rights to this film. In an industry dominated by stars whose
education, literacy, and perhaps even intelligence are limited, Shashi
Kapoor comes across as a remarkably sophisticated man, and one who
is unafraid to challenge verbally the titans of Bombay's film world.
Kapoor invited me one morning to accompany him to Bombay's
Mehboob Studios, where he was to attend the "mahuraat," or inaugural rituals, for a new film.

As we drove to the studios, Kapoor complained bitterly about how
films that lacked "commercial sex appeal" simply stood no chance
with the country's "fatcat" distributors. But India needed to encourage filmmakers of all sorts, Kapoor said. He didn't think that the
government's agency for financially backing struggling filmmakers,
the National Film Development Corporation, was as yet sufficiently
tuned in to the growing needs of such producers. Kapoor, who spoke
in a mix of English and Hindi, continued in this vein even as we
reached the studios, where a mob awaited the star. After a frenetic
session of dispensing his autographs, we were led into a cavernous
studio, where a set of a nightclub had been constructed. "Extras," or
winsome starlets, clustered about, casting provocative glances at Kapoor; servants circulated with steaming tea in tiny glasses; a brahman
priest stood in one corner before portraits of various Hindu gods,
whose blessings would soon be invoked to make this film a success.
Production on Indian films rarely starts without such a "mahuraat"
ceremony.

Kapoor later told me that he was dismayed that the outside world,
and especially American audiences, did not sufficiently understand
the realities of everyday India. One of the chief culprits in this, he
said, was the Indian commercial filmmaker, whose work rarely reflected the wondrous ethnic and regional diversity of India and who
simply did not bother to reach out to foreign audiences because his
money making was assured by tapping the mother lode in India and
among Indian emigrants in selective states abroad. "The Indian
social scene needs to be projected more effectively to foreign audi-

ences," Kapoor said. "Here is the world's biggest democracy, a real-life, alive-and-kicking democracy—and how many Americans really know how we live?" Now Kapoor has done something revolutionary in the Indian cinema: he has produced a film whose male leading character is a Sikh—the part is played by Kapoor's son, Kunal (who is not a Sikh, of course). Although Sikhs are a significant minority, no commercial film had ever had a Sikh hero. In the light of recent events, I thought Shashi Kapoor to be a brave producer indeed.

Some days later, I mentioned my conversation with Shashi Kapoor to Tina Khote, a producer of documentaries in Bombay. She agreed with Kapoor's assessment. "The commercial film industry in India has lost touch completely with contemporary reality," Khote said, as we lunched at the United Services Club one balmy afternoon. The club was a relic from the Raj: liveried waiters, well-kept lawns smooth enough to skate on, frangipani and magnolia, bougainvillea, Victorian-style bungalows, and palms that swayed gently in the brine-freighted breeze from the Arabian Sea. "Those who cannot make the time-honored commercial formula work then regress into sexploitation. Do you know what packs audiences in these days? Rape scenes. After all, over seven hundred feature films being made each year, with competition so great, producers need a new gimmick to attract audiences. Except that these Indian producers are now engaged in exploiting the problems of women."

I had sought a meeting with Tina Khote because she had acquired a formidable reputation as a producer of socially relevant documentaries. One of her films, a work on bonded labor, recently won the top award at the Delhi International Film Festival. Khote, Polish-American by birth, Canadian by nationality, and a resident of India for more than thirty years, is married to Bakul Khote, one of modern India's senior industrial managers and son of Durga Khote, a veteran actress of the Indian stage and screen. Her financial security thus assured, Khote has been able to devote much time and energy to exploring social issues. Her documentaries have focused, among other things, on the rural and agricultural scene, and on the problems of the environment and women's issues. She specializes in twenty- and thirty-minute featurettes. Khote's innovations lie in the fact that in her films she seeks ways to depict women in a nonsubservient manner; she shows girls attending school; she shows equality in relations between men and women; and she shows small families—never more than two children to a couple. Thus, all these messages—female emancipation, family planning, female literacy—are continually fed to her audiences in a manner that is not grating or proselytizing.

Like Shashi Kapoor, Tina Khote feels that the "real" India—the India of ethnic and social diversity, the India of industrial progress, the India of democracy—is not adequately projected before foreign audiences. Film can be an ideal vehicle for such projection, Khote told me. What was needed was the participation of Indian sponsors, government and private, to enable dedicated filmmakers to make socially relevant films that could be promoted abroad.

"This country is humming with action," Khote said. "Look around you. You've been traveling through India. Isn't there a new excitement in the air? Don't you think the story of this India should be told with pride?"

Tina Khote—blonde, blue-eyed, exceptionally fit for someone who was already a grandmother, passionate in her speech and reflective in her thoughts, and deeply caring about her adopted country—certainly could induce her guest to nod in agreement.

I had seen for myself how film stars reigned India's modern-day gods. The sight of scores of studio hands and fans gawking at Shashi Kapoor that day at Mehboob Studios was unforgettable. But what was it really like to work in the modern Indian film industry? And even though Hindustani films dealt so much with fantasy and escapism, how did their purveyors relate to the currents and crosscurrents of contemporary India?

I posed these questions to a long-time friend named Madhur Jaffrey. She had made a name for herself in the United States and Britain as the author of several best-selling books on Indian cuisine.

In Britain, Jaffrey had hosted a widely watched television series on Indian cooking. And she had acted in such acclaimed Western-made films as *Heat and Dust, Autobiography of a Princess,* and *Shakespearewallah.* But she had never been in an Indian commercial film.

One day in London, the well-known Indian director, Ramesh Sippy, happened to see Jaffrey in *Heat and Dust.* She played the role of a dowager, the mother of an Indian nawab. So impressed was Sippy that he decided to cast Jaffrey in his next big-budget film, *Saagar,* or "Ocean." Jaffrey had many friends in the Indian film world but she had never been exposed to the methodical madness of Indian studios. She told me that she was struck by three things: the mix of technological sophistication and strange working methods; the extraordinary status enjoyed by the director and his stars; and the fact that although modern Indian films were all glamour and glitter, they represented a continuity of ethos from the days of the village bard: good won over evil, heroes prevailed over villains—Indian films were in effect morality plays.

Jaffrey was astonished by the long hours put in by Indian stars, many of whom worked two eight-hour shifts daily in different films! And in moving from shift to shift, often in different studios, these stars would also move from character to character—sometimes from hero to villain, from saint to sinner. "For me the hardest thing was to get a proper script," Jaffrey recalled; frequently, the scripts would be given to the actors minutes before the start of a new scene. And she was surprised by the widespread use of dubbing. Virtually every Hindustani film's soundtrack is rerecorded in a studio after the movie has been completed. That is because the noise level at most Indian film studios is high, and the hum of the humanity waiting outside the studios to gain a glimpse of the stars almost always filters into the sets! Thus, says Jaffrey, she found that her fellow performers often acted with their bodies but not fully with their voices—knowing that they would have a second chance to make good in the dubbing studios!

Madhur Jaffrey, no stranger to celebrity status, was nevertheless bewildered by the pampering of film stars and directors in India.

Everything would be laid on for them—luxury hotels, fine meals, exquisite wines, unlimited liquor, all sorts of entertainment. The stars not only played the roles of gods on the screen; they were gods in real life—they could and command devotion from their fans and their producers.

But why limit such exalted, even divine status only to the film business? Now some stars have parlayed their screen reputations into political careers. India's superstar, Amitabh Bachchan, had long billed himself as one of Rajiv Gandhi's closest friends. During Indira Gandhi's funeral, Bachchan seemed to be more at his side than even Rajiv's wife, Sonia Gandhi. He was endlessly quoted by television and print journalists about how much he had admired the murdered prime minister, how she had been a true mother to him. This sort of loyalty was rewarded by Rajiv Gandhi, who asked Bachchan to run for Parliament on a Congress ticket. Bachchan took on the formidable H. N. Bahuguna, a veteran opposition Member of Parliament, in the Allahabad constituency in Uttar Pradesh. Gandhi came to campaign for Bachchan, and Bachchan won big. Still, I wondered why Amitabh Bachchan really decided to go into politics: was it because of his desire to serve people, or was it because his recent films had been flops? Politics, after all, had traditionally been a means to achieve power and pelf, and a seat in Parliament would also assure Bachchan of continued exposure to the masses.

Two other movie stars were also asked by Rajiv Gandhi to run for Parliament in the December 1984 election. In Madras, the actress Vyjayantimala defeated a senior local politician named Era Sezhian; and in Bombay, Sunil Dutt knocked out one of India's most prominent lawyers and a longtime parliamentarian, Ram Jethmalani. To be sure, these election campaigns were colorful; the star candidates were assisted on the hustings by their glamorous colleagues from filmdom. But many thoughtful people around the country asked the following questions: Were the stars really sincere in their claims that they were joining politics to serve the people? What was their record in public service? Had these stars really served the people by frequently appearing before them in films filled with lurid sexual scenes and disgusting violence? Hadn't the stars encouraged, however indirectly, by their flamboyant roles crimes like rape, murder and gangsterism?

One afternoon in Bombay, I put these very questions to Sunil Dutt. We met at the home of Murli Deora, the local Congress Party boss and another recently successful candidate for Parliament. Dutt, a tall, big-boned man, has been compared to Gary Cooper; he has graced the Indian screen for more than two decades and has also produced films with nationalist themes. He has raised money for India's defense fund. And after his wife, Nargis—herself once a movie star—died of cancer, Sunil Dutt set up a foundation for cancer research and gave millions to establish a special cancer ward in a Bombay hospital. If Indians can spend fortunes building temples, they can surely raise more hospitals, Dutt believes.

"In recent years, I have been affected deeply by two events—the death of my wife, and the murder of Indira Gandhi," Dutt told me. "When I took my wife for cancer treatment in New York, she said she felt so privileged to be able to afford the expensive care—and she said, what about the unfortunate millions back home who would never be able to afford even a fraction of such medical care? That was when I vowed to devote myself to raising funds for cancer work in India.

"The violence that followed Mrs. Gandhi's death shook me. How could we have done those things to other Indians in a civilized country? I felt that people who are sincere about healing our communal wounds should come forward and serve the nation. I know all this sounds very grand. But I really believe in our secular principles. And I consider myself fortunate to have gained a reputation because of my films. So why not exploit that reputation in the service of ordinary people? For me politics is not a passport to glory. I have already achieved all the glory a man might want in his lifetime."

I asked Sunil Dutt how it felt when he was sworn in as a Member of Parliament.

"When I walked into the Lok Sabha, at first it was just another large hall with lots of people," Dutt said. "But then my name was called to take the oath of office. As I walked toward the speaker's dais, it suddenly struck me that down these same aisles had once walked such people as Nehru and Indira Gandhi and Vallabhai Patel. That's when it all hit me—that I was so privileged to be here, that this was a historical trust that I should never abuse. This was no movie studio —it was real life, and I was part of the drama."

6

Expectations

PUNJAB, Kashmir, Delhi, Maharashtra, Andhra, Karnataka, Kerala. I had traveled in pretty much of a north to south pattern, which was the most I could do given the time constraints on my book project. I had landed mostly in the trouble spots of India, areas whose problems—rural, urban, political—were likely to prove thorny, even intractable, for Rajiv Gandhi's new government. I could sense the new expectations for better living conditions generated by the forty-year-old prime minister among everyday people; but I could also sense that the ordinary Indian was not to be so easily seized with soaring hope. After all, much of the new government's rhetoric had been broadcast before—during Indira Gandhi's time.

Among the youthful professionals of India's large cities, however, I discerned a markedly upbeat mood. A whole new generation of professionals has sprouted and succeeded in India since I first left Bombay eighteen years ago to enroll at Brandeis University in Waltham, Massachusetts. Running into some of these young men and women in cities like Bombay and Delhi and Bangalore and Calcutta and Hyderabad, I could almost see their energy—so charged up they seemed to be with ambition and drive. The architect Anuradha Parikh in Bombay, whose work involves designing housing for the needy; Mahesh Jethmalani, a Bombay lawyer who made a mark at an early age in India's highly competitive legal circles; Rajguru Deshmukh, another young lawyer, who wrote a couple of critically acclaimed books on murder trials; Pritish Nandy, a Calcutta poet who parlayed his reputation into a job that has made him one of India's most innovative magazine editors; Avinash Bendre, who has built a lucrative photography consultancy; Kuldip Saran, whose management skills have made him into a sought-after corporate prize; Dina Vakil, a clever editor who converted the moribund *Indian Express* magazine into a solid publication; Anil Dharker, who has developed new formats for television interview shows on the government network; Vinod Mehta, who single-handedly launched India's first Sunday newspaper and transformed it into a highly readable—and profitable—enterprise; Minhaz Merchant, who constructed a thriving publishing empire before he was thirty. They are India's "Yuppies," to be sure, but they are also dedicated and deadly serious about the development of India. When a Bombayite friend asked me why I didn't return to the city of my birth and plunge into, say, journalism, I very nearly replied: "And scramble to find a job? All the opportunities have already been taken—there are few vacancies." (I might add that Indian-born people also seem to be increasingly adept at seizing journalistic opportunities abroad. I cite the case of Patricia J. Sethi, who is a success story at Newsweek Magazine in New York. Her specialty has been to obtain exclusive interviews with elusive leaders.)

During my passage through India, I found that a new generation of highly motivated, achieving Indians was making its presence felt in the country. As Titu Ahluwalia, head of a market research company called Marg, said, many of these men and women received their higher education abroad; they resolved to return home and take on the system and work in India. They could have readily have found a slot in Western professional society, but for various reasons they did not want to be part of that society. They represent a reversal of the much-publicized "brain drain" that has resulted in thousands of bright Indians settling abroad because they could make more money overseas in jobs they never would be able to get back home.

The political aspirations of the post-Independence generation have now found expression in the ascendency of Rajiv Gandhi, forty years old, to the prime ministership of India. Gandhi's closest friends—among them, former business executives Arun Singh and Arun Nehru, advertising whiz Arun Nanda, and journalist Suman Dubey—are all fortyish, they went to college in either Britain or the United States, and they are now in a position to influence the country for many, many years to come.

When the election results poured in last December, I watched with admiration how Prannoy Roy analyzed on television the welter of incoming data. The psephologist, or student of elections, is only thirty-five years old. It was the first time that "instant analysis," so familiar to television viewers in America, was being tried out on the government-run Indian network; the suggestion came from yet another Indian "Yuppie," Asoka Raina, who has formed an independent television company to produce current affairs and other programs. An ambitious television series is being planned now on India's brain drain problem.

If there is a high priest of this so-called brain drain, it is an American by the name of Allen E. Kaye.

I've known him for many years, and this time I ran into him in Bombay. He was in India on a business trip, his ninth in eight years. Kaye is an immigration lawyer who has specialized in assisting Indians, of whom close to 20,000 emigrate to the United States each year. In addition to these men and women, at least 100,000 others travel to America annually for holidays or short business trips. The visa applications of another 100,000 Indians are turned down every year by the American government, among other reasons on the suspicion that once in the United States they would stay there permanently.

[The United States permits no more than 270,000 legal immigrants from all over the world to come in each year; in six so-called "preference" categories. No country can send more than 20,000 immigrants annually in these six preference categories. There is, however, no overall numerical limit on close relatives that American citizens may bring in every year as immigrants to the United States. And each year, too, several hundreds of thousands of people are allowed in as refugees. For the past few years, up to 750,000 people in all these categories have been coming into the United States every year. The highest number of immigrants to the United States each year is from Mexico, followed by the Philippines and India.]

Each time he is in India, Kaye gives lectures on American immigration. It would be no hyperbole to say that he is the most popular foreign lecturer in India today. Kaye concentrates on cities such as Bombay, Delhi, Calcutta, Madras, Bangalore, and Ahmedabad, from where his clients mostly hail. These cities have large pools of unemployed, or underemployed, educated men and women who are frustrated because there seem to be so few good jobs to go around. Tickets to his lectures cost the equivalent of $2.50. The sell-out lectures, of course, help widen his clientele.

Kaye finds himself working sixteen-hour days when in India. His Indian exposure helps him in New York and around the United States, and vice versa. The Indians who seek his help here invariably seek his professional assistance there. Moreover, one Indian talks to another, and so, with the possible exception of Rajiv Gandhi and maybe the film star Amitabh Bachchan, Allen Kaye is the most popular man in the 600,000-man Indian community in America today. His column for a weekly newspaper called *India Abroad*, which is published in New York by an enterprising Indian expatriate named Gopal Raju, is probably the publication's best-read feature. Raju and Kaye met in New York through an Indian they both knew and started an association that has proven mutually profitable. Kaye's column results in considerable business for him; other immigration lawyers envy him for it—some have scrambled to find other ethnic publications in which to write similar columns: but it is, of course, not the same; Indians are probably the fastest-growing foreign community in the United States, and Kaye has helped considerably in its growth. Now Kaye hosts radio and television programs on immigration matters for people in the New York area.

Kaye holds his consultations in the lobbies of the luxury hotels he likes to stay in. People sometimes knock on his door in the middle of the night to ask questions. He is surprisingly good-natured about such intrusions, and so is his wife, Agneta Palmblad, who usually accompanies him to India. When I saw Kaye in the marble lobby of the Taj Mahal Hotel in Bombay one afternoon, he was holding a durbar; that is, royal court! At least a dozen people had lined up in one corner awaiting their turn to meet him; the hotel receptionists occasionally looked at Kaye, no doubt wanting to obtain some advice themselves. Kaye did not dispense much good news: the United States government, he told his callers, was making it harder each year for foreigners to come and work in America. Even doctors and nurses—once welcomed with few reservations—now were finding the "green card," a permanent visa cum employment document, more and more elusive. His listeners, ever optimistic, did not seem fazed. The lure of America is very strong indeed.

I asked Allen Kaye whether his work was in effect damaging to India's well-being in the long run.

"I don't see this flow of people as a brain drain," Kaye said. "It is not that India is being deprived of skilled services. There are more engineers and doctors and scientists than actually needed in India today. The people who want to leave are those who often cannot get decent employment here because of the competition. Or they are people who can get more challenging and more financially rewarding work in the United States. In some cases, they are far too overtrained for Indian conditions. Some who go to the United States as students often stay there because they acquire skills that cannot be easily used in a still-developing society like India. Moreover, each Indian in the United States is a goodwill ambassador for India. I have found them to be very hard workers."

Not long after my meeting with Allen Kaye, I ran into Professor Jagdish N. Bhagwati of Columbia University. Professor Bhagwati is a leading authority on the Third World, and has done seminal research on the "brain drain" question. He endorsed Kaye's assertion that in reality the outmigration of skilled manpower from India under a humane open door policy enabled the country, in effect, to establish a diaspora that worked to India's advantage. "Western pluralistic societies typically respond to domestic pressure groups," Bhagwati said. "Indians abroad constitute therefore an invaluable constituency for India's interests—and a tolerant approach to the 'brain drain question' amounts to a successful application of what might be called the Trojan Horse Principle!"

Ten years ago, a young man with a shy manner, an engaging smile, and a British degree in accounting returned to his home in New Delhi from London. He was asked by his father to help him run the family's printing plant. The young man came in contact with some of his father's friends, who were in the newspaper business. He thought that the country's big newspapers were like aging dinosaurs; and the leading news magazines, once fiery and enterprising, had become toothless tigers. Journalism did not pay well, it no longer attracted the energetic and enthusiastic, and many practitioners— among them some whose writings "influenced" the masses—clearly had been seduced by their political patrons. The young man became increasingly convinced that Indian journalism was ripe for a revolution.

By coincidence, the young man's sister, a New York–based writer, was in New Delhi for an extended stay. She had herself been thinking about the journalistic scene in India and had had discussions with her father about perhaps starting a news magazine. So the young man, Aroon Purie, and his sister, Madhu Purie Trehan, teamed up and started a biweekly newsmagazine called *India Today*. The magazine is the success story of Third World journalism.

"We were there at the right time," Purie says.

The initial print run of his magazine was 5,000 copies. Now it sells 375,000 copies per issue, and has an estimated readership each issue of 3.5 million in India and overseas. This would make *India Today* one of the most widely read journals in the world. (The circulation of newspapers, and there are some 5,000 of them, is estimated to exceed 50 million. Most people do not know this, but more English-language books are published in India each year than in any country except the United States. The vernacular press is flourishing as never before.)

Published in English, Purie's magazine has color pages, is stylishly slick, and is characterized by punch-packed prose and tight editing. It looks, in fact, like a clone of *Time* magazine, a characterization that must irritate Purie, who says, "My main criterion is readability." The contrast with the country's English-language newspapers could not be greater: these papers, rooted in the staid style of the British press of the 1930s, are dull and gray. There are few feature articles; the emphasis is on pronouncements by politicians. Editorials are mostly ponderous; opinion pieces are loaded with jargon. Few newspapers are brightly laid out—the idea is to pack as much type in as possible, with little regard to style and visual appeal.

India Today has spawned a crowd of imitators in India, where people genuinely feel that imitation is the best praise. The magazine's belief is that, irrespective of the efforts by Third World leaders to force Western news organizations to portray their states more positively—efforts that have assumed sinister dimensions in such international forums as UNESCO, which has advocated a "New Information Order"—journalists in developing countries have a special obligation.

This obligation involves better coverage of their culture and societies by their own media—coverage that is disinterested yet compassionate, pithy but professional, comprehensive and, yes, objective. These are criteria that Purie acknowledges do not generally characterize publications in developing countries, where journalists are often inhibited by the heavy hand of government. *India Today* reports on the color, clangor, and confusion of India. It reports on the political shenanigans, the sophistry of policy makers and planners, police brutalities in remote villages, the growing awareness of peasants about the inequities of India's caste and class structures, the mounting aspirations of the burgeoning middle classes. And it reports on men and women in this land of 800 million people who are working quietly to bring about economic and social change.

The magazine's attitude toward the country's politicians is iconoclastic, but both Purie and his dynamic managing editor, Suman Dubey, say their publication rarely has been subjected to government harassment. Not long after the Indira Gandhi assassination in October 1984, Purie wrote in his magazine about what it was like covering the prime minister. "Mrs. Gandhi never made it an easy job for the Indian media," Purie said in his magazine. "For one, she was distrustful of most Indian publications and treated the domestic press with a certain disdain. For another, her tremendous energy made it difficult to keep up with her. What she, a lone woman, could achieve in a working day, a clutch of coordinated reporters couldn't effectively cover.

"She may have had her difficulties with the media, but it is to her eternal credit that after her return to office in 1980 it was her stated and practiced policy not to interfere with the free functioning of the press," Purie wrote. *"India Today* carried several stories extremely critical of her policies and governance, but not once was any pressure, direct or indirect, official or unofficial, brought to bear on the magazine to toe the line or desist from publishing anything. True, she declined to meet representatives of the magazine either for formal interviews or informally. But on the few occasions on which her government took exception to what *India Today* had published, the criticism was public, not covert."

Suman Dubey, a former foreign correspondent for a number of Western publications—he still contributes to the *Wall Street Journal* from New Delhi—concurs with his boss's assertion that, despite a contrary view abroad, the press has been remarkably unfettered in India. "In India we have the opportunity to write more frankly and more vociferously than in most countries," Dubey, a tall, bearded man with a pleasant manner, said to me as we sipped coffee in the lounge of the Taj Mahal Hotel in New Delhi. (The lounge is favored by Delhi's officials and journalists: several banquettes were occupied by important government officials, the sort whose doings Dubey would ordinarily examine in his magazine.) "Nobody in the government has said to me, 'Don't write this,' or 'Don't write that.' I don't think a publication like *India Today* could exist in too many other countries."

Aroon Purie's sister, Madhu Trehan, endorses this assessment. She was the one who prepared the original layout of the magazine, and it was she who helped to recruit the young staff. "The joke used to be that we ran a kindergarten at *India Today*—so young was our staff in those days," Mrs. Trehan says. Every word had to be cleared with the government censors in those days because of the "Emergency" that Indira Gandhi had imposed on the nation. This meant huge delays in production. One day, Trehan waited several hours for her layout artist to turn up and then decided to go to his house to find out why he was so late; the artist had no phone at home. When she got to his house, she found it locked. A guard explained that the artist, Pinaki Dasgupta, had left that morning for Calcutta: he was to be married the next day.

"I don't know how we put out the magazine in those days," Madhu Trehan recalls. "But it seemed to come out as if by magic."

In fact, at one point problems seemed so awesome that her brother said, half jokingly and half in despair: "There's no way this can make any money, mate!"

But make money the magazine did, and now Aroon Purie is a very wealthy man in his own right.

Madhu Trehan feels that *India Today* reflects the new, aggressive mood of India. The magazine is perfectly positioned to explore and explain the "new" India of Rajiv Gandhi, she says. The young prime minister, perhaps in recognition of this, granted his first formal press interview to *India Today*.

There are those who suggest that one way the magazine was able to flourish despite its often critical coverage of the Indira Gandhi administration was by rarely attacking Mrs. Gandhi herself. Indeed, in the ten years since *India Today* was launched, the prime minister was featured on the magazine's cover no fewer than 35 times—often enough to raise some charges of partisanship. (Sanjay Gandhi turned up six times on the cover, and now Rajiv Gandhi has appeared half a dozen times as well.) Purie responds that Mrs. Gandhi was, after all, India's leading politician and generated more news that anyone else; topicality demanded the attention given to her. I think that implicit in what Purie says is admiration, however grudging, for Indira Gandhi.

"It is said that the American presidency is the most powerful job in the world—the most difficult must be to rule the world's largest democracy," Purie says. "It was a job that Prime Minister Gandhi did at considerable personal sacrifice with seemingly effortless grace, style, stamina, and above all, with guts. For more than fifteen years, she was a living symbol of India. In spite of its differences with her, the magazine held her in high esteem—not just as the country's prime minister but also as a politician of accomplishment, a leader of unmatched stature and on the whole a remarkable human being."

Topicality has demanded that Purie and his staff of sixty men and women pay close attention to world issues—specifically those that affect developing countries. Issues such as the transfer of technology, Western aid, and the North–South dialogue are written about regularly. Special correspondents in Washington, London, Bonn, and Paris report on topics involving Indian and Third World interests. There are few sacred cows at *India Today*. Corruption in developing countries, autocratic and abusive rule, the self-indulgence of those in power—these topics are tackled with the same enthusiasm Purie and Dubey display in sending their small staff of writers to investigate charges of torture or extortion by some local political chieftan. Not long ago, a reporter named Shekhar Gupta uncovered the presence of camps in the southern Indian state of Tamil Nadu where Sri Lankan Tamils agitating for a separate state were being trained by Indians in guerrilla warfare. Gupta's story received worldwide attention.

"I am generally surprised by our success," Purie says with a smile. "I'm surprised at the way our magazine took off the way it did. We did things differently—we were younger and not rooted in the often stifling traditions of Indian journalism. Our growth therefore was attributable to the fact that we were in the right medium—and to the special circumstances around us when we started." He says this slowly, patiently, as if to ensure that his interviewer gets it just right.

What helped establish his magazine was its reporting on the alleged excesses of the Indira Gandhi government during the 1975–1977 "Emergency" period when Mrs. Gandhi, citing a national breakdown of law and order, suspended the Constitution and jailed scores of political opponents and journalists. Following the 1977 elections, which Mrs. Gandhi lost, the Janata Party government appointed judicial commissions that turned up evidence of excesses, and *India Today* thrived on the material.

"Our real contribution lies in the kind of magazine *India Today* is—it is not obliged for its existence on anybody," Purie says. In short, Purie is independent, his magazine is independent. He does not buckle under political pressure, nor under commercial strain. His independence has made him rich, and his wealth has strengthened his independence. To my mind, Purie has been one of this last decade's most extraordinary achievers in Indian society.

Characteristically, he rarely talks about his own drive and single-mindedness. When *India Today* was started, Purie's family owned one of the most modern printing plants in the country. His father had established himself as one of Delhi's most successful businessmen and film distributors. But it was Aroon Purie's ambition that has accounted for the phenomenal growth of *India Today*—that, and the efforts of young acolytes that he attracted to his magazine, like Dilip Bobb, Sunil Sethi, Shekhar Gupta, and Coomi Kapoor, men and women with a flair for writing and a keenness to examine the social issues of the day.

I went to see Purie at his office, which is squeezed into closet-size space above a warren of shops in Delhi's Connaught Place. The office had a bank of four phones, which kept ringing merrily, a red carpet, a yellow-brown sofa, three orange chairs, a circular table in lieu of a formal desk, a high-backed chair for the publisher, and a globe. There was also an enormous panel painting. His office had a sun terrace, which was edged with plants. Purie had been visiting his printing plant in suburban Faridabad and the late-afternoon traffic had held him up; but when he arrived, he seemed none the worse for the drive.

He wore a tweed jacket, a blue shirt and blue tie, and dark blue trousers, with well-polished brown loafers. He looked fit. I felt ashamed of the folds of fat on my stomach—and I was younger than him!

It had already been a remarkable week for him. A poll *India Today* had commissioned came divinely close to predicting the exact number of seats that Rajiv Gandhi's ruling Congress Party would win in the December 1984 election to the national Parliament. Envious competitors had sniped at him, and some particularly ill-informed writers of a national newspaper criticized his magazine's poll and political reporting. Ordinarily, Purie ignores attacks on *India Today;* but in this instance he felt that his publication had been so wronged by this newspaper that he responded with a strongly worded letter to the editor, which the newspaper published.

"We do what we do well, and we do it on a regular basis—we are not a flash in the pan," Purie told me. "We display consistent quality in terms of talking about what's happening in the country. This has created a certain heightened awareness in decision-making circles. Part of our constituency is the government elite—and they are affected by how we interpret events. Ours is a magazine they can trust and rely on to be consistent in its reporting and judgments."

Aroon Purie does, not, however, see himself as practicing advocacy journalism. "Our job is to reflect what is happening in society and in the world around us, to clarify issues and developments," he told me. "We hold a mirror up to society. If you concentrate just on crusading, you tend to lose your edge—you then tend to dilute your basic function, which is to inform. Journalism is only an indirect instrument of social change."

It seemed to me that *India Today* had demonstrated a unique ability to interpret and perhaps even influence the vast changes occurring in Indian society. The most dramatic recent change, of course, was the smashing victory of Rajiv Gandhi and his ruling Congress Party.

"No question that his election represented a tremendous change in our country," Purie said. "It was a psychological change as much as a political one—the change represented by a leader who's of post–freedom-movement vintage. So I feel positive about that. I think Rajiv Gandhi can set the tone, the direction, for government —he is in a position to do some streamlining. If he does that, just that and nothing else, he'd have achieved something remarkable. But I don't think he can turn the economy upside down, or root out corruption. There are a lot of overexpectations about Rajiv—and I don't go along with that."

Supposing Prime Minister Rajiv Gandhi asked Aroon Purie to write him a memorandum, a word or two of advice concerning the press and government, what would the publisher say, I asked?

Purie smiled, and paused to wipe his glasses.

"I would urge him to run an open government—a government that is open to the press and is not antipress," he said, presently. "Rajiv doesn't have to like the press, but I think there should be a certain respect toward the media. This hasn't happened in our government. Either you're with them or totally against them—that's how our leaders perceive the press. This must change. I would emphasize to Rajiv that a free press is an essential part of democracy— so let it flourish. In India, government can make life difficult for anyone owning or running the press through the control of newsprint, the wage boards, accreditation of correspondents covering government, approval of government advertisements—there are lots of measures in the hands of the Indian government which serve as knobs for harassment. I hope Rajiv is judicious in handling all these.

"And I hope Rajiv improves access to government departments, and to the prime minister's office itself. The entire government machinery needs to be opened up to the press. It would lead to a much better functioning of our system."

I thought I'd throw a curve ball to Aroon Purie. Supposing, I said, Rajiv Gandhi were to ask him to ghostwrite a speech that the prime minister wanted to deliver before a gathering of the high and mighty of the Indian media. What would *India Today*'s publisher say in his draft?

Again a pause, again a slight smile.

"I think the press in India to a large degree exercises power without responsibility," Purie said. "The press should be more aware of their responsibilities. Their performance has affected their credibility. The general newspaper coverage of this recent election was not the papers' finest hour. I also think that there must be a greater degree of professionalism in the press. There must be better pay, there must be more professional norms and standards, there must be a self-policing system.

"If Rajiv Gandhi were to address the press, I would expect him to urge the press to be socially responsible. I don't think that the press can or should be a vehicle for change—but its primary responsibility must be to tell as fairly and fully as possible what's going on in our society. Of course, the press should encourage the writing of stories that are positive. But for journalists the prime objective must be to be good journalists and not social activists. The moment they see themselves as agents of change, that leads to role confusion and to political identification."

He had lived through an extraordinary time in India, a decade of tumult and great anxiety and so much turbulence. What was the one thing about India—and about being an Indian—that really moved Aroon Purie?

There was no hesitation, no pause for thought this time.

"What really impresses me is that India is a working democracy," he said. "That is a remarkable achievement, especially in a Third World country. I am a free man, I have choice, I have options. I really believe that the roots of democracy are quite deep in our country. I don't think that anybody can rule India by dictatorship. Democracy is the only way to rule this country—democracy is deeply imbedded in our consciousness.

"You know, that really thrills me. I have been traveling a great deal around India of late, and I saw that in spite of so much poverty, in spite of the fact that there hasn't been great improvement in the lives of most people—in spite of all this, there was the determination to vote, to exercise their options, there was the clear feeling that their vote would make a difference. The feeling that the ordinary individ-

ual matters has filtered down to the grassroots, to the remotest village.
I found this heart-warming. I think this is priceless."

As he spoke, I thought I saw Aroon Purie's eyes mist. It could have
been flecks of dust that caused the misting, of course, but I didn't
think so.

Aroon Purie, in a sense, represents both the old and the new in
India. His initiative and imagination resulted in an extraordinarily
successful product, *India Today*. He pioneered a hard-hitting and
highly readable kind of magazine journalism. But his own education
reflected the traditions of upper-crust Indian families: he attended
the Doon School, an exclusive prep school that was started in 1935
by an Anglophile Indian who modeled it on the English public school
system. Purie's contemporaries included Rajiv Gandhi. Then he did
what sons and daughters of the wealthy generally did—he went
abroad for higher education; specifically, he went to the country that
attracted India's elite because of colonial ties, Britain.

The two universities in Britain long favored by Indians were Oxford and Cambridge—what in the salons of Bombay and Delhi and
Calcutta and Madras is called the "Oxbridge Connection." The
"connection" has resulted in an extraordinary old-boy network in
India, much along the lines of the Ivy League network in the United
States. If you went to Oxbridge, it is reasonable to assume that you
are doing well in contemporary India: Rajiv Gandhi attended Trinity
College at Cambridge; he worked at a bakery during his leisure hours
to make extra cash, for even though the Indian students got handsome allowances from their families, Britain was getting increasingly
expensive. Gandhi's close friends from Cambridge days remain his
close friends: among them, Suman Dubey, the managing editor of
Purie's *India Today*. Oxbridge alumni include captains of industry,
top journalists, powerful bureaucrats, filmmakers, and now the inner
circle around Prime Minister Rajiv Gandhi.

"We were a privileged lot," says Rahul Singh, editor of the Chandigarh edition of the *Indian Express,* and a Cambridge alumnus. "The
fact that we went to Oxbridge in the first place meant that we were

privileged. Virtually all of us came from highly affluent families, and affluence meant influence. It helped that we came from this privileged background—and it helped that we went to study abroad."

The sons and daughters of the privileged still go abroad, but they go to schools and colleges not only in Britain. Increasingly, they are enrolling in American universities. There are an estimated 50,000 Indian students currently in the United States, and their numbers are increasing. Not all receive scholarships, especially with many educational institutions in America desperately short of cash these days; but they seem to manage all right. Wealthy parents in India have a way of converting nonconvertible Indian rupees into hard foreign currency.

In recent years, as India's political and military ties with the Soviet Union deepened, more and more scholarships have been given by Eastern Bloc countries to Indian students. Thousands of Indians have received graduate degrees from the Patrice Lumumba University in Moscow. These Indians travel to Eastern Europe mainly to study engineering and technical subjects; and once their education has been completed, they return to India—there is no such thing as emigrating to Communist countries! There are thousands of such students who return to India every year: I wonder how they will influence Indian professional life in the years ahead. While it is fashionable to talk about the Western values and sensibilities that Oxbridge alumni bring home with them, the number of Indians who have studied in Eastern Bloc states and who return home is getting larger each year. Will we soon hear about the "Lumumba Connection"?

The unfortunate fact is that in India higher education has been mostly the prerogative of the privileged. Even more unfortunate is the fact that since independence the number of illiterate Indians has increased dramatically. One in every eight Indians has no education of any sort. As many as 76,000 villages have no primary school. There are nearly 50 million illiterate children between the ages of six and 11. The United Nations has estimated that in the year 2000, nearly 40 percent of the world's population of illiterates will be in India—

or more than 150 million people. Back in 1978, the Indian government launched an ambitious adult education program aimed at reaching 100 million illiterates between the ages of 15 and 35 in nine economically and educationally backward states. As part of this program, 200,000 adult education centers will be established to complement the 150,000 currently operating around the country. The government wants to achieve the goal of total adult literacy by 1990. No official I met in India really thought the goal would be met.

My own feeling is that it is all very well to promote such things as adult education and vocational training, especially in rural areas. But Rajiv Gandhi's real priority in education should be free, universal, and compulsory education for all Indian children. After all, the child is the father of the man.

I met a young man in Bombay who was a product of the city's municipal school system, and whose parents were not affluent enough to finance a foreign education for him. Some Indians want to grow up and become pilots; Mahendra Jain had always wanted to become a physician. His parents were thrilled with his ambition. There were no doctors in Jain's family, who were conservative Gujeratis, or members of the merchant community. His father and grandfather had run a small trading business, but it was clear that the family would not be able to send Jain to a foreign medical school as he had hoped. Jain did well in high school and fared well, too, at the K. C. College in Bombay. When he applied to medical school in Bombay, he was turned down time after time.

"Weren't your grades good enough?" I asked Jain.

"They were superb," he said. "But that wasn't the problem."

The problem was that virtually every medical school demanded "donations" of up to five lakh rupees, or the equivalent of $50,000, merely to grant admission. There were four major medical schools in Bombay, and each year they together took in 560 new students. But each year more than 70,000 applicants competed for these seats. Because it is considered very prestigious to have a doctor in the family, many parents manage to raise such incredible sums just to assure their progeny of admission to medical school. By the time graduation comes around five years later, a medical education will have cost the equivalent of another $100,000 per student.

Mahendra Jain decided he was not going to subject his parents to the humiliation of even trying to raise the money. He applied to the A. M. Sheikh Medical College in neighboring Karnataka State, where no "donations" were required for admission. He worked during his off-hours at the college's laboratory, and graduated with honors.

"All right, so I don't have a degree from a prestige university," Jain, a lanky, earnest-mannered man, said to me. "But so what? At least I have a medical degree. I am qualified to be a doctor. I have the power to shape my future with my abilities. Experience is the main thing."

He is currently serving an internship at a hospital in Bombay. The hours are continuous; there is no such thing as weekends off. Mahendra Jain has not been to a movie in a year. He lives in a dormitory within the hospital's compound. He is not a picture of good health. Hard work may not kill a twenty-four-year-old medical graduate, but it certainly gives him deep dark circles under the eyes and a pallor.

"I knew what I was in for when I made the decision to become a doctor," Jain told me. "All this hard work may tire me out, but it doesn't faze me. I know very well what this experience is worth—I know that the pain I suffer today is going to reap me rewards tomorrow. India could dispense with politicians, it can even do without Indira Gandhi—but a country of 800 million people will always need doctors. And good doctors, too."

Not long afterward, I mentioned my discussions with Mahendra Jain to another Bombay physician, Rusi H. Dastur. I told Dastur that I was horrified to hear about the extent of bribery that was allegedly involved in the field of medical education.

"Things were very different in my younger days," Dastur, who is about sixty years old, said. "There wasn't this kind of money around in those days. Who had five lakh rupees available? In those days if you wanted to become a doctor, and your grades were good, you secured admission to medical school. It was simple as that. None of

villages are entirely different. People who live in rural India still rely on ancient systems of medicine for the cure of their simple ailments —allopathy is alien to them."

Dastur points out that 80 percent of India's physicians are urban-based, while nearly 80 percent of the country's population lives in rural areas. Because these urban-trained doctors have become accustomed to sophisticated equipment such as scanners and sonograms, many of them are reluctant to relocate to the villages. But Dastur believes that in India's villages the need is not so much for more doctors as it is for social workers. He advocates the establishment of a system of "barefoot doctors," or paramedics, just as neighboring China has done. These barefoot doctors are picked from among villagers and trained to handle minor ailments common to rural life. Such personnel, Dastur feels, will be able to communicate effectively with fellow villagers.

He also advocates tackling on a war footing the pressing problems of nutrition, safe drinking water, and sanitation. Dastur told me that more than 200,000 children under the age of five become blind each year because of the lack of a proper diet. It is also estimated by UNICEF that more than 75 million Indian children go to bed hungry each night. Better nutrition from an early age will produce a better race of Indians, Dastur asserts, instead of the short and sickly millions who populate the country. He says he was encouraged by the continuing efforts of UNICEF's executive director, James P. Grant, to promote a stepped-up child immunization program in India. Grant, a tireless and irrepressible crusader for better health care for mothers and children, played a significant—but behind-the-scenes—role in persuading Rajiv Gandhi to announce recently that a $750 million child immunization effort would be undertaken as a memorial to Indira Gandhi. (Grant told me in New York that when Mrs. Gandhi died he was particularly saddened because she had been a "champion of child health care." But, Grant said, he was delighted by the alacrity with which the young Gandhi is acting to push this program to immunize all Indian children by 1990 against diseases that kill and maim, such as polio and tetanus.)

Dastur feels that India can ill afford lavishing expenditures on high-tech medicine.

"The problems which India faces today are overpopulation, malnutrition, high infant mortality, pulmonary tuberculosis, hepatitis, and diarrhea," he said. "The basic need therefore is not for advanced technology but an appropriate one suited to the indigenous ethos. It is not intensive care that is the need of the hour but extensive care that can fan out across the length and breadth of the country. Instead of a hundred new body scanners, why not establish a thousand new family-planning and family-health centers?"

In those early days after Rajiv Gandhi's resounding victory in the December 1984 parliamentary elections, India's newspapers and newsmagazines carried editorial after editorial about the challenges that the forty-year-old prime minister faced. Poverty, unemployment, fissiparous tendencies, ethnic turmoil, sinister Sri Lankans, aggressive Pakistanis, renegade Sikhs—it was all laid out for Gandhi. He was reported to be so preoccupied with fashioning a new cabinet and finding sinecures for his friends that I doubt he had the time to take in all this advice. It struck me that with notable exceptions such as Prem Shankar Jha of the *Times of India,* few of these editorial writers dealt with India's urban problems. During the election campaign, it had become fashionable for some opposition party leaders to rouse rural crowds by putting down the cities. Chowdhary Charan Singh, a former prime minister and now head of the Dalit Mazdoor Kisan Party, in effect told rally after rally in his Uttar Pradesh constituency: "The cities can go to hell. The future of India lies in its villages."

Implicit in his speeches was a sense that it was perhaps too late to do anything about urban decay, both physical and spiritual. Cities like Bombay, Calcutta, and Madras had already become unsalvageable in the opinion of many urban planners. They suffered from irremediable housing, transportation, and power problems. They had to be left to sputter along from crisis to crisis. They would somehow survive.

Sadly enough, I found, there were very few spokesmen for India's cities, very few dedicated men and women who were willing to address and redress urban woes. But in Bombay I met a woman named Bakul Patel, a management consultant who devoted several hours of her day to voluntary social work. Her emphasis was on providing proper learning environments for poor children. She has also worked to push literacy and employment projects for destitute women in urban areas. Mrs. Patel also raised funds to build a planetarium in Bombay for children; and she has initiated the establishment of several day-care centers.

"What really bothers me is that the deteriorating conditions of our urban children and women are simply not priority issues in policy-making circles," Bakul Patel said. "Child labor is rampant in our cities, even though our Constitution forbids it. Brides are burned daily because they did not fetch their husbands's families sufficient dowry. Poor widows are forced into prostitution and begging. In Bombay alone, several studies have shown that nearly 60 percent of the city's children don't even have basic immunization. Isn't it time our leaders really moved energetically to tackle such problems? Or do there have to be urban explosions before action is taken?"

Those questions were echoed in a lengthy conversation I had some days later in Bangalore with that southern city's controversial police commissioner, P. G. Halarnkar. He had become controversial precisely because he raised those very questions in public and in his private sessions with local politicians. Urban India, Halarnkar said repeatedly to whoever cared to listen to him, was sliding dangerously fast into a crisis that would affect the wellbeing of the entire nation.

I did not think that Halarnkar was sounding false alarms. Consider the growth rates of the following Indian cities over the last decade: Jaipur, 57 percent; Delhi, 56 percent; Pune, 48 percent; Ahmedabad, 43 percent; Hyderabad, 40 percent; Nagpur, 39 percent; Bombay, 37 percent; Madras, 34 percent; Kanpur, 32 percent; Calcutta, 30 percent; and Lucknow, 23 percent. The government's Census Department says that the overall rate of growth for the last decade for all of India's cities was 46 percent!

Halarnkar's Bangalore has become the fastest-growing city in

India, and one of the ten fastest-growing cities in the world. Between 1974 and 1984, its population increased by 76 percent to 3.5 million. Ten years ago there were an estimated 70,000 automobiles registered to owners in Bangalore; now there are at least 300,000. Ten years ago, Bangalore was a neat little place of parks, wide boulevards, and quaint bungalows: located in south-central India at an altitude of 3,000 feet, its climate was cool and healthful all year; people from all over the country came here for their holidays—now they come here for jobs, in the process making Bangalore even more cosmopolitan but also adding to the city's congestion. Bangalore has become the Silicon Valley of India: its professional electronics equipment companies account for more than 80 percent of the national production; there are scores of electronic component manufacturers here; eight industrial parks have sprung up in the last ten years and these estates— such as Peenya, Veerasandra, and Dyavasandra—now contain nearly 10,000 small-scale industrial units, and more than 400 large and medium-scale factories.

Such industrial growth may be good for Bangalore's economy but some of it has polluted its air beyond reprieve. Even the hardy plane trees and the bougainvillea that edge the city's roads look sick, although the fabled gulmohurs and laburnum trees have managed to resist the environmental rot. Huge government-owned enterprises such the Indian Telephone Industries, Bharat Electronics Limited, and Bharat Heavy Electricals Limited, contribute heavily to the deterioration of the environment. On the outskirts of the city is yet another government-run industrial giant, the Hindustan Aeronautics Limited, where sophisticated fighter jets are assembled or produced.

"This was largely unexpected and unplanned growth," Commissioner Halarnkar said to me as we sipped aromatic Karnataka coffee in his office. "The authorities knew that the city would expand—but what happened was beyond anyone's imagination."

Politicians come and go, as do planners. Police commissioners in India tend to have greater longevity, but the job is not exactly sought after. This is another way of saying that every official in town likes to dump his problems with Halarnkar, because his office is a handy clearing house for complaints. If the chaotic building boom results in traffic gridlock in downtown Bangalore, Halarnkar is summoned by the mayor for a dressing down; if shoddy construction results in the collapse of a factory's floor, Halarnkar is asked to explain why the police did not keep a watchful eye when the building was raised. When it was recently revealed that property owners were selling residential plots for more than $25,000 an acre, Commissioner Halarnkar was asked by the state's chief minister why speculators and peculators weren't being kept in check. But when Halarnkar moved against men suspected of violating zoning and building codes, the city's political establishment conveyed its displeasure to him. Why? Because the commissioner had cited friends of these politicians.

"Every now and then I hear rumors that I'm going to be transferred," Halarnkar, a tall handsome man with an infectious smile, said to me. "Then the rumors quickly fade. I suppose no one wants this job! I'm expected to be both a good cop and a good boy."

[Harlarnkar's remarks recalled another conversation I'd had with a man named Arun Bhatia. The Cambridge-educated Bhatia had been a rising star in the elite Indian Administrative Service until he exposed corruption in the rural Dhulia district of Maharashtra State where he was posted as chief administrator. Lower-level bureaucrats were routinely fudging the records of a multimillion-dollar government employment scheme for local tribespeople. Fictitious names were put on the employment rolls and the "salaries" siphoned off to local officials and their friends. The local police, who were in league with the bureaucrats, declined to make arrests—even when Bhatia had painstakingly documented evidence of wrongdoing.

[The state government transferred Bhatia to Bombay. There he again exposed large-scale corruption in the so-called floor space index business: wealthy builders of high-rise apartments were falsifying their applications to the local authorities, who in effect would allow these builders to raise structures bigger than the zoning regulations permitted. Money obviously changed hands. What happened to

Bhatia? He was demoted and given a minor post under a high official at whom he'd pointed an accusing finger. Arun Bhatia finally left the administrative service. He now works for the United Nations in Botswana.]

"A police officer in India is also a social worker," the commissioner continued. "And the cop's boss, the commissioner, has to be a sort of grand uncle. In India people come to a policeman for everything, not just problems of law and order. We have to be not only professional but always personable. We must deal with communal disputes. We must sometimes officiate at religious ceremonies! I even have a full-time worker who does nothing but go out and kill snakes. He's caught more than a thousand snakes so far."

Halarnkar is worried that Bangalore was rapidly losing out on three fronts: its salubrious climate was worsening because of the pollution; its pleasant physical environment was deteriorating because of the crowds and the dreadful traffic; and crime was on the increase. "I'm afraid we're headed for complete confusion here," he said. "Traffic is already nightmarish. The authorities have done nothing about building flyovers, or about widening the major arteries. The people of Bangalore laugh at the plight of Bombay—but let me tell you, we're heading in that direction. The joke may be on us if we go on like this."

The police force in Bangalore has not been strengthened as much as Halarnkar would like. Because this city is spreading out and because its residential colonies tend to consist of bungalows rather than more easily protected high-rise buildings, burglaries and house break-ins are on the rise. Halarnkar wants the authorities to increase the number of police precincts from 67 to 90 at the very least. Still, the commissioner has significantly stepped up such things as night patrols; he has formed neighborhood civilian patrol groups; he has sponsored security seminars in residential colonies. One social problem afflicting Bangalore is a form of gambling known around here as matka. Men often gamble away their property and sometimes even their spouses. The matka dens have been known to finance campaigns of politicians, which makes Halarnkar's job that much tougher.

The Indian police system came under special scrutiny following the assassination of Indira Gandhi. Many members of the 30,000-man Delhi police force participated in the widespread looting and ravaging of Sikh homes in the capital. Law and order collapsed for nearly a week after the murder of the sixty-seven-year-old prime minister by two Sikh bodyguards. Policemen in several northern Indian cities helped themselves to goods taken from Sikh homes, or they stood idly by as Sikhs were beaten and burned alive. Although thousands of Sikhs died in the violence, few arrests were made in the capital or most other northern cities. The key question that was raised by many thoughtful observers of the Indian scene was: do India's million-strong policemen have sufficient integrity? The national police force consists of the states's police officers, and the centrally supervised Indo-Tibetan Border Police, the Border Security Force, and the Central Reserve Police Force. Police officers in India are notoriously ill paid—even top officers earn no more than four thousand rupees a month, the equivalent of $400; the ordinary constable takes home less than $50 a month. No wonder policemen are susceptible to bribery and corruption.

One would think that in a country of 800 million, police manpower and budget would be items of special interest to the nation's leaders. Yet, the combined national and states expenditure annually is less than $800 million. There are fewer than 26 policemen per every hundred square kilometers—or just about 13.1 cops for every 10,000 Indians. A government-appointed National Police Commission has recommended several measures to improve the quality of police work in India; the recommendations include such things as more modern equipment, higher salaries, better training, and greater supervision of police constables in rural areas, where police atrocities have often gone unpunished. The commission has given the government eight separate sets of recommendations since 1977 —when it was formed—but nothing has been done about improving the police situation.

As Bangalore's most visible public official, Commissioner Halarnkar accepts the fact that his performance will seldom be applauded here. Behind his attitude is a very strong conviction that how he handles the problems of growth in India's boom city will significantly influence its future. I think, as I suspect Halarnkar does too, that all is not lost in Bangalore yet. It still has a chance to make order out of chaos. Dr. Rashmi Mayur, perhaps India's most articulate crusader for environmental awareness, has listed Bangalore as a city that can still be saved—unlike, say, Calcutta.

But the political leadership will have to act more forthrightly. The Rajiv Gandhi government at Delhi has given vast new prominence to environmental protection. The opposition Janata Party that rules in Karnataka has also given it more importance than its Congress Party predecessor did. Both governments will have to put into practice what they have admitted as crucial to the future of the country's cities. Bangalore is a test case for the political leadership. The priorities are clear. Growth will have to be fitted into a carefully evolved master plan. Essential services which have collapsed under the weight of unplanned development will have to be quickly restored: agencies like the World Bank are there to finance water supply and electricity schemes. An expertly designed network of roads has become imperative—and the motoring public seems willing to accept the concept of toll roads. Bangalore's city fathers must follow the commissioner's advice and enact tough legislation concerning emission control and industrial wastes; they should get the city's industrial magnates to contribute toward a beefing up of the police force; they should enforce more strictly building and zoning codes. I don't think that Bangalore's current status as India's fastest-growing city is one for anyone to covet or cherish; it is in fact one that Bangalorites are already ruing.

On the way out of Bangalore, I looked through some old newspaper clippings about the city. I came across one that described a visit that Prime Minister Jawaharlal Nehru made to this city in 1962. This, in part, was what he said:

"Bangalore, in many ways, is unlike the other great cities of India. Most of the other cities in India remind one certainly of the present, certainly of the future but essentially of the past. But Bangalore, as

I said, more than any other great city of India is a picture of the future."

And now, much more so than when Nehru spoke here twenty years ago, the future has arrived in Bangalore. The future is now.

If the future has arrived in Bangalore, it has probably come and gone in Bombay. I don't think this great commercial city, home to some eight or nine million people, can keep growing much longer at its current pace—some ten thousand people flood into Bombay each week in search of jobs and housing, according to Debjani Sinha, an editor of *Business World,* a respected biweekly magazine. These aren't just the poor people of India, the illiterate and the destitute. Many of them are graduates of schools and colleges who simply cannot find jobs in the small towns and villages where they were born. They come to Bombay because they think that Bombay still beckons those who want a decent job and a decent home. In particular, men and women who want to enter the professions emigrate to Bombay because this city, perhaps more than any other in today's India, is still perceived as a place of opportunity.

One man who did well by Bombay is N. P. Gidwani, "Nilu" to his friends. A son of the Sind province, which is now in Pakistan, Gidwani put himself through college and then journeyed to London to acquire a degree in accounting. He worked as a professional consultant for several companies and then was hired by the Great Eastern Shipping Company, India's biggest private sector shipping concern. Gidwani, a man of medium height with graying hair and a pleasant yet crisp manner of speaking, is currently the chief "adviser" to this $300-million corporation. He not only helps to manage the company's fleet of twenty-one vessels but also drafts plans for commercial expansion and diversification. His current project consists of branching out into India's booming hotel industry: Gidwani wants Great Eastern Shipping to pump some $15 million into constructing medium-grade hotels in tourist places and in India's medium-size cities. In addition, Great Eastern may soon enter the real estate business as well, with Gidwani offering advice and monitoring the company's investments.

I looked up Gidwani because I heard that he had fashioned quite a reputation in Bombay's high-power business circles for being forthright and candid in his views concerning the country's economic development. I met him at his office in the Flora Fountain section of Bombay, an area that for many years has been the city's commercial nerve center. It was a typical Indian commercial office: rows upon rows of clerks hunched over massive ledgers; secretaries pounding away at battered old typewriters; people gathered around a drinking fountain; peons languidly thumbing through newspapers or film magazines. The scene probably had remained unchanged for decades: the only concession to modernity seemed to be a set of computer terminals whose display screens glowed eerily in the dimly lit offices of the Great Eastern Shipping Company. Gidwani occupied a glass-walled cabin, which I thought was surprisingly modest for a top executive like himself. He did have access to a private elevator, though, and we used it to leave the building. The lunch hour traffic was intense. Cars moved slowly—not so much because there were other cars on the streets of downtown Bombay but more because of the dabbawallas, the lunchbox carriers who have long been a Bombay institution.

The dabbawallahs belong to a union; there are a reported 3,000 of them in the city, and each morning they fetch specially prepared but standardized tiffins, or boxes, from suburban homes. The tiffins contain food—usually a couple of curries, some rice, and yogurt—cooked by the housebound wives of commuters. The white-collar husbands who receive the food find it the most inexpensive way to eat a wholesome meal; ordinarily, an individual could wind up paying twenty or thirty rupees for a meal (the equivalent of two or three dollars in exchange rates, but considerably more in terms of an Indian's earning capacity). Moreover, a commuter is assured of a hot meal: the dabbawallah system works to such perfection that rarely do tiffins get lost or arrive cold. More than a hundred and fifty thousand office workers in central Bombay subscribe to the dabbawallahs' system.

Gidwani chuckled suddenly as we drove in his Fiat amidst the dabbahwallahs.

"You know," he said, "it occurs to me that the Indian government could learn a thing or two from these people. They could learn the art of efficiency." He cited the example of how long the central government's bureaucracy took to reach decisions concerning business or industrial proposals. The Great Eastern Shipping Company, Gidwani said, had applied for permission to own oil rigs; the proposal was especially attractive because it was to be a joint venture with the Atwood Oceanics Company of Houston, Texas, and the oil rigs would greatly complement India's accelerating exploration plans. But the company's application had been inexplicably held up for almost two years. As a result, the company's initial cost estimate had risen from $30 million to nearly $40 million: the rapidly appreciating American dollar had contributed to the rising cost of foreign material. "We can send our own satellites into space, we can build the most complex computers—but why can't we speed up project approvals?" Gidwani said, with a harassed expression.

I was particularly amazed at this instance of governmental slowness in project approval. For several years now, India's leaders have been talking about the need for self-sufficiency in oil—and, indeed, the most encouraging trend in the Indian economy in recent years has been the growth in domestic oil production. In 1982–83, for example, production doubled to 21.1 million metric tons; in 1983–84, production grew to 24 million metric tons; in 1984–85, the figure is expected to exceed 32 million metric tons. As a result of such growth, more than two thirds of domestic consumption requirements are met through indigenous production. It is estimated that if current production trends hold and further exploration is undertaken, India will produce nearly 50 million metric tons of oil by 1990, more than enough to meet its annual domestic needs. And already, the trade deficit has significantly shrunk because of the diminishing need to import oil from India's traditional suppliers in the Middle East.

As I reflected on Gidwani's experience with the government bureaucracy, it struck me that perhaps I should have not been amazed at the lethargy of officials in Delhi. I recalled a conversation with a friend named Vasant J. Sheth, the chairman of the Great Eastern Shipping Company—and Gidwani's boss—during which Sheth told me about the experiences of his father-in-law, Keshav Deva Malaviya. Malaviya is widely regarded as the father of modern India's oil industry—but it had taken him several years of strenuous efforts to convince then Prime Minister Jawaharlal Nehru to approve oil exploration. Thirty years ago, Malaviya foresaw the importance of oil for India's developing economy. Those were times when oil was plentifully available at just over a dollar a barrel from the Arabian Gulf area. The American onshore oil industry was in the doldrums. The major oil companies of the world, and even some of Malaviya's cabinet colleagues, thought it was sheer madness for India to explore for oil with such cheap crude already available from the Gulf. The critics argued that even if oil were found in India, it would cost five times as much as the imported crude from the Middle East.

Malaviya was proven right by what was to happen in the 1970s and early 1980s. He saved India from bankruptcy. This country's economic development would have been irreparably ruined by the oil price hikes posted by the oil-producing states of the Middle East, who had banded together in a cartel called OPEC, the Organization of Petroleum Exporting Countries. OPEC held the world to ransom; the industrialized states of the West were able to barely withstand the challenge, but many countries of the Third World skidded into an economic depression from which they are unlikely to recover for decades. Because Malaviya had the foresight, India's oil business helped the country to hold its own at a time of great general distress.

Prime Minister Rajiv Gandhi, soon after succeeding his mother upon her death, said that the liberalization of India's economy would be one of his priorities. Under the so-called "license Raj" fashioned under Indira Gandhi, government permission was required to start or expand all industries with a value of $2-million and more. Naturally, this bred corruption. Businessmen found themselves having to bribe everyone up and down the bureaucratic line. Even clerks in the prime minister's office had to be satisfied. Around the time I lunched with Gidwani, all of India was reverberating to the fallout of a spy scandal: several clerks in the prime minister's secretariat, along with minor functionaries in the ministries of finance and defense, had been arrested on charges of passing on documents to representatives of foreign powers. Several diplomats were recalled by their home countries following disclosures that they had overseen the espionage. It was revealed that some of the clerks were bought off with bottles of foreign liquor. Gidwani said that this was symptomatic of a deep malaise in the Indian bureaucratic and business communities; but Gidwani also pointed out that there were good people in both government and industry. However, as long as India is a country of restrictions and artificial shortages, there will be the temptation of corruption.

The whole system of licenses and controls had been initially intended to curb the allegedly avaricious private sector. The idea was to apply brakes on the commercial community so as to ensure that its activities were in the cause of the greater social good. Ironically, however, by putting severe restrictions on what businessmen could or could not do, the government ended up creating huge private sector monopolies. The Birla family, for example, got choice contracts to manufacture the Ambassador car, a version of the 1954 Morris Oxford. It was a sturdy machine, but the Birlas saw no need to change the fuel-guzzling engine's design—since so few Ambassadors were available (at one point, the waiting time for delivery was twenty years) the public was prepared to buy just about anything the manufacturers made. The Birlas, of course, retained their hegemony over the automobile industry by close political and financial relations with the ruling Congress Party. Only in recent years has the automobile business been liberalized to allow other car makers to come in. As a result, the Maruti-Suzuki car, the Fiat Automobile venture, and the forthcoming Honda and Toyota vehicles have forced the Birlas into sounder, and cheaper, products. Of course, cars are out of reach of the majority of Indians, and I hope that the new economic liberalization results in more buses for the masses.

Gidwani, like many in the private sector, is of the firm view that the government should immediately abolish all licensing and other controls. Over lunch at the Gulzar Restaurant, he told me something that I found quite amazing: every company with assets of $20 million and above is automatically categorized as a monopoly by the government: therefore, applications for any new projects or expansion were regarded in the context of extending the companies' monopolistic practices. In short, big companies were suspect in the eyes of the government and had a harder time obtaining permits for expansion. Of course, this in itself bred further corruption because big businessmen frequently bribed bureaucrats hardsomely to get approval of big projects. Gidwani also feels that the role of the country's public sector industries must now be cut down. Free India inherited a colonial economy in which the British took away raw materials at cheap prices and sold finished goods at a high profit in what was essentially a captive market. The British forced India to import everything from pencils and erasers to railway engines. Now India manufactures everything from satellites to computers, and it even exports machinery to Third World states. Jawaharlal Nehru felt that state intervention was necessary to build India's infrastructure —which is why there was such a heavy emphasis on promoting public sector industries in the two decades after independence. The building of this infrastructure—steel, heavy machinery, oil extraction, and mining, among other things—required huge investments that were probably beyond the capacity of the private sector. But Nehru's personal fascination with socialism also led him to fashion policies that promoted the public sector at the general expense of the private sector. Today, many public sector enterprises are "sick" —they operate at a loss, there is no accountability, and goods produced by this sector cannot compete adequately in international markets. [India's annual trade deficit has averaged $5 billion for the past several years, principally because export performance has been poor. According to the government's own research, in 1955 India's exports were $1.28 billion, compared to $18 million for South Korea, $444 million for Hong Kong, $123 million for Taiwan, $945 million for Indonesia, and $1.10 billion for Singapore. But these much smaller nations of East and South Asia surged ahead merrily on their free-enterprise path, while the Indian economy continued to be bogged down in socialist shibboleths and sluggish performance. By 1981, India's annual export revenues had climbed to barely $7.3 billion; but the figure for South Korea was $21 billion, for Hong Kong $21.8 billion, for Taiwan $25 billion, for Indonesia $22.3 billion, and for Singapore $21 billion. India's share dropped from 2.2 percent of world exports in 1950 to 1.05 percent in 1960 and to 0.4 percent in 1981. Among the exporting countries, India ranked 16th in 1950, 21st in 1960, 31st in 1970—and by 1981 its rank plummeted to 46th place.]

Bureaucrats do not necessarily make good corporate managers, and in fact their record as managers of public sector enterprises in India has been poor. The Reserve Bank of India—the country's central bank—has identified nearly 25,000 enterprises as "sick units"; an overwhelming number of these poorly performing organizations are in the public sector. And although 65 percent of India's industrial assets are held by public sector enterprises, they yield barely 22 percent of the total annual industrial output. Private industry contributes nearly 80 percent of the central government's revenue, excluding the direct taxes paid by the eight million individuals employed in this sector. Nani A. Palkhivala, a leading constitutional lawyer and tax analyst, says that if the public sector were to yield in taxes what the nongovernment companies do, the central government's annual revenues would increase by more than $1.2 billion. But one reason that the government has invested so much faith and funds in the public sector is that it is a source of patronage jobs. And as the public sector has grown, so has the bureaucracy necessary to administer it: Palkhivala estimates that more than 10 million men and women are employed by the central government and various state governments to administer this sector!

I hope the public sector is dismantled, and I hope the private sector's role is enhanced. The vast bureaucracy will no doubt resist any dismantling. Prime Minister Rajiv Gandhi has said that government-owned industries will be carefully monitored for performance —but I think no amount of "monitoring" is going to help. Most public sector units are sick beyond recovery.

After I left Gidwani, I remembered a quotation attributed to the late Ludwig Erhard, once chancellor of West Germany and an architect of its extraordinary economic reconstruction after World War II. "Let the money and the men loose, and prosperity will follow," Erhard said. The quotation came to mind because some people I met earlier in Delhi said they had heard Rajiv Gandhi quote Erhard at a dinner party several weeks before the assassination of Indira Gandhi.

Prime Minister Rajiv Gandhi seemed not to have forgotten Erhard. When he unveiled his first budget on March 16, 1985, he proposed unprecedented tax breaks for businessmen and for middle-income wage earners (there are about 4.5 million taxpayers in India —a country of nearly 800 million people but with a per capita income of barely $250—compared to 29 million taxpayers in Britain, whose population is about 56 million and where the per capita income is around $6,500). The chief objective of Gandhi's budget of $82.7 billion was the promotion of industrial growth. Although the tax cuts are substantial, the Gandhi administration expects to generate an additional $250 million in federal revenues because of such measures as an increase in fares on the government-run railway network. The central government's total expenditure for projects has been held at $14 billion for 1985–1986, an increase of just $1 billion from the previous year. Gandhi's budget recognizes that there will be a net deficit of $2.79 billion, compared to $3.92 billion in Indira Gandhi's last budget. I was disbelieving at first because no Indian administration had ever been so bold in rooting for the private sector; and, of course, I was delighted at the new economic direction in which Rajiv Gandhi was now taking India. According to G. S. Talwar, a senior executive of Citibank, a number of Western multinational corporations have already started looking afresh at India as an investment possibility.

Some highlights of Gandhi's budget:

- Income tax exemption has been raised from $1,250 to $1,500 on individuals—which will immediately release nearly a million taxpayers from all tax obligations on personal incomes and thus strengthen their purchasing power.

- Basic wealth tax exemption has been increased from $12,500 to $20,000. All estate duties have been abolished. The purpose of these measures is to discourage the accumulation of "black money."

- The basic tax rate for the corporate sector has been lowered by 5 percent.

- There are new measures to reinvigorate India's 13 stock markets. Among these measures is a proposal to increase from 13.5 percent to 15 percent the guaranteed interest rate on convertible debentures. The purpose of this measure is to make it more attractive for ordinary people to invest in companies.

- There will be no excise duty on computers. Gandhi is feverishly promoting computerization in government and in industry.

- A new social security program has been created under which $2.5 billion will be set aside to compensate poor families whose wage earners die in accidents.

- The asset limit for companies under the Indian Monopolies and Restrictive Trade Practices Act—which seeks to prevent excessive concentration of ownership of economic resources—has been increased sharply from $16 million to $80 million.

- The small-scale industries have received a boost: expansion of up to $280,000 now would need no prior government approval. The previous ceiling was $160,000 for new expansion. Presumably, with fewer licences now required for small businesses, the opportunities for corruption among government bureaucrats will be lessened.

The Indian budget is the government's single most important economic document because it is a statement of domestic policies and objectives. Its adoption in Parliament is assured because the cabinet—which must approve the document—is picked from Members of Parliament; the majority party gets to form the government in India, and the prime minister is also traditionally the leader of that majority party. In the United States, the administration's budget is a proposal that is then vigorously debated and even modified in Congress. In India, however, what the prime minister wants, he gets.

Rajiv Gandhi has clearly opened the doors of opportunity for the private sector. Will India's industrialists now quickly seize the baton and race ahead?

I looked up other Indians whose opinions and judgments I valued. How did they assess the challenge of change in post-Indira India? And what faith did they have in Indian's capacity for change? I went to see Vasant Sheth, Gidwani's boss, a self-made industrialist and chairman of India's biggest private shipping company. Sheth, a tall, lanky man in his fifties with bushy eyebrows and a courteous manner, invited me for a cruise on his yacht. We went out past Bombay's harbor, past a flotilla of tankers that Sheth owned, past destroyers and frigates of the Indian Navy, and down India's western coast. It was a brilliant sunny Sunday morning, and the breeze was sharp. We sat on the deck of the yacht, sipped freshly squeezed orange juice, munched peanuts, and talked.

"Modernization means, most of all, having a modern mind," Vasant Sheth said. "Rajiv Gandhi has a modern mind. But I don't know about most of his government; and I don't know if most Indians possess a modern mind. The average Indian is a low risk taker. He believes in a status quo society. And all governments are important instruments of the status quo. My biggest fear is that this monolith, this octopuslike government that reaches into every area of our lives, can't and won't be able to bring about the changes we vitally need in our country. Over the years, governments have tried to absorb discontent by thoughtless recruitment to the lower-echelon bureaucracy. These lowly and low-paid public servants, in turn, have fattened themselves on bribes and 'speed money'—gratuities they demand to push along a file toward the decision-making official. The bloated bureaucracy curbs individual enterprise and initiative."

I asked Sheth what change he would like to see undertaken the most, and who he saw as being the instrument of that change.

"The most cherished goal for India to my mind is how best to enter the twenty-first century with real economic freedom," Sheth said. "India already has the world's largest technological pool, after the United States and the Soviet Union. India is now the eighth or ninth biggest industrial power in the world. International bankers have given India Triple 'A' credit ratings.

"But I really do believe that if you want to get beyond rhetoric and the illusion of progress and want to work for honest change, only the country's elite can do it. Who are the elite? Top bureaucrats, professionals, voluntary agencies, businessmen, politicians. Members of this elite have to make sacrifices themselves in the national interest. India's economic success is only possible provided we cooperate rather than confront—we have to remove the labels that separate us, and, believe me, there are plenty of such labels. The task is gigantic."

The next day, I went to see a man who is widely perceived to be at the leading edge of India's drive to become a technological power. His name is Ratan Naval Tata, and he is chairman of India's biggest business house, Tata Industries. The Tata group consists of companies that manufacture, among other things, fertilizers, steel, locomotives, textiles, cosmetics, chemicals, heavy engineering equipment, and vehicles. The Tatas also own a chain of deluxe hotels in India and abroad. It was the Tata family which started Air India, the country's international carrier. The Tatas have long enjoyed a reputation of being socially conscious employers; they have channeled millions into charities, educational foundations, and family-planning programs. The annual turnover of the Tata companies is more than $3 billion.

Ratan Tata is a tall, handsome and amiable man of forty-seven. He has a degree in architectural engineering from Cornell University, and worked for several years with the Los Angeles architecture firm of Jones and Emmons. A few days before I met him, Tata had announced that his group would be funneling millions of dollars into the development of appropriate high-technology products for India. His announcement had been applauded in Delhi by another youthful leader, Rajiv Gandhi.

Tata received me in his fourth-floor office at Bombay House, the granite-facaded Victorian building that serves as the group's headquarters. He had just returned from a visit to one of his factories and he was in shirt-sleeves. For a man who was heir to a huge fortune and who headed a distinguished group of companies, he had a surprisingly modest office—just some beige sofas, shelves that were packed with books and files, a large picture showing the cockpit of a plane, and a modern impressionistic painting that brightened up his otherwise drab room.

I asked Ratan Tata how realistically optimistic he was about the possibility of fundamental change in India.

"Six months ago there was great frustration in India," Tata said. "There was the obstacle of ideology. There was the obsession with promoting the public sector at the expense of the private sector—despite the proven track record of failure of public sector enterprises. There was also the obstacle of those who were close to power and enjoyed clout and who could therefore swing things their way for purely subjective reasons. You concluded that things didn't happen on merit in Delhi.

"But today I sense there's been a change in ideology. The bureaucracy seems to be goaded to produce results rather than to stop progress. The sounds are different. And not only are the sounds different. I see that governmental attitudes are already changing in Delhi. There's a new courtesy that seems to be present in government. You feel it in the air in Delhi, where all the decisions that matter concerning economic progress are made. Bureaucrats have started listening to you more carefully—you're no longer kept hanging about as in the old days. What I'm saying is that if all this is sustained and expanded, then maybe we'll see a new India being fashioned from the old.

"Challenges?" Ratan Tata continued. "The challenge before Rajiv Gandhi is to mold and marshal the great store of talent that already exists in the country. The challenge really is to find the right mechanism—the tools for change are already there in the form of manpower and management skills. The challenge for Rajiv is to make the country as a whole lose its lethargy and to increase productivity and growth in all economic sectors. One of his major challenges is to make far more effective use of resources. In my view, Rajiv faces the challenge of changing the fabric of a very corrupt political environment.

"Rajiv has before him the challenge of creating a new industrial environment. Our industry must face the rigors of international competition—for too long have our industries enjoyed excessive protectionism. We have to create an environment where people are result oriented and answerable for their actions. Here at Tata, I welcome opening up to more competition. Sure there will be some shedding of blood, some pain and institutional suffering. But in the long run the new competition will make us all more healthy. Some of my colleagues obviously don't agree—but this is the way I feel."

I asked Ratan Tata what his apprehensions were for India.

He reflected for a moment, then said: "Most of all that Indians might be expecting too much of their new young prime minister. I worry that ordinary Indians, who generally assume that their government will do everything for them, now will expect that with Rajiv's ascension the Golden Age will automatically arrive."

After leaving Ratan Tata, I walked down the corridor from his office to meet an old friend named Nani A. Palkhivala. Palkhivala is a senior director of the Tata group. He is also India's most eminent constitutional lawyer and income-tax specialist. The author of several books and a sought-after speaker, Palkhivala also served as India's ambassador to the United States from 1977 to 1979, during the time that the opposition Janata Party was in power and Indira Gandhi was in the political wilderness.

Palkhivala was in a relaxed mood. His strained relations with Indira Gandhi had been much publicized by the Indian press, and it was no secret that Mrs. Gandhi smarted under Palkhivala's frequent criticism of the corruption and inefficiency of her government. Gandhi aides had ordered numerous—and unsuccessful—investigations of Palkhivala's finances. But Palkhivala has always led an open and scrupulously moral life, and given away much of his wealth to charities. One reason Palkhivala is widely respected is that his personal life-style is a model of austerity and rectitude. I thought that he was one of the best ambassadors India ever sent to Washington, and during his two years there he made many friends for India.

"Rajiv Gandhi should be quite a different prime minister from his mother," Palkhivala said to me. "I think his instincts are good. We all must wish him well because this is the most crucial turning point in Indian history."

Palkhivala's view is that Mrs. Gandhi left India in a mess, that her own rule was not beneficial to the country. His interpretation of the massive electoral mandate Rajiv Gandhi received in the December 1984 parliamentary election was that people were simply tired of the old leaders who represented the various opposition parties.

"The country clearly thinks that this young man with a fresh outlook might be the answer to all our problems," Palkhivala said. "I have always believed that if the country gets as a leader a wise man of humility, what could we not do in India? We have the manpower, we have the scientific brains, we have the industrial expertise, we have the technology, we have all the raw materials we need for rapid economic growth. This country is just yearning for the right leader —and so I hope that Rajiv shows the requisite degree of strength and

wisdom. It is not beyond a man of vision to put the country on the
right track.

"A vital point which is normally missed in political histrionics in
India is that while it is possible, in a poor country such as ours, to
have economic growth without social justice, it is impossible to have
social justice without economic growth. It seems to me that 'Economic growth for social justice' would be a more rewarding slogan
than Mrs. Gandhi's empty *'Garibi Hatao!'* ('Remove poverty!') slogan."

Nani Palkhivala had spoken about his confidence concerning
India's ability to achieve progress. I looked up one of the country's
most eminent scientists to solicit his view on the subject.

Dr. M. R. Srinivasan is chairman of India's Nuclear Power Board,
which makes him the czar of one of the country's most important
industries and one to which Prime Minister Rajiv Gandhi himself has
paid special attention. He is a man of medium height, bearded, and
with a pleasant disposition. Srinivasan invited me for breakfast at his
apartment on Malabar Hill, from where one can command a view of
virtually all of Bombay. Mrs. Srinivasan, a jolly southerner like her
husband, served idlis, the typical South Indian rice pancakes that can
fill you up without filling you out. The Srinivasans' living room
contained several photographs of the scientist receiving various high
awards from President Zail Singh and the late Prime Minister Indira
Gandhi. These photographs were tastefully displayed alongside Indian antiques.

Srinivasan told me that in the harnessing and use of atomic energy,
India had made far more progress than most people realized. Already,
India possessed what is called in the scientific jargon "control of the
complete nuclear fuel cycle"—which is to say that India now could
mine uranium, design, build, and operate nuclear reactors, extract
plutonium from spent nuclear wastes and properly handle and dispose
nuclear waste products. India is the only developing country that has
this capacity. By early 1985, India was producing more than 1,000
megawatts of power through nuclear energy, or about 2 percent of

the total power produced in the country. (By contrast, nuclear power accounts for 10 percent of the power produced in such Western countries as the United States and Britain.) The advances in the nuclear field, Dr. Srinivasan said, were largely home-grown—and he was justifiably proud of the achievement.

"In any discussion of the challenge of change I don't think that 'science and technology' are just buzzwords," he said. "If we are to improve our standard of living dramatically, then we simply must link science and technology to everyday living. By this I mean that we need to develop better industrial methods, better varieties of grain, safer and cheaper consumer products. One reason Japan has done so well is the total ability of the Japanese people to accept science and technology as integral parts of their everyday life. In India we have to cultivate the scientific temper. For this we need an accelerated education program that emphasizes the role of science. I think where we've failed as a society is that we've not been able to transform or motivate people to incorporate scientific habits so that they live in a healthier and more hygienic way. The key to this is education."

The day after I met Dr. Srinivasan, Rajiv Gandhi announced that his government would initiate a comprehensive review of India's educational system.

In Bombay, I also sought out a man named Anil K. Malhotra. Like Dr. Srinivasan, Malhotra is in a field to which Rajiv Gandhi is paying special attention. Malhotra, at forty-five, is the youngest yet senior-most member of India's Oil and Natural Gas Commission (ONGC). He is in effect the man who supervises the country's entire offshore and onshore oil and gas exploration and production program; Malhotra is the man who also decides where to drill for oil—he controls a budget of more than $3 billion. In the last five years, the ONGC, largely under the direction provided by Malhotra, has shown not only that its six thousand employees could master the latest in world oil and gas technology. More importantly, the ONGC's work has resulted in a dramatic reduction in India's annual oil imports.

Malhotra, a stocky man with a Vandyke beard, gave me the following figures: in 1980, India imported $5.2 billion worth of crude oil and petroleum; the foreign oil accounted for 42 percent of all imports, and gobbled up 85 percent of the country's export earnings. But in 1984, oil imports had tumbled to $2.9 billion, or barely 18 percent of all of India's imports; the oil and petroleum imports consumed, in 1984, only 25 percent of all export earnings. Why? Because the country's oil production—largely under the guidance of Dr. Malhotra—rose from about 10 million metric tons in 1980 to nearly 30 million metric tons by the end of last year. Self-sufficiency in oil has thus increased from 33 percent to 75 percent. Malhotra is confident that if the current trends in hydrocarbon production continue, India is within sight of self-sufficiency before the end of this decade.

A remarkable possibility indeed! And one that is the consequence of the extraordinary and unusual autonomy that was granted by Indira Gandhi to Malhotra's operations. Malhotra, who is skilled at cabinet presentations, persuaded Mrs. Gandhi to approve a budget in 1980 that would enable him to increase the ONGC's staff from 1,500 to 6,000. Instead of recruiting from India's fusty bureaucracy, Malhotra made the deliberate decision to hire new college graduates so that he could mold their attitudes on productivity; he gave responsibility to young officers, thus building up a team spirit and morale rare in the Indian government. He did not hesitate to bring in foreign consultants when necessary. Malhotra also introduced the concept of consortium bidding for offshore projects which enabled a number of countries like Japan, South Korea, and Singapore to enter into the highly restricted international offshore industry, which resulted in better value for every dollar spent. India now has twelve offshore rigs, and onshore oil production and exploration in twenty of the country's twenty-two states. The ONGC drills 200 new oil wells a year, with the figure expected to rise to a thousand. (This figure still is considerably short of the 12,000 new oil wells drilled annually in the United States, and 4,500 in China.) India's offshore oil production has risen from 100,000 barrels per day in 1980 to nearly 500,000 barrels a day in 1985. India's proven hydrocarbon deposits are estimated at 4.2 billion tons, according to Vikram Singh Mehta, an adviser to Oil India, a

government-owned oil and gas exploration company. Mehta told me
that there are an additional 13 billion tons of hydrocarbon deposits
in sedimentary bases—but the challenge will be to tap these deposits
because they are in marginal or hard-to-reach offshore and onshore
fields.

Malhotra has shown that a Third World country can make rapid
strides in oil production by retaining full indigenous control over its
oil industry and by instituting sophisticated management measures.
Now Malhotra has been asked by the Vietnamese government to
send in an ONGC team to explore for oil in the Mekong River Delta
(Vietnam's political and economic patrons, the Soviets, apparently
do not possess the kind of sophisticated technology necessary for
major offshore drilling); he sees India being able to assist other developing countries in exploring for oil.

"The challenge of change?" Malhotra said. "Well, I see it as a call
to achieve economic self-sufficiency for India. The challenge is to
bring about institutional reforms so that we establish modern management practices in all our public enterprises."

The *eminence grise* of India's bureaucrats is a man named L. K.
Jha. A member since 1937 of the Indian Civil Service—which was
created by the British as an elite administrative apparatus—he has
had a very distinguished career indeed: secretary of the finance ministry; ambassador to the United States; chairman of the economic
reforms commission; head of the Reserve Bank of India; governor of
Jammu and Kashmir State; and economic adviser to every Indian
prime minister since Nehru. Jha, now in his mid-seventies, has long
wanted to lead a less hectic life—but Rajiv Gandhi insisted that he
continue as his economic counselor. It is the fashion in India these
days to assume that the economic liberalization proposed by Prime
Minister Gandhi is the handiwork of his young aides such as Montek
Singh Ahluwalia and Arun Singh; but in fact, Jha has been more than
influential in shaping some of these plans.

I was keen to meet Jha. I had last seen him in the early 1970s in
Washington, a few days before he ended his stint as India's envoy

to the Court of Richard Milhous Nixon. It had not been a particularly happy assignment for Jha because of Nixon's general antipathy toward India and his favoring of Pakistan. A mutual friend, Mohan Shah—an Indian businessman who is based in New York—agreed now to arrange a lunch interview for me. Jha, a tall, soft-spoken man with a craggy face and a shock of graying hair, had just about an hour to spare, and he quickly got to the point.

"It's all very well to promote the private sector—but in a country where incomes are as skewed as they are in India, you cannot take the view that what is good for the House of Tata is also good for India," Jha said. "What I'm saying is that to a certain extent you will have to continue to have a planned economy." Although he was solidly behind Gandhi's promotion of the private sector, the government would need to play a major role in the development of India's many backward and economically deprived areas, Jha said.

It was Jha who drafted the Industrial Regulation Policy of 1956, which many critics say eventually resulted in the gargantuan system of controls and licenses that hampered India's private sector. When I asked Jha about this, he said that he had never intended the policy to be rigid, that he had hoped it would be calibrated and adjusted. "But the policy was pre-empted by the ideologues," he said. "The ideologues distorted the policy."

Jha believes that various officials entrusted with the management of India's economic ministries successfully resisted Indira Gandhi's efforts to ease bureaucratic controls over the Indian economy. "Rajiv Gandhi instinctively favors a freer, but not an unplanned, economy," Jha said, "and I think he will be successful in his ambitions. Overall, bureaucratic controls have been a major factor in holding back economic growth."

In addition to lessening the grip of the bureaucracy, Jha believes that Gandhi will have to vigorously promote better efficiency on the part of the public sector enterprises. He acknowledged that many of them had been a drag on the economy. The prime minister must also concentrate on accelerating agricultural production, Jha said, and he must energetically push for the development of power facilities.

Had he said all this to Rajiv Gandhi?

"What I'm telling you I also say to him," Jha said, tartly. "Rajiv is a man brought up in free India. He does not have the same hang-ups as the old Freedom Fighters, who, more than anything else, were identified by what they were against—against colonialism, against foreign domination. He has no hangups of this kind. For Rajiv, it's a question of preparing India for the twenty-first century."

Jha accompanied Rajiv Gandhi on his first formal state visit to the United States in mid-June. Gandhi met with President Reagan and other top American officials, as well with captains of industry. The message he broadcast on the five-day trip was: he was preparing India for the twenty-first century. In words that reminded me of the language used by Jha, Prime Minister Gandhi told his audiences that "technology" did not mean simply computers and sophisticated electronic gear; the hi-tech age he wanted, Gandhi said, also applied to agriculture. "India still lives mostly in villages—and that's where technology has to go," the prime minister said. "We have to be careful that we don't get carried away with 'hi-tech.' The technology we use has to be such that it helps the average Indian."

I encountered L. K. Jha in the lobby of the Washington hotel where he was staying during the Gandhi visit. I asked him if the visit was going well. With a large smile on his craggy face, Jha said that he was very happy indeed with the things the young prime minister was saying.

In Lonavala, a small town about 80 miles from Bombay, I met a man named Hemant Khairay. He works on his father's vegetable farm, and twice a week transports tomatoes and greens in a small, battered van down to Bombay. The income from the farm will not make the Khairay family millionaires, but it supports Hemant, his wife and infant son, his two younger brothers and three sisters, and his parents. Khairay is a pleasant man of twenty-two, and he has obtained a bachelor's degree in accounting. He wants to buy more land and expand his agribusiness.

We were sitting one afternoon in his house, a modest one-story structure that overlooked his vegetable acreage. Khairay's wife, Snehelata, had served us a simple but delicious lunch of dal—or lentil curry—rice, and a dry concoction of potatoes, peas, and onions. Snehelata had also cut up fresh tomatoes from the Khairay farm. It was a pleasant afternoon, and beyond the farm were the serrated hills of the Sahyadri Range. I asked Khairay if it made any difference to him who India's prime minister was.

"Not really," was his answer. "How is my life going to change on a daily basis?"

I flew down to Bangalore to meet Ammu George and her husband, T. J. S. George. The Georges were among the most courageous people I know—they decided to give up a flourishing publishing business in Hong Kong and return to India to start afresh. Why? Because in India they would not be second-class citizens. George and a partner, Michael O'Neill, had started a successful magazine called *Asiaweek* in Hong Kong, which set the standard for many publications covering the clangorous political scene in East and Southeast Asia. But he had had his fill of success; George now wanted to return to his first love, writing books in his native language of Malayalam. He and Ammu decided to settle in Bangalore, where they had land. But when I met them, George had been once again drawn into the fray of publishing—his friend, the newspaper magnate Ramnath Goenka, asked him to take over the languishing Bangalore edition of the *Indian Express*. So now T. J. S. George was back, as an adviser, in the world of deadline meeting, headline fitting, and lead writing. Except that working conditions at the *Express* were far more primitive than at *Asiaweek;* and the type of ultramodern technology George had been accustomed to in Hong Kong's presses was simply unheard of in Bangalore.

I asked George why he accepted Goenka's offer.

"Once a newsman—" George replied, elliptically, and with a smile.

"He must have promised you lots of money, no?" I said.

"Yes," George said. "My salary is one rupee a year. This is essentially a labor of love. I like a chance to train young journalists."

George, a chunky, balding man with a low-key manner, seemed both buoyant and cautious when I met him. He had looked upon Indira Gandhi's later years as disastrous, but now he felt that her son Rajiv was displaying encouraging qualities of leadership. He thought Rajiv Gandhi had the nation's goodwill with him and that most people wanted to give him a chance. In his comments he echoed what Nani Palkhivala had said to me in Bombay.

"Journalistically speaking, I cannot think of a more exciting country to be in than India," George said. "I think we have an unstoppable future. But what really saddens me is that until now India hasn't become a great country because of unimaginative and low-grade leadership. We have ample resources. Now if only we have truly inspired and civilized political leadership, this is going to be a great country."

I asked George if he honestly believed that lethargic Indians could be so disciplined that they worked in unison for the national good.

"Look, I was never a supporter of Indira's 'Emergency,' but just think about what happened during those three years," George replied. "One day this country was hopelessly inefficient. The next day? Well, the next day the trains started to run on time, people started to report punctually for work, and so on. So while the 'Emergency' was a political tragedy, it also proved to Indians that they possessed the intrinsic ability to do things well.

"I think one of Indira Gandhi's great failures was that she concentrated excessively on India's external role, when she should have focused on developing the country's internal strength. But I feel that you cannot expect to have a meaningful external role unless you have solid internal strength. Whatever leverage and strength you have in foreign affairs has to be a reflection of your internal strength. I think we should have taken a lesson from the Chinese. They first attended to their internal consolidation."

The challenges to Rajiv Gandhi?

"I worry whether communalism in India will ever be contained,"

George said. "The way it has been allowed to grow—it's become a cancer. I think the biggest question facing us is: will India be able to rise above its communalism? I really worry about this. Can the majority Hindus live in peace with Muslims? And with the Sikhs? I don't think you can solve communalism through public speeches. Will the demands of electoral politics allow the containing of religious passions? No one knows the answers. What is encouraging is that democracy has taken deep roots in India. But Rajiv must not allow those roots to be consumed by the cancer of communalism."

We broke for lunch. Ammu, a skilled cook, had prepared a savory fish curry, which I polished off with zest. Ammu does not discuss politics, preferring instead to spend her time doing social work among the poor of Bangalore. But she seemed heartened by the fact that Prime Minister Rajiv Gandhi had recently done something that his mother had failed to do: he created a new Ministry for Women and Social Welfare. And Gandhi announced that henceforth education would be free for girls up to high school. Moreover, the prime minister had included five women in his cabinet, and had also elevated several more women to high positions in his ruling Congress Party. As Ammu George saw it, Rajiv Gandhi clearly had calculated the benefits of thus appealing to half of the country's population.

Her husband was not surprised by Rajiv's actions concerning opportunities for women. The young Gandhi had always impressed him as a man who was sophisticated and modern in his sensibility.

"If first impressions are anything to go by, then I'm optimistic about Rajiv's prospects for success—and optimistic for India," George said.

He paused to sip coffee.

"I'm not a man given to hyperbole," George said, presently. "I'm cautious by nature. But I can't but help feeling that the kind of India there was at Indira Gandhi's death may have died with her—the India of political cynicism, the India where the masses had nothing to look forward to but more frustration.

"I think what we are seeing now is a completely new India. This is a rebirth."

EPILOGUE

The Challenge of Change

M Y father died during the writing of this book. The eldest son
of a Hindu family is required by tradition to set fire to his
father's funeral pyre, and I flew from New York to Bombay to
discharge my duty. I am an only child; in addition to comforting my
widowed mother, I had to organize the religious rites and attend to
death taxes and property settlements. My father, a lawyer and ac-
countant, had left behind a modest amount for my mother, and I had
to find my way through a nettlesome bureaucratic labyrinth to ensure
her financial security. My father's cremation was held up for more
than an hour because some obscure clause in the local municipality's
rules book called for the filling out of a certain form; but the municipal office had run out of blanks, and I had to wait until the one
remaining form could be photocopied. In India bureaucracy rules
supreme in death as it does in life.

A brahman priest invited me to chant Sanskrit hymns. On the
plane to Bombay, I had read up on the origins of these hymns. In
lyrical language which went back to ancient Aryan times, these
hymns invoked the blessings of the gods for the soul of the departed.
They asked the gods not only to forgive him for his mortal sins but

also to release him from the cycle of death and rebirth. In the thirteen days of mourning that were to follow, I volunteered for every religious pooja and ritual that Hindu sons traditionally performed in India— not because I felt obliged to go through the motions but because these ceremonies revealed to me the significance of symbolism in everyday Indian life. I sat through rites before tiny mounds of rice and sweetmeats, which were symbolic offerings to the soul of my dead father and to the spirits of my ancestors; I washed the feet of the officiating brahman priest in acknowledgment of the brahmans' centuries-old stewardship of Hinduism; and I poured milk and rose water over coconuts to solicit the blessings of my own male forefathers for continuation of the male line in the family (the coconuts symbolized the collective bodies of my ancestors). They were complex rituals, and the priest, a cheerful man named Pandurang Gulwani, patiently explained the significance of every one of them.

As I lit the sandalwood heaped on my father's funeral pyre and watched the flames soar toward the cloudless blue February skies, I thought about what extraordinary changes my father had seen during his lifetime. He was born in the first decade of this century, when India was a colony of an imperial power that was indifferent to the economic wellbeing of its subjects. My father lived through the founding and flowering of India's nationalist movement, through two world wars in which Indian soldiers served the Empire heroically, and through a time which saw the rise and triumph of Mahatma Gandhi and Jawaharlal Nehru. Indeed, I was conceived after India achieved her independence from Britain—my parents, who had been married for nearly ten years by then, were determined that their first child should be born in a free India. My father, who believed in destiny, lived to see the establishment of modern India's great political dynasty—Nehru, his daughter Indira Gandhi, and her son Rajiv Gandhi. He was proud of this dynasty, and I always felt that he was a trifle disappointed that I did not share all his enthusiasms.

On that balmy February morning after the cremation, I gathered my father's ashes in a small brass urn and consecrated them to the high tide of the Arabian Sea, on whose shores my father took me for long walks when I was a child. During those walks he would often tell me how proud he was that I would grow up in a free India where men could dream limitless dreams. He talked about the certain possibility that in my lifetime I would see more change than he and his forebears combined. Such change would bring with it great challenges, my father often said when I was a child and in his subsequent letters to me after I had settled abroad. But always he would add that it was not the change that really mattered, or even the resulting challenges to the traditional ways of an ancient land. What mattered was the capacity of Indians to deal with the change and the challenges it brought. About that capacity there was, in his mind—and now in mine—a big question mark.

And so, when I think about the legacy of my father what comes to mind is not only his warmth, his gift of love and caring, his profound moral conviction that work was the best form of worship, and that good will ultimately triumph over evil. I also reflect, especially in these times of head-spinning change in India, on the questions he often raised during his remarkable lifetime: are we, as Indians, really capable of meeting the challenges to our timeworn attitudes and life-styles? And can we seize the time and transform our society to ensure a better life not just for the privileged few, but for us all?

I stayed on in India after my father's funeral because, in the early months of 1985, India was plainly charged with a special electromotive force. The new prime minister, Rajiv Gandhi, was barnstorming the nation by helicopter and airplane not only to urge Indians to vote his Congress Party into power in various state legislative assemblies that had been scheduled for March, but also to exhort his countrymen to set aside their ethnic and communal differences and work for the national good.

Everywhere there was talk of a "new technological age." Prime Minister Gandhi's youthful aides were quoted in newspapers and magazines as saying that their forty-year-old leader would guide India toward an unprecedented era of economic growth and social justice.

It was not all political rhetoric. Gandhi's government moved swiftly to liberalize import policies for the automobile industry, opening up that cobweb-ridden industry for vigorous new competition that would surely result in more, better, and cheaper cars for the average Indian. Industrialists petitioning for new licences for expansion or joint ventures with foreign firms were now finding their applications being acted on with greater alacrity. There was a sense in the business community that Rajiv Gandhi was not merely mouthing platitudes about change: he meant to hold his administrators accountable for their actions; he seemed determined that government should be a good manager.

The budget that the Gandhi administration unveiled on March 16 further reinforced people's belief that the prime minister would alleviate crushing tax burdens and also stimulate industrial growth. Gone were the habitual references to socialism. So revolutionary was Gandhi's budget in the kinds of tax and other concessions it offered, that Indians went berserk with delight: they held rallies, they organized parades, they took out processions to hail the new savior.

At first I was troubled by what I perceived to be the excessive adulation of the young prime minister. Of course, I could understand the reasons for such adulation: here was a handsome young prime minister who spoke well; he especially appealed to those Indians been born after Independence—and there were now more than 400 million of them. It occurred to me that Indians had forgotten that when Rajiv Gandhi's mother, Indira Gandhi, won her huge electoral victories more than a decade ago, there had been similar public outpourings of enthusiasm for her; she was seen as the leader who would pull India into a new age of modernity. She fulfilled few of her promises. Were Indians now again setting themselves up for similar disappointment? Was Rajiv Gandhi simply promising too much to his eager millions?

One evening in India, I telephoned my friend T. J. S. George in Bangalore. I reminded him of a conversation we had in the turbulent days following the assassination of Indira Gandhi. George, a veteran journalist, had said then that the ascension of Rajiv Gandhi and his post-Independence team was a "rebirth."

Did he still think so?

"Of course," George said, "how else would you characterize the situation? This new budget, for instance, really calls for a total restructuring of Indian society—Rajiv wants liberalization, an open-door attitude toward investment, he is drastically lowering taxes for business and for the middle classes. There has never been anything like this before. There's a whole new attitude of openness in the government. Those in power are giving the impression that they mean to actually serve the people who placed trust in them. Of course I would call it 'rebirth.' "

Rebirth or replay? I pondered the question one evening in Bombay as I watched Rajiv Gandhi address a massive rally in Shivaji Park. The same placard-waving and slogan-shouting crowds that used to turn up at his mother's public appearances around the country were again in attendance here, and they cheered Rajiv repeatedly. Pictures of Indira Gandhi were hung on bamboo poles so that her handsome stern face was everywhere. It was eerie seeing those pictures: in the dying light of a cool February evening, Indira Gandhi's face seemed to be floating above the multitudes. Was she smiling in benediction, or was she mocking those of us who remained mortals? Were her pictures strung up as talismans? Or were they meant to be grim reminders of India's greatest tragedy in modern times? There seemed to be as many security personnel in Shivaji Park as there were ordinary citizens. The young prime minister spoke about the great dream of development, and about how India would enter the twenty-first century a proud and prosperous nation. Change the voice, and it could have been Indira Gandhi speaking.

Clichés. Already Rajiv Gandhi had become a skilled employer of them. But say this much for him: in his own quiet manner, he spoke with conviction and compassion.

It occurred to me as I listened to the prime minister that perhaps he and his youthful coterie might just be single-minded enough to

forge ahead and make a success of their plans. That evening in Shivaji
Park I recalled the words of a friend, Bradford Morse, who heads the
United Nations Development Programme. Morse once said to me
that the chief responsibility of national leaders was to enlarge the
capacity of their people.

As I looked at the young man on the platform, his unlined face
smiling and acknowledging the accolades of his people, his eyes
glinting with ambition, I wondered how often he thought about his
mother; I wondered how Rajiv Gandhi would avenge his mother's
murder. Would his be the politics of divisiveness and confrontation
in the manner of his mother, or would he apply a healing, soothing
hand to the nation, as his grandfather, Jawaharlal Nehru, did?

Nothing that Rajiv Gandhi said that evening in Shivaji Park was
memorable. I do not know whether it was his youth, or the simple
fact that he looked so poised and confident—but I somehow came
away with the feeling that this young leader would flower. Somewhere in the recesses of my mind there echoed a passage whose words
I was not able to immediately identify. As I inched my way through
the departing crowd toward a bus stop, someone accidentally stepped
on my foot. Perhaps it was the sudden pain, or perhaps it was simply
my subconscious finally bubbling to the surface—but I now clearly
remembered the words I was groping to grasp. They were something
that Rajiv Gandhi's grandfather, Nehru, had once said. In a cele-
brated speech to the Indian Constituent Assembly minutes before
India became independent in August 1947, Prime Minister Nehru
said:

"Long years ago we made a tryst with destiny, and now the time
comes when we shall redeem our pledge. . . . A moment comes, which
comes but rarely in history, when we step out from the old to the new,
when an age ends, and when the soul of a nation, long suppressed,
finds utterance."

My father had been among the privileged people who actually
watched Jawaharlal Nehru speak. Years later, he told me that as he
heard Nehru the sentiment that kept swirling in his mind was: "I
wish him well—for his sake and for the sake of India."

Both Nehru and my father are gone, and it is now almost forty years since India made that first tryst with destiny. But what Nehru said then, and what my father felt at that heady time of independence, are especially appropriate today as Rajiv Gandhi leads India into a new age.

He will need a sense of history to guide him—that, and the humility to realize that in the ultimate analysis no one person can shape India's destiny. India cannot be changed by public-relations gimmicks, nor only by the jargon of hi-tech. A prime minister can inspire his people by his vision, but India is a large country, and terribly complex, and whatever reforms a prime minister has in mind must be presented in socially acceptable forms. To put across his modern ideas, Rajiv will have to adapt them to local cultural idioms; and while change in a huge country like India cannot be instituted overnight, the prime minister will also have to visibly accelerate the push for modernization and deliver on his pledges. Rajiv Gandhi, more than his mother and grandfather, is going to have to contend with increasingly assertive regional leaders and movements—and he is going to have to draw the best out of them if the country is to move into a more progressive era. His will have to be the politics—and, indeed, the economics—of consensus. Cooperation, not confrontation, will have to be the basis of development.

As a journalist I have been privileged to visit most of the Third World. And I believe that of all the big developing countries I have seen, India still has the best chance for getting its people out of the rut of poverty. I am encouraged by the rising levels of education, and by the solid underpinnings of cultural richness; I am encouraged by the fact that the infrastructure for wider economic growth is now in place; I am encouraged by India's self-sufficiency in food. But Indians need to be freed of the maze of senseless controls that have proliferated and plagued the economy with Soviet-style inefficiency. India has made impressive economic progress despite such controls, to be sure, but now Rajiv Gandhi has an extraordinary opportunity to shift the country's economy into still higher gear, and to slice away at the inequities that have persisted since independence. He has made a heartening start, but the test will be in the sustained translation of good intentions into programs and policies. And here the danger is that Rajiv Gandhi and his well-intentioned band of associates might be overwhelmed by the daily realities of governing India.

Not long after my father's death in February, I was going through his papers when I came across an ancient notebook. It was a diary that he had kept during the independence struggle. He had jotted his impressions about the titans of his time—Mahatma Gandhi, Jawaharlal Nehru, Maulana Azad, Vallabhbhai Patel. It was a time of excitement, and it was a time of hope. I moved down the pages to the post-Independence entries, and one particular section caught my eye.

"Indians are clamoring for deep, constructive change," my father had written in Marathi. "They have suffered for so long, but they are a patient people. How much longer will they suffer, how much longer will they be patient?"

He wrote those words just around the time I was born. But the questions he posed then are even more valid today.

Glossary

THERE are a number of terms peculiar to India—words and phrases that are not quite English, or pure Hindi either, but what visiting foreign correspondents wryly call Hindlish, which really means a melange that has slipped into contemporary usuage. Some of these Hindlish terms originated during the days of the British Raj. I offer the following words and phrases not only because many Indians who turn up in my narrative mouth them, but also because visitors to India are certain to encounter Hindlish.

A

ACCHA: Okay!

ACHKAN: a long coat buttoned up to the neck, usually worn on formal occasions

ADIVASI: a tribal or aboriginal person

AGNI: fire; ancient Aryan god of fire

AHIMSA: nonviolence; originally a Jain concept, reinterpreted by Mahatma Gandhi as a political doctrine

ARAAY: I say!

ARYAN: Indo-European language group of tribes who invaded and conquered north India thousands of years before the birth of Christ

ASHRAM: a hermitage
AYAH: a nursemaid or maid servant
AZAD: free

B

BACHHAA: literally, "child"; used to mean naive
BAAS: Enough!
BABU: a somewhat disparaging term for a clerk or lowly official
BADMASH: a rascal or rogue
BAGH: a garden
BANDH: a total strike, these days generally accompanied by violence
BANIA: A Hindu merchant caste, originally from the western state of Gujerat
BANYAN: the traditional holy Indian tree, usually old and huge
BEGUM: honorific for Muslim woman, usually a noblewoman
BHANG: Indian hemp
BIDI: a cheap Indian cigarette in which the tobacco is rolled in leaves instead of paper.
BRAHMAN: member of the highest Hindu priestly caste
BRINJAL: eggplant
BUDDHA: Enlightened One; Gautama Buddha, the former Prince Siddharta, was the founder of Buddhism
BURKHA: a long veil, usually used by conservative Muslim women
BURRA: big

C

CANTONMENT: military station, or community
CHAPPRASI: office boy, or servant
CHOR: thief
CHOTTA: small
CHOWKIDAR: security guard, usually nightwatchman

COOLIE: a manual laborer

CRORE: ten million; a crore of Indian rupees is equivalent to a million American dollars, at current exchange rates

D

DACOIT: bandit; the hotbed of banditry has long been in the Chambal Valley in central India

DARSHAN: literally, a glimpse; an audience with a holy man; audiences with Indira Gandhi were often called darshan

DARZI: tailor

DHOBI: washerman

DHOTI: white garment worn like a sarong and drawn up between the legs in the manner of a loincloth

DOWRY: usually a cash payment given by a bride's family to the bridegroom at the time of marriage

DURBAR: royal court

DUREE: rug

F

FAKIR: mendicant, usually someone living on charity

FIRINGHI: usually a put-down term for a white

FLEETFOOTS: canvas sneakers, usually the sort worn for tennis or jogging

G

GARIBI: poverty

GHATS: steps leading into a river, such as the Ganges in Banaras; also a word used as a synonym for hills

GHEE: clarified butter used in cooking and for religious ceremonies

GHERAO: literally means to surround; a form of protest perfected by leftist unions in West Bengal who surround a factory and refuse to let management out until their demands are met

GOONDA: a bad character, or hooligan

GURKHA: one of the class of Nepalese mountain people who have long served with distinction as mercenaries in the British and Indian armies

GURU: spiritual adviser, saint, or mentor

GYMKHANA: a club

H

HARAMI: a person who does harm or evil

HARIJAN: member of the "untouchable" class; means "child of God," a term used by Mahatma Gandhi to characterize untouchables, many of whom still live in overwhelming poverty and suffer from social discrimination

HARTAL: a local strike, usually a wildcat or lightning strike

J

JAI: victory

JIHAD: Muslim holy war

K

KAFFIR: infidel

KALI: the mother goddess

KARMA: the Hindu doctrine that holds that every deed, good or bad, entails certain consequences that may appear during successive incarnations of the soul; it is sometimes called the doctrine of retribution

KHADI: homespun cloth; Gandhi advocated the wearing of khadi garments as a form of protest against British colonial rulers under

whom India became a lucrative market for British textiles; khadi
is cool and comfortable, and thus ideal in India's heat and dust;
khadi, or khaddar, has long been the symbol of allegiance to the
Congress Party

KHANSAMA: a cook

KIRPAN: a dagger carried by many Sikhs

KOTWALI: local police station

KURTA: a long, loose tunic, usually worn with pyjama trousers

L

LAKH: 100,000 units, such as a lakh of rupees

LATHI: a stave carried by Indian policemen and used as a baton to
disperse crowds

LOK: people; the lower house of the Indian Parliament is called the
Lok Sabha, or Assembly of the People

LUNGI: a saronglike wrap, favored in the Tamil south

M

MAHARAJA: king; also Raja

MAHATMA: great-souled one; the honorific by which Mohandas
Gandhi, founder of modern India, was widely known

MALEE: a gardener

MANDAPAM: central shrine of a temple

MANTRA: a Hindu hymn or psalm

MAYA: illusion

MEMSAHIB: European married woman, from "madam-sahib"

MITHAI: greasy Indian sweetmeats, usually offered at auspicious
times

MORCHA: a protest march

MULLAH: a Muslim religious or social leader

MUNNAH: young son, or sometimes daughter

N

NAGAR: city

NATARAJA: "King of the Dance"; one of the names by which Shiva, a Hindu god, was known

NAUTCH-GIRL: dancing girl

NAWAB: nobleman, usually a Muslim; also, nabob

NETA: leader

NIRVANA: the goal of salvation, or eternal liberation, to which Buddhists aspire

P

PAAN: betel leaf, highly favored as a digestive; usually available with a variety of savory fillings and sometimes with narcotics

PADDY: rice in the husk

PAKISTAN: Land of the Pure

PANCHAYAT: an Indian village council originally supposed to consit of five elders

PANCH SHEEL or PANCH SHILA: the so-called Five Principles of Co-existence first enumerated in the preamble to the Sino-Indian treaty of 1954 on trade with Tibet. The principles are: mutual respect for each other's territorial integrity and sovereignty; nonaggression; noninterference in each other's internal affairs; equality and mutual advantage; and peaceful co-existence and economic cooperation. The treaty has now lapsed, but the principles are frequently cited by Indian policy makers in their dealings with other nations

PARSI: a descendant of Zoroastrian Persians who migrated to India as religious refugees after the Arab invasion of Persia in the eighth century A.D. The Parsis are now concentrated in Bombay; an enterprising community, many Parsis are engaged in commerce and the professions. India's most famous Parsi is Zubin Mehta, conductor of the New York Philharmonic

PEON: a gofer, or office boy

POOJA: a holy ritual, the Hindu form of mass

PRASAD: religious offering, usually a sweet dish, blessed by the gods

PUKKA: "the real thing," or the "real McCoy"; also solid

PUNKAH: large cloth fan, usually worked by servants pulling cord attached to a wood frame

PURDAH: literally, curtain; but commonly means a form of segregation of the female in a conservative Muslim household

R

RAJ: literally, kingdom or empire; used in such expressions as the "British Raj"

S

SADHU: a holy man, usually a wandering mendicant

SAHIB: respectful term for sir

SARDAR: sobriquet for a Sikh; "sard" is usually the derogatory term

SATI: outlawed Hindu ritual where widow burned herself on her husband's funeral pyre

SATYAGRAHA: literally, force of truth or soul force; nonviolent civil disobedience originally used by Mahatma Gandhi as a weapon against the British, now employed for political and economic causes

SEPOY: old term for a soldier

SHAKTI: strength

SHETHJI: word used to address a wealthy person or a big shot

SHIKAAR: a hunt, usually for tigers or elephants

SIKH: literally, a disciple; a member of the martial religious community that sprang up in the Punjab in the sixteenth century in the time of Muslim rule as a reformist monotheistic sect. The founders of Sikhism borrowed heavily from both Islam and Hinduism. Sikhism's holiest shrine is the Golden Temple in Amritsar

SWAMI: a saint, or spiritual leader

SWARAJ: independence

T

TAMASHA: a spectacle; generally a word used to connote farce

TAMIL: a member of the largest linguistic group in south India. Tamils are also found in Sri Lanka, Burma, Malaysia, and Singapore. The word also denotes their language, the oldest and most highly developed of the southern Indian Dravidian tongues

TIFFIN: literally, box; means lunch, usually a packed lunch for white-collar workers

TIKKA, or TILAK: forehead mark of red paste, or vermilion, worn by Hindu women, usually to denote married status

TONGA: a two-wheeled pony cart

V

VARNA: the ancient word for caste, signifying the four traditional Hindu social divisions: the brahmans, or priests; kshatriyas, or warriors and administrators; the vaishyas, or traders and merchants; and the shudras, or laborers; the "untouchables" were traditionally outside the caste system

W

WAH: Wow!

Z

ZAMINDAR: landowner; popular usuage denotes someone who exploits

AUTHOR'S NOTE

I HAVE long admired the writings of A. M. Rosenthal, who covered India during the 1950s for the *New York Times,* and who later became the paper's executive editor. Few foreign newspapermen or writers before or since have understood India so well, or written about it with such depth and compassion.

Consider the following passage from a Rosenthal reminiscence of India: "When I was young, and writing from India, I embraced the gift of each day. Each day was filled with sound and movement, with thought and action, with a delighted awareness of the present, hope for the future and the sense of the rolling of history.... When I think of my four reporting years there, I see myself surrounded by people and motion and color and joys and horrors and kindly friends, by heat, rain, the scent of dung and of the marigold, snow on the mountain, muck in the village, anger, laughter, elegance, decay.

"When I tell my friends about my love for India, they say, but how about caste and filth and poverty and stenches and disease, riot and death?

"Yes, I tell them, of course, of course. But that is not all of India, and it is the rest, I say, the huge infinite variety of the rest, that lifted my heart and still does. It is the sense of color and dash in the dress of every Rajasthani woman brick-carrier. It is the music everywhere, the dozen different countries and the races and religions roiling in the one India. It is the warmth of the people you meet who are so kind, so loving, the adventure in travel and the still-existing greatest adventure—the Indian adventure in freedom."

It was reading and rereading Abe Rosenthal's dispatches from India—he was there when I was still a child—that made me resolve years ago to write a book on India. I wanted to take a crack at it because Abe's reporting made me terribly thrilled about the country where I was born and where I spent the first eighteen years of my life. In Abe's dispatches, India came alive: it was a place of magic. It was not that he overlooked the underbelly of India, its warts, its degrading poverty, its permeating miseries; but he put these things in perspective. In his reporting, you could see everyday Indians living, loving, laughing, weeping, breathing—you could see them do the things everyday people do elsewhere all the time. Yet you could also see how Indians were different—how special were their struggles to achieve modernity, how hard they had to scrape to survive.

Abe Rosenthal saw India through his special vision, and it was, of course, one foreigner's view of what this extraordinary place was like at a particular time in his and its life. I was determined to write a book that showed how one Indian-born man saw the country of his birth and breeding, a sympathetic book but one that also—as Abe's dispatches did—accurately and fairly reflected contemporary reality. But how to go about it, how to structure a book about so large a land? Ideas came and went, ambitions rose and fell, reporting trips to various parts of India were undertaken—but still no clear sense of what the India book would ultimately be.

On a balmy October morning in 1984, I found myself in Bombay, where I was born. I was visiting my father, who was seriously ill and confined to a hospital room. On that day, October 31, the news of the assassination of Prime Minister Indira Gandhi by two of her trusted Sikh security guards hit us all like a thunderbolt. Later that day, my former employers, the *New York Times,* telephoned to ask if I would travel up to the Punjab and report from there for newspaper. The caller was John Darnton, the deputy foreign editor, who knew I was there. He diplomatically did not point out that foreigners were forbidden from traveling to the Punjab since the Indian Army's invasion of the Golden Temple in Amritsar—so presumably the newspaper's American staff members could not travel to this troubled state. In my case, of course, it helped to look Indian in India and also to carry an Indian passport, facts that were implicit in Darnton's request and which would enable me to journey without hindrance to the trouble-torn Punjab, the home state of Prime Minister Gandhi's assassins. My father urged that I at once speed up north, never mind his condition, for this was history in the making.

In the event, I was the only foreign correspondent who was able to report from the Punjab in the immediate wake of the assassination. Worshipping at the Golden Temple in the company of Sikh friends was one of the most moving experiences I ever had; and as I visited with Sikhs and non-Sikhs around the Amritsar area, it struck me that a book was finally taking shape in my head.

I decided that I would write not only about the assassination of Indira Gandhi and its aftermath; most importantly, I would write about where Indians, who had gone through a remarkable seventeen years of her political rule, now saw their country going. I did not wish to be a soothsayer, but I did want to find out from ordinary Indians and from their leaders what sort of future they thought lay in store for them. And so I embarked on a fresh round of reporting.

This book is the result of that reporting trip, which took me between November 1984 and March 1985 from the northern Indian state of Kashmir to Kerala at the southern tip of the country. I traveled to India's great cities and booming towns, and I journeyed to rural areas, where more than 70 percent of India's 800 million people live. I interviewed politicians and peasants and political scientists; I talked with young professionals, movie stars, teachers, farmers, businessmen, technocrats, journalists, musicians, artists, social workers—most of all, I looked up ordinary Indians. I observed firsthand the December 1984 national elections in which Prime Minister Rajiv Gandhi's ruling Congress Party won 401 out of 508 seats contested for Parliament, an unprecedented achievement for any political party since India became independent from Britain in 1947.

This book was made possible because of the receptivity and help of my longtime literary agent, Timothy Seldes of Russell and Volkening, Inc., in New York. I am also especially grateful to Starling Lawrence, my editor at W. W. Norton. Star has always been wonderful to work with, and his suggestions about the structure of this book were invaluable. I also thank Nina Bouis, the line editor for this book, whose counsel was very beneficial.

My deep gratitude also to Tarzie Vittachi. Tarzie is the best guru any writer could have: he is patient, he has a sharp eye, and he is a man of vision and insight.

A great many people were generous with their time and hospitality during my reporting trip, and I want here to acknowledge their contribution to my book and to thank them:

The *New York Times* asked me to go to the Punjab in the wake of the Gandhi assassination—a reporting trip which helped develop this book. In particular, my thanks to Abe Rosenthal; Seymour Topping, the managing editor; Arthur Gelb, the deputy managing editor; Warren Hoge, the foreign editor; John Darnton, the deputy foreign editor; and Marie Courtney. And special thanks to Assistant Managing Editor James L. Greenfield and to William Stockton, assistant to the executive editor.

Romesh and Raj Thapar of New Delhi, two of the loveliest and warmest people I've had the privilege of knowing, shared with me many insights and gave me so much of their time. My deep gratitude to them.

Special thanks also to Dr. Rajni Kothari of Delhi's Center for the Study of Developing Societies who spent long hours with me and offered extraordinary analyses of the contemporary scene in India.

Also in New Delhi, my thanks to: H. Y. Sharada Prasad, information advisor to Prime Minister Rajiv Gandhi; Salman Haidar of the External Affairs Ministry; Manmohan Singh, chairman and managing director of Frick India; Kris and Brinda Srinivasan; Ajai and Indu Lal, who offered me shelter; Vijay and Bunty Dhawan; Aroon Purie, editor and publisher of *India Today;* Khushwant Singh; Professor Ashis Nandy of the Center for the Study of Developing Societies; Professor Dharma Kumar; Arun Bhatia; Jalabala Vaidya, Gopal Sharman and Anasuya Vaidya of the Akshara Theater; Pandit Ravi Shankar; Vichitra Sharma of the *Hindustan Times;* Gautam Phillips; Noni and Nilima Chawla; Jerry Brennig; Zahed and Laila Baig; Prem Shankar Jha; Hugo Corvalan of the United Nations Fund for Population Activities; Prabha Krishnan; P. A. Nazareth, secretary of the Indian Council for Cultural Relations; William K. Stevens, Sanjoy Hazarika, and P. J. Anthony of the *New York Times* bureau; Inder Mohan and Rani Sahni; Babulal Jain, and Tasneem and Vikram Singh Mehta.

In Andhra Pradesh, my warm thanks to Anand Mohan Lal, my father-in-law, for his suggestions and his insights into the Indian condition; and to my mother-in-law, Malati Lal, for her encouragement. Special thanks also to Pramila and Lessel David for their time and their assistance in arranging for visits to the countryside. And thanks to Chief Minister N. T. Rama Rao; to Ramoji Rao, publisher of *Newstime;* and to Potla and Nandita Sen, also now of Hyderabad, for their trenchant assessments of the Indian scene.

In Bangalore: my special appreciation to T. J. S. George, the veteran journalist who is now resident editor of the Indian Express, and to his wife, Ammu.

In Kashmir: C. B. Kaul of the *Indian Express* was enthusiastically helpful in setting up appointments and in providing expert assessments of the local political scene. Thanks also to Begum Abdullah and to Moulvi Mohammed Farooq, the religious leader of Kashmir, who generously gave me their time and thoughts.

In the Punjab: Inder Mohan and Anjali Khosla; Karuna and Satish Mahajan; Janak Raj Seth; Bhagwant Singh Ahuja; Mickey and the entire Ahuja clan, and Raman and Rajeev Mehta, all went out of their way to help me. My profound gratitude to them.

In Cochin: Kutty Narayan and his family were, as always, wonderfully helpful.

In Calcutta: my thanks to Bikash and Debjani Sinha; and to M. J. Akbar, editor of the *Telegraph,* whose book, *India: The Siege Within,* was particularly useful to me.

In Bombay: warmest thanks to my parents, Balkrishna and Charusheela Gupte, who patiently put up with my unpredictable comings and goings. Rahul Singh and Niloufer Billimoria were very generous with their time, as were Vir and Malavika Sanghvi. My gratitude to Shri Prabhakar Korgaonkarsaheb and his sister, Tai. And thanks to: H. P. Roy; Protima Chowdhury; Shri Vaidyanathan; Pritish Nandy; Dr. Rusi H. Dastur; Dr. D. C. Patel; Dr. Mahendra Jain of Bhatia General Hospital; Bakul Rajni Patel; Anil Dharker of *Debonair* magazine; Titu Ahluwalia; Geeta Kanar; Nalini Kunte; Anil and Jaymala Bhandarkar; Neelu and Ava Gidwani; Ava Viegas of Panam; Dilip and Nina Sardesai; Vasant and Asha Sheth; Anil and Ena Malhotra; Shyam Benegal; Tina Khote; Shashi Kapoor; Dom Moraes and his wife, Leela Naidu; Ramchandra Moray; Murli and Hema Deora; Ram Jethmalani and Mahesh Jethmalani; Hari Jaisingh; Dr. M. R. Srinivasan and Geeta Srinivasan; Ratan N. Tata; and Ambassador Nani A. Palkhivala, one of India's most distinguished lawyers and thinkers, who shared with me his thoughts on the Indian scene. And warm thanks to Shobha Rajadhyaksha, editor of celebrity Magazine, and an astute analyst of Indian affairs.

In New York: warm thanks to Ralph Buultjens, who offered his assessment of Indira Gandhi, who was his close friend and mentor over many years; Madhur Jaffrey and Sanford Allen; Jill Bialosky, Assistant to Starling Lawrence at W. W. Norton; Madhu and Naresh Trehan; Anil Walia; Bradford Morse, administrator of the United Nations Development Programme; Rafael M. Salas, Dr. T. N. Krishnan, and Jyoti Shankar Singh of the United Nations Fund for Population Activities, who gave useful perspectives on India's population problems; Edmund Kerner, also of the UNFPA, who offered a Sri Lankan point of view concerning Mrs. Gandhi's ambitions in Asia; Barbara Bender; Barry Sahgal of Ladenburg, Thalman and Company, investment bankers; and Jerry Flint, assistant managing editor of *Forbes* magazine, whose general advice has always been a great help. And a special thanks to Janki Ganju of Washington, D.C., for his unfailing good humor and splendid counsel.

Thanks to Tina Brown, editor-in-chief of *Vanity Fair* magazine, and to senior editor Patricia Towers. And a very warm thanks to Gina

Maccoby of Russell and Volkening, Inc., and to her assistant, Mariam Altshul.

I also thank my friends Hugh O'Haire Jr., editor of the United Nations's *Populi* magazine, and Shehbaz Safrani, a New York–based scholar and painter, for offering useful suggestions concerning parts of the manuscript. Thanks, too, to Chanchal Sarkar in Delhi, and Professor Jagdish N. Bhagwati of Columbia University, for scrutinizing the manuscript.

A very fond thanks to James W. Michaels, editor of *Forbes* magazine, for writing such an extraordinary foreword to this book.

In London: my thanks to Michael Thomas of A. M. Heath, Inc.; to Swraj and Aruna Paul; and to Elizabeth Allen.

I am deeply grateful, as always, to my wife, Jayanti. She showed great patience during the researching and writing of this book; taking care of a five-year-old son as well as a thirty-six-year-old husband were formidable tasks indeed! Jayanti also read the manuscript with her keen and observant eye, offering suggestions and pointers that were of great value to me. Our son, Jaidev, is too young now to read this book, and India to him is only a place to enjoy marvelous holidays with his grandparents. But I hope some day he will look up what his father learned about the country in which both of us were born.

How I wish that my own father, Balkrishna Gupte, had lived to see the publication of this book. One of his fondest ambitions was for me to write a book about India. My father died on February 5, 1985, after a long illness.

Pranay Gupte
New York City
June 1985.

BIBLIOGRAPHY

T HERE is a treasure trove of literature on India and the subcontinent and on Asia. Establishments such as Barnes and Noble and the Strand Book Store in New York, and Foyle's and Hatchard's in London have long shelves devoted to fiction and nonfiction about the region. Here are books and publications I have found particularly useful:

Abbas, Khawja Ahmad. *Indira Gandhi: Return of the Red Rose.* Bombay: Popular Prakashan, 1966.
——. *That Woman.* Delhi: Indian Book Company, 1973.
Ahluwalia, B. K., and Ahluwalia, Shashi. *Martyrdom of Indira Gandhi.* Delhi: Manas Publications, 1984.
Akbar, M. J. *India: The Siege Within.* London: Penguin Books, 1985.
Ali, Tariq. *The Nehrus and the Gandhis: An Indian Dynasty.* London: Picador Books, 1985.
Allen, Charles, and Dwivedi, Sharada. *Lives of the Indian Princes.* London: Century Publishing, 1984.
Azad, Maulana Abdul Kalam. *India Wins Freedom.* New York: Longmans, Green, 1960.
Baig, M. R. A. *Muslim Dilemma in India.* Delhi: Vikas Publishing House, 1974.
Barnds, William J. *India, Pakistan, and the Great Powers.* New York: Praeger, 1972.

Bhagwati, Jagdish N., and Desai, Padma. *India: Planning for Industrialization.* London: Oxford University Press, 1970.

Bhatia, Krishan. *The Ordeal of Nationhood.* New York: Atheneum, 1971.

——. *Indira.* New York: Praeger, 1974.

Blaise, Clark, and Bharati Mukherjee. *Days and Nights in Calcutta.* New York: Doubleday and Company, 1977.

Bobb, Dilip, and Raina, Asoka. *The Great Betrayal: Assassination of Indira Gandhi.* Delhi: Vikas Publishing House, 1985.

Bose, Mihir. *The Aga Khans.* London: World's Work, 1984.

Bowles, Chester. *Ambassador's Report.* New York: Harper and Row, 1954.

——. *Promises To Keep.* New York: Harper and Row, 1972.

Brecher, Michael. *Nehru: A Political Biography.* London: Oxford University Press, 1959.

Bright, J. S. *Indira Gandhi.* Delhi: New Light Publishers, 1984.

Brown, Judith. *Modern India: Origins of an Asian Democracy.* Delhi: Oxford University Press, 1984.

Cameron, James. *An Indian Summer.* London: Macmillan, 1973.

Campbell-Johnson, Alan. *Mission with Mountbatten.* London: Robert Hale, 1951.

Chaudhuri, Nirad C. *Autobiography of an Unknown Indian.* London: Macmillan, 1951.

——. *The Continent of Circe: Being an Essay on the Peoples of India.* New York: Oxford University Press, 1966.

——. *To Live or Not to Live.* Delhi: Indian Book Company, 1973.

Chopra, V.D.; Mishra, R. K.; and Singh, Nirmal. *Agony of Punjab.* Delhi: Patriot Publishers, 1984.

Collins, Larry, and Lapierre, Dominique. *Freedom at Midnight.* New York: Simon and Schuster, 1975.

Coolidge, Olivia. *Gandhi.* Boston: Houghton Mifflin, 1971.

Coomaraswamy, Ananda K. *The Dance of Shiva.* New York: H. Wolff, 1957.

Critchfield, Richard. *Villages.* New York: Doubleday/Anchor, 1983.

Crocker, Walter. *Nehru: A Contemporary's Estimate.* New York: Oxford University Press, 1966.

Das, Durga. *India: From Curzon to Nehru and After.* London: Collins Publishers, 1969.

Erikson, Erik H. *Gandhi's Truth.* New York: W. W. Norton, 1969.

Fischer, Louis. *The Life of Mahatma Gandhi.* New York: Harper and Row, 1950.

Fishlock, Trevor. *India File.* London: John Murray, 1983.

Galbraith, John Kenneth. *Ambassador's Journal: A Personal Account of the Kennedy Years.* Boston: Houghton Mifflin, 1969.

———. *John Kenneth Galbraith Introduces India.* London: Andre Deutsch, 1974.

Gandhi, Indira. *On Peoples and Problems.* London: Hodder and Stoughton, 1983.

Gandhi, Mohandas Karamchand. *The Story of My Experiments with Truth: An Autobiography.* Boston: Beacon Press, 1970.

Glyn, Anthony. *The British: Portrait of a People.* New York: G. P. Putnam's Sons, 1970.

Greer, Germaine. *Sex and Destiny: The Politics of Human Fertility.* New York: Harper and Row, 1984.

Gross, John. *Rudyard Kipling: The Man, His Work and His World.* London: Weidenfeld and Nicolson, 1972.

Gupte, Pranay. *The Crowded Earth: People and the Politics of Population.* New York: W. W. Norton, 1984.

Hangen, Welles. *After Nehru Who?* London: Rupert Hart Davis, 1963.

Harrison, Paul. *Inside the Third World.* London: Penguin, 1979.

———. *The Third World Tomorrow.* London: Penguin, 1980.

Harrison, Selig S. *India, the Most Dangerous Decades.* Princeton: Princeton University Press, 1960.

Hibbert, Christopher. *The Great Mutiny: India 1857.* New York: The Viking Press, 1978.

Hobbs, Lisa. *India, India.* New York: McGraw-Hill, 1967.

Hutheesing, Krishna Nehru. *Dear To Behold: An Intimate Portrait of Indira Gandhi.* New York: Macmillan, 1969.

Illustrated Weekly of India. Edited by Pritish Nandy. Bombay: Times of India Publications.

Imprint. Monthly magazine edited by Vir Sanghvi and published by R. V. Pandit. Bombay.

India Today. Fortnightly magazine, edited by Aroon Purie. Delhi.

Joshi, Chand. *Bhindranwale: Myth and Reality.* Delhi: Vikas Publishing, 1984.

Karanjia, R. K. *The Mind of Mr. Nehru.* London: George Allen and Unwin, 1960.

——. *The Philosophy of Mr. Nehru.* London: George Allen and Unwin, 1966.

Kaye, M. M. *The Far Pavilions.* New York: St. Martin's Press, 1978.

Keay, John. *Into India.* London: John Murray, 1973.

Khan, Mohammed Ayub. *Friends, Not Masters: A Political Autobiography.* London: Oxford University Press, 1967.

Kothari, Rajni. *Politics in India.* Boston: Little, Brown and Company, 1970.

Lapierre, Dominique. *The City of Troy.* New York: Doubleday, 1985.

Lewis, John P. *Quiet Crisis in India: Economic Development and American Policy.* Washington: The Brookings Institution, 1962.

Malgonkar, Manohar. *The Devil's Wind.* London: Hamish Hamilton, 1972.

Mansingh, Surjit. *India's Search for Power: Indira Gandhi's Foreign Policy 1966–1982.* Delhi: Sage, 1984.

Maxwell, Neville. *India's China War.* New York: Pantheon Books, 1970.

Mehta, Ved. *Portrait of India.* Delhi: Vikas Publications, 1971.

——. *Walking the Indian Streets.* Delhi: Vikas Publications, 1972.

——. *Mamaji.* New York: Oxford University Press, 1979.

——. *The Ledge Between the Streams.* New York: W. W. Norton, 1984.

Menon, K. P. S. *The Flying Troika: The Political Diary of India's Ambassador to Russia, 1952–61.* New York: Oxford University Press, 1963.

Menon, V. P. *The Story of the Integration of the Indian States.* Calcutta: Orient Longmans, 1956.

———. *The Transfer of Power in India.* Princeton: Princeton University Press, 1957.

Mohan, Anand. *Indira Gandhi: A Biography.* New York: Hawthorn Books, 1967.

Moorhouse, Geoffrey. *Calcutta.* New York: Harcourt Brace Jovanovich, 1971.

———. *India Britannica.* London: Harvill Press, 1983.

———. *To the Frontier.* London: Hodder and Stoughton, 1984.

Moraes, Dom. *A Matter of People.* New York: Praeger, 1974.

———. *Voices for Life.* New York, Praeger, 1975.

———. *The Great Cities:* Bombay. Amsterdam: Time-Life Books, 1979.

———. *Mrs. Gandhi.* Delhi: Vikas Publishing House, 1980.

Moraes, Frank. *Indira Gandhi.* Delhi: Directorate of Advertising and Visual Publicity, 1966.

Morris, James. *Pax Britannica.* London: Faber and Faber, 1968.

———. *Heaven's Command.* New York: Harcourt Brace Jovanovich, 1973.

———. *Farewell the Trumpets.* New York: Harcourt Brace Jovanovich, 1978.

Morris, Jan. *Stones of Empire: The Buildings of the Raj.* With photographs and captions by Simon Winchester. New York: Oxford University Press, 1983.

Myrdal, Gunnar. *Asian Drama: An Inquiry into the Poverty of Nations.* New York: Twentieth Century Fund, 1968.

———. *The Challenge of World Poverty.* New York: Pantheon Books, 1970.

Naipaul, Shiva. *From the Dragon's Mouth.* London: Hamish Hamilton, 1984.

Naipaul, V. S. *An Area of Darkness.* London: Andre Deutsch, 1964.

———. *The Overcrowded Barracoon.* London: Andre Deutsch, 1972.

———. *India: A Wounded Civilization.* New York: Alfred A. Knopf, 1977.

———. *Finding the Centre.* London: Andre Deutsch, 1984.

Nanda, B. R. *The Nehrus: Motilal and Jawaharlal.* London: George Allen and Unwin, 1962.

———. *Mahatma Gandhi: A Biography.* New York: Baron, 1965.

Nayar, Kuldip. *India: The Critical Years.* Delhi: Vikas Publications, 1971.

———. *The Judgment: Inside Story of the Emergency in India.* Delhi: Vikas Publishing House, 1977.

Nayar, Kuldip, and Singh, Khushwant. *Tragedy of Punjab: Operation Bluestar and After.* Delhi: Vision Books, 1984.

Nehru, Jawaharlal. *Autobiography.* London: Bodley Head, 1936.

———. *The Discovery of India.* New York: John Day, 1946.

———. *India's Freedom.* London: Unwin Books, 1965.

Palkhivala, Nani A. *We, the People.* Bombay: Strand Book Stall, 1984.

Pandit, Vijayalakshmi. *Prison Days.* Calcutta: Signet Press, 1945.

Paul, Swraj. *Indira Gandhi.* London: Heron Press, 1984.

People magazine. Edited by John Rowley and published by the International Planned Parenthood Federation. London.

Raghavan, G. N. S. *Introducing India.* Delhi: Indian Council for Cultural Relations, 1983.

Rajagopalachari, Chakravarti. *The Mahabharata.* Bombay: Bharatiya Vidya Bhavan, 1951.

———. *The Ramayana.* Bombay: Bharatiya Vidya Bhavan, 1951.

Reeves, Richard. *Passage to Peshawar.* New York: Simon and Schuster, 1984.

Rushdie, Salman. *Midnight's Children.* New York: Alfred A. Knopf, 1980.

Sahgal, Nayantara. *Prison and Chocolate Cake.* New York: Alfred A. Knopf, 1954.

Salas, Rafael M. *People: An International Choice.* New York: Pergamon Press, 1976.

——. *Reflections on Population.* New York: Pergamon Press, 1984.

Scott, Paul. *The Raj Quartet.* New York: William Morrow, 1976.

Sen Gupta, Bhabani. *The Fulcrum of Asia: Relations Among China, India, Pakistan, and the U.S.S.R.* New York: Pegasus, 1970.

Shaplen, Robert. *A Turning Wheel: Thirty Years of the Asian Revolution.* London: Andre Deutsch, 1979.

Sheean, Vincent. *Lead, Kindly Light.* London: Cassell, 1950.

——. *Mahatma Gandhi: A Great Life in Brief.* New York: Alfred A. Knopf, 1970.

Sheth, N. R. *The Social Framework of an Indian Factory.* Manchester: Manchester University Press, 1968.

Singh, Jyoti Shankar. *The New International Economic Order.* New York: Praeger, 1977.

Singh, Karan. *Contemporary Essays.* Bombay: Bharatiya Vidya Bhavan, 1971.

Singh, Khushwant. *India: A Mirror for Its Monsters and Monstrosities.* Bombay: IBH Publishing Company, 1969.

——. *The Sikhs Today.* Bombay: Orient Longmans, 1967.

——. *Train to Pakistan.* London: Chatto & Windus, 1956.

——. *We Indians.* Delhi: Orient Paperbacks, 1982.

——. *Delhi: A Portrait.* With photographs by Raghu Rai. New York: Oxford University Press, 1983.

——. *The Sikhs.* With photographs by Raghu Rai. Delhi: Rupa and Company, 1984.

Singh, S. Nihal. *My India.* Delhi: Vikas Publishing House, 1982.

Spear, Percival. *A History of India.* London: Penguin Books, 1970.

Sunday. Weekly newsmagazine, edited by M. J. Akbar and published by Ananda Bazar Patrika publications. Calcutta.

Thapar, Romila. *A History of India.* London: Penguin Books, 1966.

Theroux, Paul. *The Great Railway Bazaar: By Train Through Asia.* Boston: Houghton Mifflin, 1975.

Traub, James. India: *The Challenge of Change.* New York: Messner, 1985.

UNFPA. *State of the World Population 1984.* New York: United Nations Publications, 1984.

UNICEF. *The State of the World's Children 1984.* New York: Oxford University Press, 1984.

Vadgama, Kusoom. *India in Britain.* London: Robert Royce, 1984.

Vittachi, Tarzie. *The Brown Sahib.* London: Andre Deutsch, 1962.

Walvin, James. *Passage to Britain: Immigration in British History and Politics.* London: Penguin, 1984.

Watson, Francis. *A Concise History of India.* London: Thames and Hudson, 1979.

Willcoxen, Harriet. *First Lady of India: The Story of Indira Gandhi.* New York: Doubleday, 1969.

Wirsing, Giselher. *The Indian Experiment.* Delhi: Orient Longman, 1972.

Wolpert, Stanley. *A New History of India.* New York: Oxford University Press, 1977.

Index